PRACTICAL HUMAN RESOURCES FOR PUBLIC MANAGERS

A Case Study Approach

American Society for Public Administration
Series in Public Administration and Public Policy

Advancing excellence in public service . . .

PRACTICAL HUMAN RESOURCES FOR PUBLIC MANAGERS

A Case Study Approach

NICOLAS A. VALCIK
TEODORO J. BENAVIDES

CRC Press
Taylor & Francis Group
Boca Raton   London   New York

CRC Press is an imprint of the
Taylor & Francis Group, an **informa** business

CRC Press
Taylor & Francis Group
6000 Broken Sound Parkway NW, Suite 300
Boca Raton, FL 33487-2742

© 2012 by Taylor & Francis Group, LLC
CRC Press is an imprint of Taylor & Francis Group, an Informa business

No claim to original U.S. Government works

Printed in the United States of America on acid-free paper
Version Date: 20110713

International Standard Book Number: 978-1-4398-4143-3 (Hardback)

Visit the Taylor & Francis Web site at
http://www.taylorandfrancis.com

and the CRC Press Web site at
http://www.crcpress.com

The authors would like to dedicate this book to Jo Valcik, Manuel T. Benavides, and Maria M. Benavides.

Contents

Foreword

For a number of years, Nicolas A. Valcik and Teodoro J. Benavides have developed a set of key ingredients to show how evolving human resource trends can be successfully managed and taught to anyone. They have developed and documented *case studies* over the years through their personal varied employment situations in private, public, and academic settings. Their combined experience comprises the decades of knowledge and experience that are found in this book.

Practical Human Resources for Public Managers: A Case Study Approach is a keystone for evaluating choices and making decisions that have been absent or difficult to ascertain from most organizations. We learn in most information technology and management endeavors that people are the most valuable resources that any company or public organization can have. Today's employer faces myriad issues when hiring an employee: how to recruit, whom to select, how to interview, Equal Employment Opportunity policies, fair salary offerings, health issues, performance evaluations, behavior/disciplinary actions, turnover, and the list goes on and on. Valcik and Benavides take us step by step into the "real world" with examples of historical events that lead us to "What Happened" and "What Could Have Happened" as well as suggested readings for more in-depth analysis and important points to remember. This book attempts to bridge the gap between human resource theory and what actually occurs in the world.

The importance of this book cannot be overlooked by professionals and students alike. The real case studies allow the reader to form his or her own opinions about the particular case while understanding the many outcomes possible. In this case study approach, students can make the right or wrong decision without the usually drastic consequences, such as lawsuits, dismissal, probation, salary adjustments, civil service censure, or other varied punishments that can arise from poor heuristics. Many human resources professionals can also benefit from this book by reviewing cases that rarely occur, especially in different regions or between public and private organizations. Most readers will find Chapters 11 and 12, on organized labor and morale and motivation, particularly interesting because these topics are rarely taught to the human resources professional; rather, they are touched upon by outside consultants or implied by memorandums of understanding or some other bulletin-like correspondence.

Valcik and Benavides have finally provided a tool for human resources professionals to scrutinize their discipline and begin to analyze the "what ifs" in their world. I hope you find this work as informative and beneficial as my colleagues and I have.

Stuart B. Murchison, PhD
Clinical Associate Professor
Geospatial Information Sciences and Geography
The University of Texas at Dallas

Foreword

After more than 30 years' work in public administration, I clearly understand that the most critical building block of success is the effective management of the human assets. And while a foundation in the principles of human resource management may establish the infrastructure for this success, only the practicalities and complexities of the real-world experience can provide the complete structure. Dr. Nicolas Valcik and Mr. Teodoro Benavides are particularly qualified in this approach with their broadly ranging backgrounds and wide variety of work assignments.

The unique perspective of public entities and nonprofits is especially challenging. The occasionally onerous legal requirements, the expected transparency, and the public accountability bring much more complexity to public versus private human resources administration. The authors' field experiences greatly enhance the case studies approach of this text with real-life situations, reflecting the practical application of all aspects of human resource management.

For the full- or part-time student, the in-service trainee, or the practitioner, both the structure and the content of this book function to develop and enhance proficiencies while providing a discussion format for interactive group instruction. Make use of this powerful tool to build and improve skills in the essential management of human resources in public administration.

Mary K. Suhm
City Manager
City of Dallas

Preface

The inspiration for *Practical Human Resources for Public Managers: A Case Study Approach* came from an experience in the classroom. Dr. Nicolas Valcik, an instructor in the Public Affairs program at The University of Texas at Dallas, was unable to find a suitable case study book for his class on human resource management in the public sector. To resolve the deficiency, he wrote a booklet of case studies drawn from a variety of actual events that occurred either in his professional life or in the lives of other professionals, altering the names and locations to protect identities. He wrote the case studies in a way that could suggest multiple possible endings, thus fostering in-class discussion and critical thinking. Some case studies were written to provide no perfect solutions, mirroring what one would find in a real-world professional setting.

When the course was complete, Dr. Valcik felt that these case studies were a successful instructional tool and could prove useful to other instructors. He wanted to incorporate experiences from municipal management and expand the potential audience to practitioners searching for pragmatic ways to deal with human resource issues in their workplaces. Dr. Valcik approached Teodoro Benavides, who had worked as a city manager for much of his professional life, for his expertise.

Both authors bring experience from a wide array of working environments that include teaching and administrative experience in public universities and management in municipalities of various population sizes from a few thousand to more than a million. The authors have also worked in a variety of capacities within these organizations, which allows them to see a variety of perspectives on how different departments handle similar situations. Dr. Valcik has written municipal risk management policies for the City of McKinney in Texas, worked as a university recruiting analyst for Nortel Networks, and taught undergraduate and graduate-level courses in human resource management for the Public Affairs program at The University of Texas at Dallas since 2007. Dr. Valcik has worked as an administrator for The University of Texas at Dallas since 1997 and currently (2011) holds the position of associate director at the Office of Strategic Planning and Analysis.

Teodoro Benavides has worked for the Fire Department of the City of Fort Worth, Texas, where he was responsible for the administrative and budget matters.

He also served as the city manager of Denton, Texas, where he supervised more than a thousand employees. However, his longest tenure of employment was the 24 years he served with the City of Dallas, Texas. While in Dallas, he held a variety of professional and managerial positions, which included budget analyst, capital budget administrator, assistant budget director, director in the Office of Budget and Research, assistant director of Health and Human Services, assistant city manager, and the city manager from 1998 to 2004. After his retirement, he worked from 2006 to 2008 as an executive recruiter for governmental clients while employed by the firm Waters Consulting Group. He is currently on the faculty of the Public Affairs Department in the School of Economic, Political, and Policy Sciences at the University of Texas at Dallas; and he is a senior consultant with the firm Government Strategic Resources, for which he does executive recruitment, organizational analysis, and leadership training.

Practical Human Resources for Public Managers: A Case Study Approach is meant to provide insight into human resource trends and to demonstrate how real-world situations can be successfully managed by public sector practitioners. It provides students and practitioners with the means to work through various situations and the freedom to try new ideas and to make mistakes in the safety of a classroom setting. Public administrators often face situations that are too complex and nuanced to be adequately addressed in most human resources textbooks on the market today, most of which focus on a legalistic framework rather than on solutions to common workplace issues. The authors have the sincerest hope that this book will be used for both training as well as a reference for practitioners and academics in the field of public administration.

Acknowledgments

The authors would like to acknowledge many people for their time and effort in assisting with the production of this book. We would like to thank Dr. Evan Berman for his continued support of the book and the constant feedback that he provided us throughout the project. We would like to thank several individuals who provided invaluable feedback to us throughout the process of determining what aspects were important to academics, to administrators, and to students themselves. The administrators we would like to extend thanks to are Larry Wilson, Dr. Karen Jarrell, and Dr. Melvin Letteer. We would also like to thank two students who provided feedback for the book, Krysten Carrera and Tamera Brinkley. Most importantly, we would like to thank our proofreader and illustrator, Andrea Stigdon, who did a phenomenal job with all aspects of this book.

Nicolas Valcik would also like to thank Dr. Stuart Murchison for the training and support he provided with ArcGIS. Nicolas would like to thank his students, coworkers, and colleagues who provided positive feedback so that he could work on a book of this magnitude. Nicolas would like to thank Dr. Doug Watson for giving him the opportunity to teach Human Resources at both the undergraduate and graduate levels in the Public Affairs program. Nicolas would like to thank his mother, Jo Valcik, for all the support she provided, as well as his siblings, Erik and Heather. Most of all, Nicolas would also like to thank his wife, Kristi, who has always been there to provide moral support and who has believed in him in all aspects of his career.

Ted Benavides would like to thank his mother, Maria M. Benavides, and his father, Manuel T. Benavides, who encouraged him to go to college and become the first one in his family to receive a college degree. Ted would also like to thank his mentor, Dr. N. Joseph Cayer, who inspired him to seek a career in public service. Most of all, Ted would like to thank his wife, Aretha, who is always on his side and has been the inspiration to continue his new career and passion, which is teaching.

About the Authors

Nicolas A. Valcik currently works as an associate director of Strategic Planning and Analysis for the University of Texas at Dallas and serves as a clinical assistant professor for Public Affairs for the University of Texas at Dallas. Nicolas received a doctorate degree in public affairs from the University of Texas at Dallas in 2005, a master's degree in public affairs from the University of Texas at Dallas in 1996, a bachelor's degree in interdisciplinary studies from the University of Texas at Dallas in 1994, and an associate's degree in political science from Collin County Community College in 1994.

Prior to 1997, Nicolas worked for a number of municipalities, across different of departments, as well as for Nortel. In 2006, Nicolas authored *Regulating the Use of Biological Hazardous Materials in Universities: Complying with the New Federal Guidelines*, published by Mellen Press. Nicolas has served as editor for three volumes of *New Directions for Institutional Research* (Volumes 135, 140, and 146) in addition to writing numerous articles and book chapters on institutional research topics and homeland security issues. Nicolas specializes in several areas as both a researcher and a practitioner: higher education, information technology, human resources, homeland security, organizational behavior, and emergency management.

Ted Benavides currently serves as a faculty member for the University of Texas at Dallas (UTD) in the School of Economic, Political, and Policy Sciences' Public Affairs Program. In addition, he is currently affiliated as a senior consultant with the firm Strategic Government Resources, which does executive search and organizational analysis for local government entities. He also served as a senior vice president for the Waters Consulting Group from 2006 to 2008, which does executive search, compensation studies, and organizational analysis for public sector organizations.

Ted Benavides served from 1998 to 2004 as city manager of Dallas, Texas. Mr. Benavides was responsible for administering all programs and services for the city's 1.2 million people, for overseeing an annual $1.9 billion municipal budget, and for directing a workforce of 12,000 employees.

From 1996 to 1998, Mr. Benavides was city manager of the City of Denton, Texas, and from 1990 to 1996, he served as one of five assistant city managers in Dallas. Prior to that, he held a number of other positions with the City of Dallas, including director of the Budget and Research Department, assistant director of the Health and Human Services Department, assistant director of capital budget programs, capital budget administrator, and budget analyst. He joined the City of Dallas in March 1978.

Ted Benavides earned a bachelor's degree in education, political science, and history from Texas A&I University (now Texas A&M University—Kingsville) and a master's degree in public administration from Southern Methodist University. He is also a graduate of both Leadership Dallas and the Executive Institute of the Texas Municipal League at the Lyndon B. Johnson School of Public Affairs in Austin and is a fellow of the National Academy of Public Administration. Benavides serves on the board of directors of the National Forum for Black Public Administrators and is the vice chair of the Texas City Management Association University Relations Task Force.

Chapter 1

Introduction

Human resource issues can provide some of the biggest challenges to a manager in an organization. Books pertaining to human resource issues often provide little information beyond legal statutes, offer only the most basic guidelines for formulating human resource decisions, and are generally not focused on concerns faced by public sector institutions. The lack of resources available to guide managers in public organizations for formulating policies, making decisions on personnel issues, or crafting strategic goals in recruiting, hiring, or retaining personnel prompted the creation of this book.

The intended audience for this American Society of Public Administrators Series book is applied practitioners who work primarily in the public sector, nonprofit organizations, and medical services. The book is not designed to replace a textbook but is intended to supplement existing human resources textbooks. For specific regional issues (e.g., organized labor), an instructor should assign a textbook that contends with those specific areas that are required for public managers. This case study book is intended to give students and practitioners practical guidance as well as provide real life situations that occur in the workplace.

The environment and culture of these organizations require a different focus than private sector organizations like Raytheon or IBM because of civil-service statutes and other legal realities that do not apply to private organizations. This book contains case studies that have actually occurred in various organizations. The purpose of these case studies is to allow the reader to review a human resources situation and see the eventual outcome. Reality-based case studies have been used because the authors believe that truth is always better than fiction when training managers or human resources personnel to contend with personnel issues in their organizations.

Administrators must be aware of federal, state, and local laws when they make human resources decisions for their organizations. However, this case study book is designed to give guidance to administrators in addition to the legal statutes that will assist them in making human resources decisions not only that are legally tenable but also that will enhance organizational capabilities and reduce civil liabilities. Administrators need to be aware of both internal and external relationships when determining policies and procedures for management and human resource issues. Administrators must be attentive to internal organizational needs and requirements that will enhance their organization's ability to fulfill mission-critical objectives while simultaneously paying attention to how the organization is impacted by federal, state, and local statutes and how customers serviced by the organization can hold the organization liable for employee actions. In other words, the *soft skills* take on greater importance to administrators in public, medical, and nonprofit organizations where effective interpersonal communications are required.

Administrators of medical organizations and higher education institutions have unique human resources issues they must address. Medical organizations can be nonprofit (e.g., American Association for Cancer Research), for-profit (e.g., HCA Medical Center of Plano), or public (e.g., the University of Texas Southwestern Medical Center) organizations, thus placing medical organizations in different environments or cultures depending on the mission of the institution. Two issues that bind almost all medical organizations are providing health care and addressing medical liability. Medical organizations employ specialized personnel who have extensive training, degrees, or certifications required to perform their job responsibilities, creating additional benefits and complexities regarding human resources issues. Higher education institutions also have several unique characteristics that can affect human resources issues. Colleges and universities can either be public or private organizations that typically provide a wide array of services that include educational services, research, and community outreach programs. Higher education institutions also have different cultures and environments that affect how faculties are managed, particularly if tenure is available for their faculty. Throughout this book the reader will be provided some basic terminology that is specific to different public organizations.

Overview of Chapters

The chapters that follow in this book can be grouped into three major areas: how legal statutes impact public organizations, core human resources issues in public organizations, and special human resources topics that affect the public sector in unique ways.

Chapter 2 provides an overview of federal, state, and local legal statutes that directly impact human resources issues within a public organization. This chapter also addresses right-to-work and employment at will and demonstrates how these issues affect public organizations. Chapter 2 provides the framework upon which all other topics discussed later in the book will build.

The next five chapters deal specifically with issues pertaining to the core functions of human resources offices: obtaining, managing, and terminating employees. These chapters will explore how the development of superior interpersonal and communication skills can add value to the organization. The ability of an administrator to understand the various federal human resources statutes (Equal Employment Opportunity, Americans with Disabilities Act, etc.) will be explored throughout the informational text of the chapters as well as within the case studies.

Chapter 3 discusses recruitment and the different methods that can be used to attract and retain good applicants for public organizational positions. As Chapter 3 will point out, administrators must understand what their organization requires when recruiting for particular positions. Chapter 4 analyzes the hiring process for public organizations and provides practical tips for administrators regarding the advantages and disadvantages of various hiring methodologies. Administrators should take note of the applied techniques that can be used positively when an organization is going through the hiring process. Chapter 5 explores the efficacy of performance evaluations and how performance evaluations can be used to more effectively evaluate employee performance in the workplace. The issue of how to use performance evaluations as a proper management tool will be discussed, as well as the ethical implications of using a performance evaluation inappropriately. Chapter 5 will also discuss how to construct an effective performance evaluation instrument to get an accurate appraisal of employee performance.

Chapter 6 discusses what administrators can and cannot do when rewarding and disciplining public sector employees. Public organizations are bound by many more statutes than their private industry counterparts with regards to monetary incentives. However, public administrators can provide other types of incentives for employees who perform exemplary work on a consistent basis. Public administrators are also legally constrained in how they can contend with difficult employees or with behavioral problems. This chapter provides tactics for reprimanding employees in a fair and legal manner. The case studies in Chapter 6 provide guidance for administrators on how to best proceed with rewarding and reprimanding employees and provide real examples on how situations can become complex in the work environment.

In Chapter 7, the authors discuss retention and termination. The issue of retention is discussed at length because retaining good employees is crucial for maintaining an effective organization. Tactics for correctly dismissing a poorly performing employee without incurring liability for the administrator and his or her organization are also discussed. An often overlooked aspect of being an administrator is the intangible element of gathering organizational intelligence, which is incredibly important in regard to personnel retention. Organizational intelligence enables administrators to make more informed decisions on which human resources policies and procedures should be implemented to benefit their organization. An administrator who lacks organizational intelligence is likely to make costly long-term mistakes that can negatively impact the organization's personnel assets.

The remaining chapters deal with special human resources topics that impact public organizations. Chapter 8 focuses on workplace violence and hostile work environments, what specific threats a public organization may have to contend with, and measures that administrators can take to diminish their organization's vulnerability. While most organizations have not faced major challenges associated with workplace violence and hostile work environments, an administrator should be aware of the dangers and potential violence that can occur. The case studies will provide real examples of workplace violence and threats that managers have had to cope with in the past. Chapter 9 will discuss health benefits as well as mental illness in the workplace.

Chapter 10 focuses on the benefits of mentoring and mentoring programs for employees and the organization. Administrators should be aware of the benefits to having a mentoring program and what type of resources an organization should dedicate to make a mentoring program successful. A successful mentoring program can lead to improved training, retention, and morale for the organization as a whole.

Chapter 11 discusses how to negotiate with organized labor associations. Due to legal considerations, public organizations must use different tactics for negotiating with unionized employees than a private organization might use. This chapter also addresses liability risks associated with employees. This topic is of special concern for medical organizations, particularly if an administrator has not taken steps to ensure that personnel are trained properly, that proper operating guidelines are in place, and that the guidelines are being followed by employees. The case studies will also provide insight into how real situations can become quite complex when administrators must negotiate between organized labor and their own organizations.

Chapter 12 discusses employee morale, motivation, and how to aid employees through organizational transitions. While positive employee morale is important to an organization under normal operating environments, good morale becomes crucial when an organization undergoes a dramatic transition. Chapter 12 discusses the management aspect of human resources as well as the importance of having excellent interpersonal communication skill sets.

In the final chapter, the authors discuss trends in human resource management and a final notation for this case study book. This chapter discusses where administrators will need to be aware of new trends and how workplace environments are evolving.

Chapter 2

Equal Employment Opportunity Situations

In the United States, federal statutes, state laws, local ordinances, and agency rules provide supervisors in public organizations with a framework in which they can address personnel issues. The federal, state, and local guidelines were formulated by congressional acts, state statutes, and local ordinances to protect employees from discrimination by employers during recruitment, hiring, management, and termination processes. Other countries have rules and regulations that bind supervisors and organizations to their culture's values and definitions of fairness. For example, Turkey not only maintains standard regulations for all employees but also has regulations that are gender specific (e.g., females are not allowed to work after certain hours). Regardless of the country, if federal regulations, state statutes, or local ordinances are violated by employers, the organization faces the possibility of being fined or facing litigation in a civil action suit.

In the last 50 years, the trend is for more intervention by government agencies and managers in the relationship between individual employees and their governmental employers. This trend has resulted in an increasing number of employment statutes and court decisions to regulate the line between governmental managerial decisions and individual employee rights. This chapter will focus on several areas that managers in the United States should be aware of when contending with personnel matters. This chapter deals with the rights and responsibilities of government employees and how Equal Employment Opportunity (EEO) laws and regulations have impacted the workplace.

Employment Laws and Regulations

Public services managers must keep many personnel issues and laws in mind while managing their complex workforces. Governmental agencies can be considered the last of the big conglomerates as federal, state, and local agencies provide a huge array of services, including education, health, public safety, human services, capital improvements, and environmental protection, just to name a few. To effectively manage public agency workforces, public service managers must keep in mind the legal framework that allows them to lead their workforces, produce the desired results, protect their employees' rights, and make the work environment enriching and challenging. We will explore issues such as at-will employment, compensation, health and safety, individual liability, privacy issues, discrimination, civil service, freedom of speech, and grooming and dress codes.

The EEO statutes have several provisions that state that no class of people will be discriminated against based on race, ethnicity, religion, national origin, disability (reasonable accommodation), age (over 40 years old), or gender when applying for a position, hiring for a position, or being terminated from a position (Kulik, 2004). The EEO statutes, however, protect organizations as well as applicants and employees. The statutes provide organizations with clear guidelines that will protect them from civil liability as long as the guidelines and protocols are followed and the organizations have acted in good faith with hiring and termination practices. If organizations do not act in good faith, then applicants and employees are protected by civil legal actions as well as through the Equal Employment Opportunity Commission (EEOC), which has the power to take action against infracting organizations (e.g., fines) to hold organizations accountable for their actions.

The employment relationship in American governmental agencies is affected by whether the employee is at will, has civil-service protection, or is exercising rights such as freedom of speech, freedom of associations, or right to privacy at work. Throughout U.S. history the at-will statute has fluctuated due to political and economic influences. In most organizations, at-will status is limited to midlevel and executive management positions, which represent a minority of public service positions (Figure 2.1).

Workers with civil-service protection or academic tenure cannot be dismissed from employment without procedural due process. These types of employees are considered to have property rights to their positions, and any governmental agencies that operate under these principles must show cause for the discharge of an employee. Employees with civil-service protection must be given an opportunity to receive the reasons for their discharge and a hearing process to refute the charges or to disprove the cause of the discharge action. Even employees who are at-will are often provided some form of procedural due process before being discharged.

Thus it is quite common in governmental agencies for some of the workers to fall under protection by civil-service rules while others do not. This distinction is important when dealing with issues such as discharge or other adverse actions,

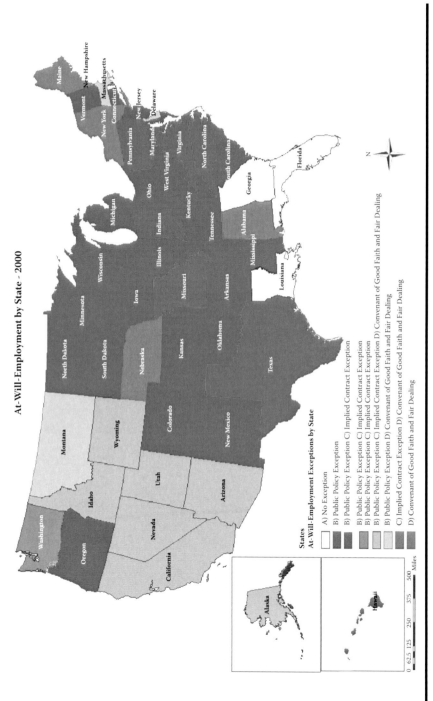

Figure 2.1 U.S. Map—HR at-will employment.

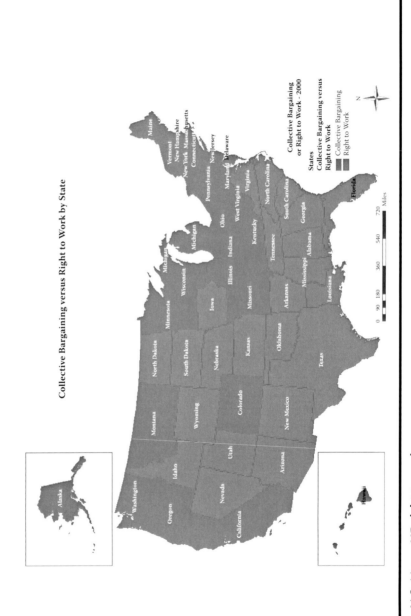

Figure 2.2   U.S. Map—HR right to work.

which can include verbal counseling, written reprimands, suspensions, salary reductions, demotions, and terminations. At-will and probationary employees would not usually be provided due process protection. The lower-level personnel actions may only be appealed to one or a few levels up the organizational chain, and some can be appealed to the highest level of a public agency or even to the courts.

Employees do not forfeit their right of free speech when they accept employment in the public sector. Public sector employees may, and often do, write letters to newspaper editors or speak to their elected or appointed legislative bodies outside work hours to express their opinions on their agencies' actions. These rights, if practiced according to rules and regulations, cannot be curtailed even if the employee's opinions run counter to the public organization's official position.

Discrimination

There are three major federal antidiscrimination statutes: Title VII of the Civil Rights Act of 1964, the Age Discrimination in Employment Act, and the Americans with Disabilities Act. These laws state that governments may not discriminate against employees on the basis of race, color, national origin, religion, sex (gender), age (40 years or older), or disability. The basis of the Civil Rights Act of 1964 was a civil rights speech given by President John F. Kennedy on June 11, 1963, in which he asked for legislation guaranteeing that all Americans have the right to be served in facilities that are open to the public—hotels, restaurants, theaters, retail stores, and similar establishments—as well as a greater protection for the right to vote by ending unequal voter registration requirements. This act emulated the Civil Rights Act of 1875, which had guaranteed that everyone regardless of race, color, or previous condition of servitude was entitled to the same treatment in "public accommodations" like inns and theaters but was struck down as unconstitutional by the U.S. Supreme Court in 1883. The Age Discrimination in Employment Act protects individuals who are 40 years of age or older from employment discrimination based on age. The protections in this act apply to both employment and job applicants. This act was passed to rectify the fact that age discrimination was not included in the 1964 act and to address age discrimination that tends to occur during times of economic downturns or recessions when jobs are more difficult to acquire.

The Americans with Disabilities Act of 1990 (ADA) was the result of work by hundreds of advocacy groups and was originally signed by President George H. W. Bush. In its simplest terms, it is patterned after the Civil Rights Act of 1964 and works to prevent discrimination against a qualified individual with a disability within the hiring, training, promotion, and separation processes. All employers with more than 15 employees must be in compliance with the terms of ADA. Disability is defined by the ADA as "a physical or mental impairment that substantially limits a major life activity." Certain medical conditions can be defined as a disability on a case-by-case basis. For example, the State of Illinois was sued based on the claim that a person suffering from infertility had a disability and thus must be provided with treatment under this law. The 2008 ADA Amendment Act, which was signed by President George W. Bush, was created to give broader protection for disabled workers and address court rulings that Congress deemed too restrictive. This law and its amendment have had a profound impact on human resources management.

Authors' Experience

Having worked for government agencies that served communities with a great deal of diversity in its citizens, customers served, employees hired, appointed and elected officials, and contractors and vendors employed, we quickly realized that equal treatment above the requirements of the law was not only required but demanded by these communities. It is important for managers to be fair and equitable to everyone from the employees and vendors to the appointed and elected officials while ensuring that those who serve the community resemble the community's citizens and be held accountable to them. While we did not have quotas for hiring or for selecting vendors, we were constantly striving to foster diversity in all governmental functions and at all pay grades. Even when we had budget reductions and layoffs, substantial efforts were made to ensure the cuts and/or layoffs were fairly distributed among the diverse workforce, at all levels of the organization, and at all levels of age and tenure.

Maintaining this level of sensitivity sometimes made it more challenging to operate a business, but the benefits to the community were enormous as these actions communicated to our citizens, leaders, and employees that our organization was more like a family. We wanted to have a reputation as an employer of choice, committed to fairness and equity well above the requirement of equal opportunity legal requirements. The organizations that I worked for believed that diverse workforces were qualitatively better because through these diverse employees we were able to tap into a wide variety of experiences, training, educational backgrounds, and circumstances that strengthened and invigorated the workforce.

Final Notes

This chapter introduces federal, state, and local statutes pertaining to equal employment opportunity and discrimination. Ignorance or willful disregard of these statutes can result in severe consequences for a public organization and its leadership. It would be unwise for a public administrator to regard these legal statutes as pointless political correctness. When faced with a hostile work environment arising from unregulated conflicts over appearance, religion, health, privacy issues, disparate treatment, and retaliation, the public agency's credibility and effectiveness is at risk. Formulating effective personnel policies, clear guidelines, and training will ensure compliance with employment laws. Compliance will, in turn, cultivate safe, productive work environments and create a diverse, effective agency that can earn the confidence of the community.

Important Points to Remember

1. Because public organizations work for their citizens, and their revenue and resources derive from the governed, diversity practices must be implemented and sustained so that public servants resemble the citizens they serve.
2. Public agencies should endeavor to employ a diverse workforce at all pay levels, job classifications, and skills.
3. When responding to the needs of a continuously changing and diversifying society, it is a competitive advantage to have a diverse workforce.
4. While it is in the best interests of all public agencies to have a diverse workforce, it is also essential to have employment policies and practices that comply with the law and that provide everyone with fair access to employment.
5. Public sector agencies need to also have an explicit marketing strategy to attract and employ the most qualified and diverse workforce possible.
6. The development of a diverse workforce is an excellent way to broaden and strengthen the capacity of public organizations to deal with the rapidly changing world that public agencies must operate within during these volatile times.
7. Equal treatment of employees applies not only to hiring but to all human resources processes and policies such as benefits, opportunities for promotion, training, reduction in force, pay, and many other similar issues.
8. The elected and appointed boards of public agencies also need to be included in their organization's diversity and Equal Employment Opportunity policies and procedures.
9. It is important that vendors and contractors of public agencies reflect the diversity of the public agencies that are employing their services.
10. Public agencies can be successful by exhibiting the equal employment and diversity behavior that we would like to see in our society.

CASE STUDY 2.1
Equal Employment Opportunity Issue

SITUATION FOR CASE STUDY 2.1

The year is 1969 and you are the manager of a state highway department in a rural north Texas city that specializes in maintenance and construction of state highways.

This department is one of hundreds across the state with more than 17,000 employees. The town where your department is located has a population of around 3,500 people and is the county seat of government. Everyone in town knows each other. Your organization consists entirely of male construction workers who range from 18 to 65 years of age. Your facility is small with a minimal amount of corridor space at the entrance of the building. Your department needs an employee to perform dispatching and secretarial work. After interviewing several potential job applicants, you have decided to hire your first female employee, Flossie. Flossie had previous experience working as a drug store clerk, thus demonstrating an ability to work well with different types of customers and supervisors. You feel confident about this hiring decision because Flossie was outspoken, confident, and thick-skinned, qualities you felt would serve her well in a male-dominated work environment. However, you quickly learned that having a female employee required adjustments for your department and its other employees. Flossie was a recently widowed 52-year old who had never learned to drive a car. Since this town has no public transportation, she will have issues getting to and from work. Furthermore, you do not have any gender-specific facilities, for example, a women's restroom, for female employees.

1. As a hiring manager what steps need to be taken?
2. What other issues may be brought to the forefront with this situation?
3. What are the costs involved in renovating a facility for both genders? Would there be any other potential costs involved with renovating a 50-year-old facility to comply with modern statutes?
4. What are the advantages of hiring a more diverse staff?

WHAT ACTUALLY HAPPENED IN CASE STUDY 2.1

Flossie was a widow who had spent much of her adult life as a homemaker and mother. Her highest level of education was a high school diploma. Her only work experience was as a clerk in the town's drug store prior to her marriage many years ago. This woman became the first female employee to work for the state highway department office in a town that, at the time, was located in a remote, rural area in Texas. Today the district where Flossie worked employs 630 maintenance and construction employees, has a population of more than two million (as of 2008), and covers an area of over 6,900 square miles.

When the state highway department hired Flossie, it constructed a female restroom to accommodate her. In addition, a highway department employee was selected to transport her to and from work every day. A woman in an all-male office in the 1970s was quickly exposed to juvenile male behavior. When Flossie was first hired, she became the butt of practical jokes by the construction crew (they once stretched plastic wrap over the toilet seat). While this behavior is clearly not acceptable in today's workplace, Flossie understood that she was breaking a new barrier for women in her community and accepted the jokes with good humor, affection, and a sharp wit. Flossie referred to the other employees as "her boys" and assumed a motherly role within the department, using her years of experience as a homemaker and mother to navigate the sometimes juvenile environment and win the respect of her coworkers. When Flossie retired, the highway department hired another female employee, thus establishing a trend in the previously all-male organization.

KEY ISSUES RAISED IN CASE STUDY 2.1

While equal employment opportunity is at the core of Case Study 2.1, this case study also brings up hostile work environment issues. Soon after the women's rights movement of the 1960s and 1970s, women were accepting jobs in predominately male environments and, in some cases, accepting jobs that had previously been occupied only by men. These women did not have adequate protection from hostile work environments or from sexual harassment as employees do today. Flossie had to find her own way to deal with the male-dominated environment at her workplace. There were age-related issues as well because Flossie was much older than many of her coworkers. Finally, there are issues regarding unusual workplace accommodations for employees, in Flossie's case employer-provided transportation.

WHAT COULD HAVE HAPPENED IN CASE STUDY 2.1

The hiring manager should be commended for hiring a woman at a time when that was not very common. The fact that the applicant was also much older indicated that the hiring manager saw her as someone possessing knowledge, skills, and abilities. The local state highway department made extraordinary accommodations for Flossie by arranging transportation and building restroom facilities for her. Male applicants would not have needed these accommodations.

The atmosphere of practical jokes perpetrated on the lone female employee is a different matter. Could the state highway department have done a better job of preventing the practical jokes? In today's workplace, these jokes would have been perceived as sexual harassment or the creation of a hostile work environment. In Flossie's case, she knew these people who were part of her small community and was familiar with the relaxed culture. She also understood that how she handled the office politics would determine not only her ability to interact successfully with her coworkers but also whether this department would consider hiring other women in the future based on their experiences with her. Today with the increased risk of litigation by employees, many organizations are highly motivated to prevent unprofessional behavior from occurring. Employers must balance the need for a professional environment free from bullying and discrimination with employees' desire for camaraderie and some level of informality with each other. Any activity that clearly interferes with the productivity of the office must be stopped.

CASE STUDY 2.2
Low Salary Levels for Minority and Women Executives in a City Located in the Southwestern United States

SITUATION FOR CASE STUDY 2.2

A city located in the southwestern part of the United States had done a remarkable job of hiring an executive workforce that was representative of the community that it served. The city's demographic profile was as follows: 37% white, 36% Hispanic, 25% black, 2% Asian and Pacific Islander, and 0.4% Native American. The 145 employees who comprised the executive workforce included the city manager, 5 assistant city managers, 35 directors, and 104 assistant directors or assistant chiefs. The table below provides the demographic profile of the executive workforce.

Executives—145				
White	Black	Hispanic	Asian/ Pacific Islander	Native American
60 (41%)	36 (25%)	45 (31%)	3 (2%)	1 (0.7%)
Male	Female			
76 (52%)	69 (48%)			

By making an effort to reflect the community's ethnic and gender makeup, the city hoped to instill confidence in its citizenry that the city respected the diversity and beliefs of the community.

Not only were gender and ethnicity data open to public scrutiny, but so were pay grades and salary information. Several of the minority and women executives conducted an analysis of the executive employee information to ascertain if the pay for all the executives was comparable and fair. Their initial analysis seemed to indicate that their pay was much lower than those of their white colleagues within the same pay grades. However, one of the executives pointed out that they needed more analysis on the information to confirm if minority and women executives were really being underpaid. It was determined that the resumes of all the executives had to be reviewed and their length of service with the city factored into the analysis before any solid conclusions could be made.

The analysis concluded that most of the minority and women executives were being underpaid. A small but vocal subgroup did not concur with the evaluation, pointing out that the pay for the police and fire executives distorted the data. The police and fire executives had longer tenure than the average city executive, and the fire executives had the longest tenure of any group of executives in the organization. However, even when police and fire executives were excluded, the information clearly showed that the salaries of the minority and women executives were below that of their white male counterparts. The minority and women executives took their findings to the human resources department and asked them to conduct a salary analysis to determine if minority and women executives were underpaid relative to their white executive colleagues even when factoring years of service and qualifications.

WHAT ACTUALLY HAPPENED IN CASE STUDY 2.2

The human resources department analyzed the years of service of all executives, the number of employees supervised, budgetary and departmental responsibilities, educational qualifications, and professional certifications such as CPA, PE, and ACIP. The analysis clearly showed that 79% of the minority and women executives regardless of rank were on average paid 15% less than their white male counterparts. The city manager, upon reviewing the empirical data, accepted the report but, given the sensitivity of the situation, requested that human resources hire a compensation firm to review all the data and the methodology used by human resources. In this way, the analysis could be validated by an independent organization. The decision to use a third party to validate the salary analysis displeased the minority and women executives, but the city manager was able to convince them of the need for a second opinion on the matter.

After an extensive review of the information, the outside compensation firm came to the same conclusion as the human resources department. The compensation firm pointed out that almost all the most recently hired executives who were predominately minority and women had been offered pay in the lower ranges of the executive pay grades. The city manager acknowledged the accuracy of the data and issued an executive order to correct the pay imbalance for minority and women executives over a three-year period until the pay inequalities were eliminated, thus providing equal treatment to all employees and averting a discrimination lawsuit. The city manager also directed human resources to establish new pay policies to police pay practices for all city employees to ensure that there would be no further pay inequalities. He also requested that the city auditor conduct a performance audit of human resources' new procedures and policies every three years to ensure compliance with the new pay system. The city manager informed the members of the city council individually of the findings and that the pay for the minority and women executives was going to be adjusted. The city council members approved the city manager's recommended course of action.

However, when the pay adjustments were made public, there was a negative reaction to the news by the city's workforce and the community. The executives who were not eligible for pay adjustments were also very displeased with the city manager's remedy. The negative response took the city council by surprise. The city council in turn no longer openly supported the pay adjustment solution, with a few council members claiming that they had not given the city manager approval for the pay adjustments.

KEY ISSUES RAISED IN CASE STUDY 2.2

This organization provided an equal opportunity hiring plan but forgot to include a plan to ensure that all city executives were compensated in a fair, consistent, and equitable manner. This case study also illustrates how human resources should have detected the pay inequity and addressed the issue promptly without the need for employees to point out the inequity with upper management. This situation also highlighted the importance of transparency when dealing with pay issues for public employees, especially with high-ranking public officials. The city manager should have presented his pay adjustment solution to the city council and to the public in an open forum to explain the necessity of the action and to assess the public's reaction to the plan.

WHAT COULD HAVE HAPPENED IN CASE STUDY 2.2

The city should have established internal controls through its human resources department to identify inequities in compensation. The city should have had a written salary policy in place for executives. Finally, human resources should have conducted regular salary audits to detect pay inequities. The only reason the city averted litigation was because the executives who were directly impacted by the salary inequities gave the city time to assess the situation and implement a speedy remedy.

CASE STUDY 2.3
The Case of the Inaccessible Job Training Office and Intake Center

SITUATION FOR CASE STUDY 2.3

An executive from the budget office was transferred to the Health and Human Services Department to assume the post of Human Services assistant director. The Human Services Division was in disarray because the last two assistant directors had been fired for lying on their resumes. The division was dogged by a long list of organizational shortcomings including the state of the division's job training office. The Job Training Office had recently failed a U.S. Department of Labor performance audit. The new assistant director had several operations that were in need of his attention, such as the Senior Affairs Office, the Martin Luther King Jr. Community Center, the Handicapped Services Office, the Childcare Assistance Office, the Homeless Program, and the Youth Services Office. However, the city manager and the assistant city manager over the Health and Human Services Department had informed the new assistant director that his primary focus should be the Job Training Office because the U.S. Department of Labor had informed the city that they would return soon to conduct a follow-up audit on the Job Training Office, and they expected to see substantial improvement in the operation of the city's federally funded Job Training Office and Program.

On the first day at his new position, the assistant director asked his staff where the Job Training Program, which had recently been moved from the southeast section of the city near the Martin Luther King Jr. Community Center, was now located. His staff informed him that the Job Training Office and Intake Center was on the south side of the central business district near the main bus routes to make it more accessible to all city residents. The new Job Training Office and Intake Center building had been recently selected by the Job Training Program manager. The assistant director drove to the job intake center and made an unannounced tour of the facility. He discovered that the new facility was not very customer friendly. The facility was not easily accessible for handicapped customers, citizens, and employees.

The assistant director requested the city's Handicapped Services manager, who was a friend and a direct report, to visit the city's job intake center and assess the facility to determine if it was in compliance with the Americans with Disabilities Act (ADA) requirements. The Handicapped Services manager, who was confined to a wheelchair due to injuries suffered in a car wreck when he was a child, would be the best person to test any access issues with the new facility and to certify that the Job Training Program was in compliance with all ADA requirements.

WHAT ACTUALLY HAPPENED IN CASE STUDY 2.3

The Handicapped Services manager visited the city's job training and intake office, which was just south of the central business district. When the manager arrived at the intake facility, he found that the facility did not meet any accessibility requirements of federal employment law. The manager was able to park his automobile in the site's parking lot but was unable to get onto the sidewalk that provided access to the front of the facility because there was no wheelchair-accessible ramp on the sidewalk. He was assisted by some job training applicants onto the sidewalk to get to the front door. When he got to the front door, he found that the door did not have an automatic access feature. Several of the job training center applicants had to open the doors and keep them open so that he could enter the facility in his wheelchair.

Once inside the office, he learned that administrative offices were on the first floor but the processing officers who determined eligibility of the job training applicants were located on the second floor. However, the building only had stairs and no elevator. In addition, the restroom facilities were not handicapped-accessible even though the restrooms had signs indicating that they were. The Handicapped Services manager submitted his written report to the Health and Human Services assistant director describing all the shortcomings of the intake office and how it was noncompliant with federal equal employment and ADA requirements.

The Health and Human Services assistant director used the report to secure funding to have the Public Works Department make the parking lot and sidewalks accessible to handicapped citizens, clients, and employees. The Building Services Department modified the facility's doors to make the intake center compliant with ADA facility requirements. The assistant director instructed the Job Training Program manager to move the applicant processing operation from the second floor to the first floor and to modify the restrooms to make them accessible. The Job Training Program manager was demoted for selecting an intake facility that was not compliant with equal employment and ADA requirements. The assistant city manager notified the Health and Human Services Department director that staff would not be eligible for a merit increase for the next 12 months because the job training intake office was noncompliant with ADA requirements.

KEY ISSUES RAISED IN CASE STUDY 2.3

Public organizations need to prioritize issues that affect the ability to serve all of its citizens, including individuals with disabilities. Access to all public facilities and programs needs to be at the top of any checklist when opening a new facility or renting a facility. Not only is it the right thing to do, but equal access is the law. This incident highlighted the need for training to instill a culture that values treating all citizens with dignity and fairness, even if that means sacrificing personal convenience (having one's office on the first floor) for basic handicap accessibility (locating services on the first floor).

WHAT COULD HAVE HAPPENED IN CASE STUDY 2.3

When the department requested the Property Management Department to find them a new centrally located intake office for their Job Training Program, the department should have realized the facility would need to be fully accessible to all job training applicants as required by federal law. It should have been made clear to the Property Management Department that any facility they secured and recommended to the Health and Human Services Department should be ADA compliant. In addition, the Property Management Department also needed to include a requirement for ADA compliance in its checklist of requirements for leasing facilities for the city. The Human Resources Department needed to ensure that requirements with city ordinances and state and federal laws are covered in all supervisory training so that the mistakes made by the job training manager and the property management supervisory personnel would not happen again.

Suggested Readings for Chapter 2

Burstein, Paul (Editor), 1994. *Equal Employment Opportunity: Labor market discrimination and public policy.* ISBN: 0-202-30475-2. New York: Aldine De Gruyter Hawthorne.

Burstein, Paul, 1998. *Discrimination, jobs, and politics: The struggle for Equal Employment Opportunity in the United States since the new deal.* ISBN: 0-226-08136-2. Chicago: The University of Chicago Press.

Miller, Frederic, Vandome, Agnes F., and McBrewster, John, 2010. *Equal opportunity employment.* ISBN: 6130880693. Mauritius VDM Publishing House Ltd.

Chapter 3

Recruiting Employees

Recruiting is a key component for the successful development of an organization's human capital. Public and nonprofit organizations traditionally only actively recruit for positions within upper administration or that are very specialized. Municipalities in particular tend to actively recruit police, fire, and civil/traffic engineer positions. School districts in some areas (e.g., Dallas Independent School Districts) expand recruitment activities nationally, and even internationally, for certain areas of study like Spanish, math, and science. Higher education institutions tend to recruit for positions that are administrative and professional as well as any faculty position that is tenured or tenure track.

Medical organizations recruit actively since medical positions require specialized personnel that are in high demand in the industry. Many medical organizations have recently recruited international applicants for certain positions, like registered nurses, that are difficult to fill domestically. For lower-level, classified staff positions, public and nonprofit organizations tend to use other recruitment methods that are not heavily dependent upon staff or resources unless economic times dictate otherwise. With good recruiting and hiring decisions, an organization can improve its organizational capability and overall retention. Ineffective recruiting can destabilize and demoralize an organization and make retention of good employees very difficult. In Chapter 3 the reader will see several different aspects that need to be taken into account when recruiting for public, nonprofit, or medical organizations.

Recruiting Obstacles for Public Organizations

Recruiting for a public, nonprofit, or medical organization can present a few obstacles. For example, if a public organization resides in a region that has several high-tech corporations that traditionally pay higher salaries than public organizations, recruiting personnel will be more difficult because the public organization may not be able to compete with private industry salary rates. However, in poor economic times when private industry is either laying off employees or not hiring, public organizations will be able to draw in more applicants with higher skill levels than usual.

Another aspect that can affect recruitment for public organizations is media coverage. When organizations face scandals or negative media coverage, some employees may leave the organization and potential applicants may no longer wish to apply. Although most organizations do not face negative publicity often, when problems do arise, they can be very damaging to the organization's reputation. For example, in 2003, it was determined that a hospital was responsible for accidentally giving a patient too many drugs, which resulted in the death of the patient (Dallas Morning News, 2009). In 2005, hired the hospital a new medical center director to direct the cancer center after the family successfully litigated against the hospital for malpractice. This incident directly led to the medical center's hiring of the new director since (Dallas Morning News, 2005). While there is no direct evidence to link the incident to Dr. Levinson's hiring or having a negative impact on recruitment, the incident generated negative press for the organization.

Public organizations can draw in new applicants when they receive positive media attention. For example, the U.S. military received an increase in recruiting after the movie *Top Gun* was released in 1986 (Campbell, 2001).

Taking an Inventory of Needs for the Organization

A hiring manager should always be aware of the needs of the organization in regard to skills or abilities before any recruiting is initiated. For example, if an organization needs budget analysts who have a minimum level of computer proficiency, then whoever is recruiting or advertising for that position should make this requirement known to potential applicants. The applicants save time by not applying for positions that they are not qualified for, and the employer saves time by not having to review applications that do not meet the minimum requirements for the open position.

That being stated, a manager should also be able to recognize that an applicant may be able to adapt to other job requirements and help the organization in ways that may not have been foreseen. An example of this would be an employer hiring an applicant who had very little computer programming experience in his or her background but was able to learn and develop into a good programmer due to other skills that the applicant possessed, like a demonstrated ability to think in a step-by-step fashion, an attentiveness to detail, and an eagerness to learn new skills. This allows the organization to obtain an employee who, with minimal training, can become the programmer the organization needs.

Taking Organizational Culture into Account

A key factor to keep in mind when recruiting is organizational culture and which applicants will best fit within that culture. Organizational culture arises from the mix of personalities and skill sets of the people who work for that organization. Many organizations have a mixture of both experienced and novice employees in their workforce. When recruiting for open positions, an organization should take into account not only what type of person will fit the job requirements for the organization, but also if the applicant's personality will synchronize with the existing core of employees. Take, for example, an organization with an open entry-level position; two applicants apply for the position, one a recent college graduate with no work experience and the other a recent retiree. Both applicants are willing to work for the same amount of money and both appear to be a good fit personality-wise with existing employees. Which applicant does the organization need to hire? Either hire will have advantages and disadvantages for the organization. The new graduate will require on-the-job training and initially take up more resources. The other applicant, having worked a particular way for many years, may or may not follow set procedures as well and may require oversight to ensure compliance. Furthermore, the older applicant might not work for the organization for very long before permanently retiring from the workforce. Then again, the college graduate might leave in a few years to take a job that offers more money. Does the organization have the resources and time to invest in training, or does it need an impact employee in a short amount of time? Will a candidate's experience be beneficial or a hindrance in a field that now uses different procedures or operates under new guidelines? Every organization will have a different perspective on the potential of fresh skills versus the known variable of experience.

Strategy for Recruiting

This leads to another question that should be reviewed when recruiting for an open position: should the organization recruit short-term employees or employees who want to make a career in the organization? Again, there are advantages and disadvantages to recruiting either type of employee. A short-term employee can bring valuable skills that can be applied immediately, provide instant efficiency gains, and give the organization the time and flexibility to find a better replacement after the short-term employee leaves. However, there is a risk that a short-term employee will require more training than anticipated and, once trained, will leave before the organization can realize a return on its training investment.

Where to recruit is another issue that needs to be considered. A manager should look at a wide array of recruiting avenues such as job fairs, new graduate career fairs at high schools and higher education institutions, online advertisements, and the traditional newspaper postings. Even if no positions are currently open, managers may want to attend career and job fairs to maintain their organization's visibility for when positions become available in the future. Using interns from high schools and higher education institutions is another good way for managers to assess knowledge, skills, and abilities of entry-level workers. By using interns, the manager does not have to commit to a permanent position for the individual who might not have the aptitude for the position, lacks key skills, or does not fit in with the culture of the organization. Furthermore, interns gain real-world experience working for the organization and add a valuable reference to their resume.

Public, nonprofit, or medical organizations need to evaluate how much they are willing to pay for specialized services. Due to high demand from the private sector and the cost of education and training for specialized personnel such as doctors, engineers, police officers, and so on, public organizations need to be prepared to pay somewhat close to market value for specialized personnel. Some public organizations will offer a certain percentage of standard private industry salaries for certain specialties in order to be competitive for available applicants; however, this approach may not be feasible politically. A city council may find it difficult to justify why the city's attorney makes more than the city manager. To avoid these conflicts, a public organization may need to outsource specialized services to a third party.

Advantages in Public Organizations Recruiting Applicants

Public, nonprofit, and medical organizations have several advantages over the private sector when recruiting top-quality applicants. One of the biggest advantages is the generous benefits that public organizations can offer. In a time when many companies are slashing medical benefits and retirement options, public organizations can offer reasonably priced group insurance packages that can more than compensate for the lower salaries typically offered by public organizations. Another huge benefit is that the mandatory workweek for most public organizations is usually set at 40 hours with legally mandated monetary compensation or time off for overtime. Many private organizations require employees to work well over 40 hours each week with no compensation for overtime. Public organizations are also much less likely to outsource or lay off employees. The main advantage that public organizations traditionally have over their private industry counterparts is stability.

When Managers Should Be Cautious

Organizations should be very cautious of hiring an employee who is seeking a higher salary than what is advertised for the position. In some cases an organization may want to consider the applicant's request if the skills and experience warrant the additional pay for the position. However, if the requested salary is out of step with the skills of the applicant or the skill level of the position, it would be in the organization's best interest to keep the job search open with the hope that the right applicant will meet both the skills and salary expectations of the organization. Sometimes it is preferable to keep a position vacant than to hire an overpriced employee who may not do enough work to justify his or her salary or may create conflict within the organization, particularly when that salary, becomes known to other employees who are performing similar work for lower pay.

A delicate subject to consider is whether an organization should target certain groups of applicants to increase diversity. Public and nonprofit organizations should always be aware of the Equal Employment Opportunity laws and conform to those guidelines. However, there are underutilized groups that have not been recruited actively that can benefit the organization with fresh skill sets and new ideas. If hiring directors want to see more gender or ethnic diversity in their departments, they can hire based on other attributes and still fulfill their diversity goals. Many colleges and universities maintain diverse populations of bright, hard-working young people. Student labor has been seen as a benefit for higher education institutions because students need employment to begin accruing work experience while they are working toward a degree.

Student workers are frequently paid much less than traditional employees, which can offset any training they require, and typically provide a good infusion of skills and knowledge to the organization. Another source of skilled, diverse employees is former military personnel. The armed forces have been seen as a gateway to a better life for impoverished and underserved populations and thus recruit a diverse group of citizens from across the country. Former military personnel also bring fresh skills as well as self-discipline and work ethic and are highly trainable.

Funding and Effort Level for Recruiting

An important consideration for recruiters is how much funding and effort public, nonprofit, and medical organizations should put forth to recruit applicants. For higher-skilled positions, public and nonprofit organizations will need to recruit heavily to ensure that the correct person for the position is hired. Often, public organizations use search firms and contract the recruiting process out for positions such as university presidents and city managers. The cost of recruiting applicants for higher-skilled positions will be greater than for entry-level positions that are frequently advertised on the web or in newspapers.

Recruiting internally for open positions is another option. Often public, nonprofit, and medical organizations have good personnel employed in other positions who could be recruited for an open position. If an organization places value on its employees and wants the employees to stay with the organization for the long term, then recruiting employees (and ultimately hiring them) for internal positions could be a good policy. The advantages of internal recruiting are having previous knowledge of the applicant's work history, work ethic, and skill levels and having an applicant with knowledge of the organization's inner workings. The disadvantage is that hiring internally can create discord and dissension if the recruiting and hiring process is driven by politics and self-interest. If the applicant who is being recruited lacks the knowledge, skills, or abilities that are required for the position, then that person (and the employers who made the hiring decision) might not be able to earn the respect of their peers, which can lead to organizational discord. The hiring manager must make every effort to be completely unbiased throughout the hiring process, particularly if more than one internal applicant applies for the position.

It is important to manage the recruiting process carefully. Good applicants will apply to many organizations and will most likely receive multiple offers. If the recruitment process is too arduous or if the organization waits too long to make a decision, the best applicants will be lost to other organizations. Managers should regularly monitor the recruitment progress and assess how long it takes for applications to be processed through their human resources office. Once the applications are submitted, the manager must be decisive and begin the selection process quickly (see Chapter 4).

Executive Recruiting

Recruiting for higher-level executives is a more complicated process than for the standard public service. This process is further complicated if the position is of great importance or has a high level of public exposure within the organization and in the community. Hiring a high-level position such as a university president or a police chief will involve more steps in the selection process than would hiring a facility manager or a city building services director, who would not have a high community profile.

When hiring a high-profile executive, it is advisable to involve the elected and appointed leadership of the organization, the public, employee groups, and community organizations. Media coverage of the selection process and requests for information on the process and the candidates will likely occur. In the public sector, there is usually very little that can be withheld from the public about the process and the identity of the candidate pool. Therefore, a media strategy is vital to the selection and placement process. It is advisable to hire an executive recruitment firm to assist in the identification of the best possible candidates, to ensure a thorough and transparent process, and to assist with all the due diligence requirements of high-level executive selection. Patience and persistence is required because executive positions with high public visibility and community importance could take months to fill.

Whether recruitment is conducted internally or through an executive search firm, typically the organization will develop a position description and an organization and community profile, which will be incorporated into the recruitment materials used in the selection process. High-level executive searches require active recruitment of top candidates to supplement the more passive procedures such as want ads and Internet job sites. Executive placements require substantial coordination to identify candidates, select top candidates to be interviewed, arrange the interviews, check references, and complete due diligence issues such as credit checks, education verification, and criminal background checks. In the executive selection process, it is critical to allow sufficient time for all interested parties to be involved so that the process cannot be questioned and so that everyone feels that they had a role in selecting the best candidate for the position.

Author's Experience

Nick was recruited from Nortel Networks by the executive director of the Office of Strategic Planning and Analysis at the University of Texas at Dallas. He was initially hired to create PowerPoint presentations and analytical charts. The executive director had known Nick when he was a student at the University of Texas at Dallas and was familiar with his work ethic and high-quality output, which was what the department needed when the executive director began recruiting employees. Because of Nick's ability to learn programming languages, the executive director was able to provide a person to perform critically needed job functions. Nick was soon performing work that was very different from what he was hired to perform. Because the executive director sought out job applicants on their ability to learn, adapt, and work in a fluid environment, the organization benefited highly from the executive director's approach to recruiting personnel for his department.

Final Notes

The recruiting process is extremely important to public, nonprofit, and medical organizations because it enables organizations to obtain skilled employees who can bring fresh skills and knowledge that can revitalize and improve the organization. Since budgets are usually tight for public and nonprofit organizations, those organizations should be careful to allocate funds judiciously to attract the best applicants for the least amount of cost and effort. Recruitment efforts need to emphasize the organization's strong points and refrain from promising opportunities, benefits, and pay that the organization cannot provide. By keeping in mind such issues as competitive pay, nonmonetary incentives, organizational culture and diversity, when to outsource, when to hire internally, and when to consider the political ramifications of a hiring decision, recruitment managers in public organizations can streamline the hiring process and improve their chances of getting the best personnel for the job.

Important Points to Remember

1. Recruiting can bring new talent to a public organization.
2. When recruiting, keep in mind not only current organizational needs but future challenges that the organization may face.
3. Point out the benefits of working for a public organization over private industry, particularly if the salary is noncompetitive with the private sector. Be sure to mention nonmonetary benefits like medical and dental coverage or guaranteed 40-hour workweeks, federal holidays, and competitive vacation time and sick leave.
4. The population that you are recruiting from may have hidden advantages. An example of this would be college students or recent graduates who lack experience but are trainable, are satisfied with lower pay, and will bring the latest knowledge and skills to the job.
5. When recruiting, make sure that the organization is well marketed so that potential applicants understand exactly what the organization does and the important role that the organization plays in the community.
6. If recruiting at a conference or job fair, send personnel that are energetic and outgoing and can sell the organization's strong points.
7. Remember to balance the need for data on the application process with the time and cost that it takes to complete the application process. If the application process is too confusing or time consuming, qualified applicants will not complete the process.
8. If you meet someone who is a strong potential candidate for an open position in your organization, provide the person with a business card and information on the open position.
9. Make sure that potential applicants understand the culture of the organization and that the culture is accurately represented by recruiters. For example, if employees wear suits and ties to work every day, do not allow recruiters to wear business casual attire.
10. If possible, make it easy for potential applicants to see what positions are open at the organization. This reduces time and effort for both the applicant and the organization.

CASE STUDY 3.1
Rebuilding an Organization

SITUATION FOR CASE STUDY 3.1

You are the director of the Economic Development Corporation (EDC) for Stallion, Texas, which is essentially a bedroom community of a major metropolitan city. The city has no historical buildings or landmarks and is fully built out. The population of your city in 1996 is about 40,000 people with an average household income of $90,000, and since the city has very little undeveloped land remaining, your only real choice is to redevelop areas that have been sitting vacant or have fallen into disrepair. The city's main points of entry are an abandoned railway line that cuts through the center of town and two interstate highways. Suburban cities flank three of Stallion's borders, and the fourth border is adjacent to a high-crime area that is a part of Stallion's large metropolitan neighbor. The city recently elected to apply a one-half-cent sales tax toward funding the EDC instead of the mass transit system expansion from the metropolitan city.

The EDC currently operates out of an old military installation that was abandoned and had become the property of the City of Stallion. In addition, the EDC coordinates and is housed with the Chamber of Commerce for the City of Stallion. Your economic development staff is very small: one person for the Visitor's Center, an administrative assistant, a Main Street manager, and an intern provided to you by the city manager.

Your Main Street manager has been highly involved with the Main Street Commission, which is charged with developing a strategic plan for Main Street for the City of Stallion. The project has experienced resistance from local business owners, who do not support the Main Street program because they fear that their properties will be negatively impacted. This project has the Main Street manager working to capacity, and she has limited resources and no help. The administrative assistant and Visitor's Center employee are working on other projects that are currently pressing issues as well. You have put the intern on the job of collecting information on vacant and lease property in the city so that you can form a strategy for attracting potential businesses, an assignment she has successfully completed ahead of schedule. In addition, your relationship with the Chamber of Commerce and with the Visitor's Center employee is strained at best.

1. What are you going to do about the increasing requirements on the EDC?
2. How are you going to contend with a municipality that appears to be very limited in resources?
3. How are you going to utilize your intern?
4. How are you going to deal with your relationship with the Chamber of Commerce and your employee at the Visitor's Center?

After finishing her previous task, your intern is completing her schoolwork in her cubicle because you have not assigned her to work on another project. Your Main Street manager commandeers the intern to calculate depreciation values on property and perform survey work. You are under pressure from the city manager and the city council to create jobs in the City of Stallion because you have created very few since you were hired six months ago. In addition, the city manager who hired you is about to resign under pressure from the city council.

1. How do you feel about the Main Street manager utilizing the intern?
2. Do you need to think about expanding your departmental staff to handle the increases in tasks that need to be completed?

The city council has just forced their city manager to resign and promoted the assistant city manager to city manager. There are now increased expectations on you from the new city manager and the city council to successfully bring in new industry to Stallion. However, you are faced with several problems, not the least of which is that your Main Street manager has resigned and very soon you will be without your intern since she is graduating at the end of the month. This leaves you with only an administrative assistant and one person over the Visitor's Center. The Chamber of Commerce feels that you have underutilized some of the personnel that worked for the EDC, in particular, the intern.

1. What is your next step as director?
2. What is your strategy for bringing in more personnel?
3. What human resource issues will you face during this time of rebuilding?
4. Since you have to work with the Chamber of Commerce, do you want to involve them in the rebuilding process of your organization?

You realize that you have not effectively utilized your existing employees. The intern was willing to work full-time for the EDC, but you were not interested in extending an offer of employment to her. The intern has since earned a master's degree and now works in a good public sector position elsewhere. Personnel issues have not improved in the three months that followed the resignation of the city manager. When the Main Street manager accepted a higher paying job at another city, Main Street efforts ground to a halt. The City of Stallion still lacks an identity and is known primarily as a residential community with very little revenue coming in from businesses. In essence, you have not improved the situation that will attract jobs or companies to the area.

As the EDC director, you are advertising the vacant Main Street manager position. This person must be able to interface with local business leaders and community leaders on Main Street. Additionally, the Main Street manager must be able to present a professional appearance at public functions and implement recommendations set forth by the Main Street Commission.

1. What kind of person do you want to hire for the position?
2. Which recruitment issues should you be aware of when going through the hiring process?
3. How long should you advertise the position, and how many people should be interviewed?

WHAT ACTUALLY HAPPENED IN CASE STUDY 3.1

Case Study 3.1 illustrates the problems that occur when personnel are not managed well and no plan is implemented to retain existing personnel or recruit new personnel for the organization. From the given situation it is obvious that internal methods for recruiting and retention were not followed by the director, which left only the external methods. In 1996, the Internet was just beginning to be used to advertise job postings, so this particular method was not an option at the time. That left only print advertising for external recruiting. As stated by Carol T. Kulik:

> For the cost of a stamp, any Tom, Dick, or Sally can submit a resume in response to your ad. As a result, unless you have written a very specific, very focused ad, you may find that your help-wanted ad elicits applications from individuals who are poorly qualified for the position. In other words, help-wanted ads can be a very inefficient recruiting method. (Kulik, 2004, p. 31)

Mismanagement and lack of recruitment are at the heart of the problem for this case study. The EDC director should have advertised the position widely using both internal and external recruiting methods. The recruitment for such a position was not aggressively pursued and therefore the number of qualified applicants applying for the position was minimal. As Kulik states:

> Your current recruiting strategies may not be attracting the attention of these nontraditional applicants. In some cases, the new strategy may simply be variations on your existing strategy. You may want to supplement your newspaper advertisements with ads in publications directed toward more specialized audiences (e.g., *Working Woman, The Advocate, Hispanic Times*). (Kulik, 2004, p. 42)

No efforts were made by the economic development director to expand the applicant pool by advertising to nontraditional applicants. In addition the director did not take much initiative in attempting to fill the position, despite the fact that an intern could have performed the job and was available to do so. The lack of action steps taken by the director therefore limited the number of qualified applicants that applied for the position and ultimately left the organization depleted of talent.

The Main Street manager was the driving force behind the economic development in the historical areas. Once the Main Street manager resigned to take a position at another municipality, the position sat vacant for while. Soon the EDC director left the municipality. The Main Street manager became the director of a nonprofit group that performed charity work for an entire region of the state. The economic development director worked from city to city before eventually leaving the state.

KEY ISSUES RAISED IN CASE STUDY 3.1

There are three main issues raised in this case study: employee management, retention, and recruitment. Why the Main Street manager and intern were allowed to leave without some attempt to retain them through promotions or other incentives could be attributed to several factors. The EDC director might have placed little importance in the Main Street program or felt her own position and credibility with the city manager or city council were threatened by the program. Another reason the Main Street manager was not retained might have been because there was no additional money to offer for a pay raise. Promoting the intern to the Main Street manager position was not considered by the economic development director even though the intern was capable of performing the job. Some managers are intimidated by employees who have advanced education. Instead of attempting to find the best employee for the organization, sometimes managers attempt to find employees who will not outperform them and will not question their decision-making process. Unfortunately, these insecurities can deplete an organization of talent and cause applicants to work elsewhere. Case Study 3.2 will demonstrate the positive outcomes of good recruitment tactics under difficult circumstances.

WHAT COULD HAVE HAPPENED IN CASE STUDY 3.1

The economic development director could have retained the intern by utilizing her on more projects. This intern had proven herself a valuable worker and was willing to work for lower pay than someone with greater experience. The intern might have had fresh ideas for bringing new business to the city, including businesses that might appeal to people her own age. If the intern had been offered the position vacated by the Main Street manager, continuity and momentum could have been preserved in the Main Street program. This point leads to another regarding the Main Street manager: no incentives were provided to retain the Main Street manager. However, if the economic development director could not provide a pay increase or some other incentive, then plans to find a replacement that could fill the Main Street manager position for the existing pay scale should have been made.

CASE STUDY 3.2
Starting from Scratch

SITUATION FOR CASE STUDY 3.2

You have just been hired as a director of a reporting department for a state agency. The state agency you work for employs approximately 2,000 employees, and the department that you have been hired to oversee is very small but important to the organization. You have been with the state organization for more than 20 years, but this new position is a completely different experience for you. When you inherit the department, you find out that the former director was fired for reasons no one is willing to reveal, and two of the department's employees resigned two months after you were hired as the new supervisor. The department experiences a high turnover rate due to burnout and lack of leadership by the previous three directors.

The department is currently in shambles, and a variety of business operations that the department was doing have now ceased. Several of the resources you need are in complete disarray. For example, one of the former computer programmers wrote his documentation in Mandarin (which no one else in the organization can read). Most of the programs written for the organization's mainframe computer, which are needed for reporting and analysis, are completely inoperable. The programs that do exist have multiple copies, and you are not sure which copies are the most current or comply with state and federal mandates. In addition, no one is sure how much of the old data is accurate. The location of some of the data is unknown to the agency, much less known to you or your department. The state auditors are on their way, and you are now the only one in the department.

1. What is your first action?
2. What kind of personnel do you need to recruit?
3. What is your recruiting and strategic hiring plan?

You decide that you need help immediately simply to get control of the situation. The first two people you hire are graduate students, Greg and Paul, from a nearby research university. The first interview with Greg was conducted informally in his laboratory. Paul (who you have known in the past) needed a job to support him through college and was willing to do the necessary tasks required by the director. One of the students has a wide variety of technical skills and can automate key reporting functions, while the other student can obtain data, document procedures, and restart reporting processes. You choose to proceed with electronic reporting and automation, even though the state agency is accustomed to paper reports and is resistant to converting to electronic methods for reporting and accessing data.

You also interviewed and hired Steve, who was previously employed in the private sector. You have known Steve for a long time and you are familiar with his work ethic and training. You were going to have Steve perform a specific job responsibility. However, upon further evaluation, you decided Steve has the ability to learn computer programming on the job and would be able to produce reports and provide information for the state auditors. You feel a bit overwhelmed, but slowly and surely things are beginning to look much brighter than when you first took the job.

WHAT ACTUALLY HAPPENED IN CASE STUDY 3.2

The director hired people from private companies, graduate students he knew, and part-time workers to get the office into some type of order as quickly as possible. In some cases the director hired personnel that, on paper, were not the best fit for departmental operations. They lacked experience and key skill sets and did not come from fields that typically engaged in the kind of work this department did. However, the personnel were loyal, reliable, and hard working. Two of the employees had advanced technological skills and could adapt to new requirements. The director's approach did allow the department to reestablish itself, make progress on setting new operational standards, and automate certain functions. During the first six months, the director had a number of challenges, including migration to a new information system and a state audit, but those challenges were met successfully.

KEY ISSUES RAISED IN CASE STUDY 3.2

This case study contends with the issues of recruitment, interviewing, hiring, and leadership in a nonfunctioning department. When an incoming director is new to the situation, the director must assess personnel, functionality of the department, and resources. In this particular situation the director needed to understand quickly the functionality of the department before the proper personnel could be hired. As a stop-gap measure, the director hired graduate students and other people that he knew could be trusted and would take orders without question. At the time the director was recruiting (1997), the job market was weak and it was difficult for new college graduates to find employment. The director took advantage of this situation and hired several new graduate students over the next three years. His decision to hire skilled but inexperienced workers benefited the department in the long run; those students provided high-quality work and unique solutions that reestablished the department's functionality within a few months.

Retaining those employees became difficult when the job market became more attractive, and the employees were able to find better paying, private industry positions. Out of the original hires, only one of those students is still employed with the organization and has been promoted at least three times since initially hired. The other two employees took other positions, one with a large private corporation and the other with the federal government.

The director exemplifies several different strategies. The first strategy was to use an underutilized workforce that consisted of new graduates. The second was to take advantage of the strengths of that workforce by using their advanced skills to streamline the organization's business processes and to automate certain functions. Using graduate students enabled the director to obtain new skills at lower pay than what someone established in their professional career would accept. The director provided the graduate students with a chance to complete their studies toward an advanced degree while earning job experience, thus providing an incentive that compensated for the low pay.

WHAT COULD HAVE HAPPENED IN CASE STUDY 3.2

This case study illustrates the difficulties that a manager faces when attempting to rebuild a department. The director did a commendable job under very difficult circumstances to rebuild the department and get operations underway quickly.

CASE STUDY 3.3
Hiring with Noncompetitive Pay

SITUATION FOR CASE STUDY 3.3

The budget director of a large city in the southwest was having difficulty recruiting new budget analysts because the pay scale was not competitive. The annual turnover for budget analysts had averaged 33% over the past decade. The budget director documented the turnover rate in a detailed impact report that included where budget analysts went after leaving the Budget Office, which was typically to the surrounding suburbs. The only way that the budget director was able to retain experienced budget analysts was to promote them to supervisory positions. The Budget Office had the following budget analyst and budget supervisor career ladder:

- Budget Manager
- Budget Analyst III
- Budget Analyst II
- Budget Analyst I

The Budget Office had six budget groups: three operating budget groups, one grant budgeting group, and two capital budget groups. There were 6 budget managers and 18 budget analysts in total in the Budget Office. The city Budget Office required all its analysts hold at least a master's degree. The surrounding suburbs usually had one or two budget analyst positions, but their pay scales were 20% to 30% higher than the entry-level budget analyst position in the large southwest city. The suburbs found it beneficial to allow the large city Budget Office to hire and train the entry-level analysts and then hire the analysts away once they had gained sufficient on-the-job experience.

The budget director grew tired of constantly recruiting and training new budget analysts. In addition, the 33% annual turnover rate was starting to create continuity issues within the city's budget process. There was a significant burnout issue with the analysts because the workload was heavy and there was constant pressure to reduce costs and streamline city business processes while maintaining current service levels. The budget director took his impact report directly to the human resources director to ask for higher pay scales for all his budget analyst and budget manager classifications.

The human resources director conducted a pay and classification study of the budget analyst and budget manager positions. Human resources determined that the budget analysts and budget manager positions were underpaid compared with similar positions in the surrounding metropolitan area. However, while there was evidence of employee burnout and high turnover, there was insufficient evidence to suggest that the attrition was causing any substantial negative impact in the Budget Office. Furthermore, human resources determined that the Budget Office was filling all its openings rather quickly in spite of the lower pay for the entry-level budget positions. The fact that all the budget analyst selections met the job requirements, which included holding a master's degree, indicated that these requirements were not deterring qualified candidates.

The human services department recommended against upgrades to the budget analyst and budget manager positions and rejected adjustment to the pay ranges for these positions to better compete with their suburban competitors. While they did validate the high turnover rate in the Budget Office, they believed that if the pay for the Budget Office personnel were adjusted, then the city's entire pay plan would need to be adjusted. The ramifications of such an action would require the concurrence of the city's top management team, and the elected officials would need to sign off on the policy decision to pay more than the market average in the metropolitan area.

WHAT ACTUALLY HAPPENED IN CASE STUDY 3.3

The budget director appealed the human resources department's pay and classification study to the city manager's office. After reviewing all the data from the study, the city manager's office upheld the findings of the study. The city manager's office determined that the turnover rate had a beneficial by-product in that the inexperienced budget analysts brought new perspectives to their assignments. They also believed that promotions retained the best and most experienced budget analysts. They considered the loss of entry-level budget analysts to surrounding suburbs was manageable and an acceptable cost of doing business in a competitive metropolitan labor market. The high turnover rate allowed for the quick promotion of the most promising budget staff in order to keep the quality and expertise that management was attempting to achieve.

KEY ISSUES RAISED IN CASE STUDY 3.3

The key issue in this study is the toll that high turnover takes on a department. High turnover affected the continuity of work processes within the department and depleted the time and funds allotted for training. However, the budget director needed to have a wider organizational view when it came to this personnel issue. The budget director offered only one solution—increase the pay scale—and did not research other solutions nor ask for feedback from his superior and the human resources staff to determine the organization's attitude and strategy about the salary scales and career ladders for the Budget Office positions. By asking the human resources department to conduct a pay and classification study, he bypassed his supervisor and challenged the organization's compensation strategy, thus costing him political leverage.

WHAT COULD HAVE HAPPENED IN CASE STUDY 3.3

Budget directors are high enough in the organizational structure to be expected to have a global perspective on the needs and demands of their organization. This budget director should have discussed his turnover issues with his supervisor before making a formal request to human resources for the pay and classification study for his budget analysts. By asking human resources to conduct a pay and classification study, he caused a paper trail of publicly accessible documents that could have caused personnel issues in other departments. Fortunately, there were few repercussions from the study. This episode taught the young executive to better assess the needs of the organization and his supervisors and that his primary mission was to solve problems, not create new ones. It turned out to be a great learning experience for the budget director, and he later went on to be a city manager in several communities.

Suggested Readings for Chapter 3

Authur, Diane, 2005. *Recruiting, interviewing, selecting and orienting new employees*. ISBN: 978-0814408612. AMACOM. New York, New York.

Dubinsky, Alan J., and Skinner, Steven J., 2003. *High-performers: Recruiting and retaining top employees*. ISBN: 978-0324200966. South-Western Educational Publisher, Florence, Kentucky.

Johnson, Gail, 1991. *Recruiting, retaining and motivating the federal workforce*. ISBN: 978-0899305622. Quorum Books, Westport, Connecticut.

Chapter 4

Selection of Employees

Selection is the process of hiring personnel into the organization. This process applies to permanent employees and to independent contractors. The selection process for any public organization must be legally defensible and cost effective, and any tests that are used in the selection process must pass a certain criteria of validity to ensure that the selection process will be viable for an organization (Kulik, 2004). Employee selection within a government agency is a multistep process that begins with identification of a need within an organization, includes the recruitment and interview process, and continues after the candidate has been hired. Although much of the process is similar to employee selection in private enterprise, two distinct processes are used to hire *civil-service* and *non-civil-service* governmental employees.

In the 19th century, civil-service hiring had developed a reputation for nepotism. Reforming the hiring process took on great importance in 1883 after U.S. President James Garfield was assassinated by Charles Julius Guiteau, a disgruntled lawyer who felt he should have been awarded a position in Garfield's administration because of a speech he wrote supporting Garfield's candidacy. As a result of the assassination, the Pendleton Act was passed in 1893, which established the U.S. Civil Service Commission (Ingraham, 1995). This organization created a classification for government jobs and a merit-based employment system to avoid appointments made through political connections. Since that time, all levels of government, including city, county, and state, have some form of civil-service hiring and selection programs. Jobs in these systems can rank from maintenance worker to senior manager. The hiring process for civil-service positions strictly defines how the organization can legally hire, discipline, and terminate employees. One example with potential litigation issues is the use of physical agility tests for police and firefighter candidates. The hiring process must determine not only which candidates are the most qualified for the position but also which would be the best fit with the department's personnel.

Non-civil-service positions include senior and executive management positions that serve at will. Although qualifications for the positions are essential, they are not the only determining factors in selection for these positions. Many of the original political patronage positions were non-civil-service positions. As a result of past nepotism, non-civil-service jobs have become subject to greater scrutiny, greater transparency of the hiring process, and more competitive hiring. Within the federal government, the president directly appoints cabinet and many senior-level agency officials, and these posts are then ratified by Congress. Gubernatorial appointments at the state level follow similar procedures. In local government, however, the process is influenced by the type and form of government. In a strong mayoral form of government, senior-level appointments tend to have greater political influence, although many city charters require a confirmation process by governing bodies like councils or commissions. In a council/manager form of government, the appointment process is directed by the city manager and his or her designates, and may also require some form of confirmation.

The Hiring Process

The hiring process for both civil- and non-civil-service positions includes the following key steps: needs assessment, recruitment, vacancy announcement, prescreening, obtaining applications and resumes, interviewing, validation of qualifications, and extension of job offer. Legally, civil-service positions at the federal, state, and local levels are required to be posted as open positions for a certain length of time as well as advertised in two or more sources. Depending on the organization, positions can also be posted for internal applicants only.

Needs Assessment

The hiring process is triggered by a vacancy or by a perceived need for a new position due to departmental expansion or alteration of departmental priorities. If a vacancy has occurred, it is prudent to determine if the position remains necessary to the organization and if funding is still available to support the position. Civil-service positions may require an assessment of position description, classification, title codes, and salary review. It is important to maintain documentation on the needs assessment stage as it might be required by the organization's fiscal and human resources departments. Prior approvals for recruitment will be necessary for civil-service positions, although this step is less likely with executive and senior management positions.

Recruitment

The recruitment mechanism is determined by whether the vacancy is a civil-service or non-civil-service position. For non-civil-service positions, the hiring manager will need to determine if recruitment will be conducted through an internal process managed by departmental staff or with an external recruitment firm. It may be necessary to use an external recruitment firm to demonstrate that the selection process is open and transparent.

In the case of executive and other non-civil-service positions, an organizational assessment is generally conducted as part of the recruitment process. The recruiting official will work with the hiring official to review the community profile, pay plans, dominant issues, and position background. This assessment is used to develop recruitment brochures by identifying organization characteristics as well as key competencies, traits, and qualifications desired in a candidate. Due to the high-level nature of these positions, the assessment is often extended to both internal and external stakeholders. It is often critical to obtain the input of elected officials, appointed officials, employee associations, community groups, and citizens during this process. A salary survey is generally conducted to look at market and organizational trends to identify a target point for the salary being offered. The appointed position will typically have some salary flexibility; however, legislative approval may be required to make changes to the overall salary range.

Within the civil-service structure, individuals are generally prequalified through an established method that creates pools of qualified candidates for vacant positions. The prequalification process begins when the organization opens a position and accepts applications for the position. Various examinations, such as written tests, questionnaires, oral interviews, training and experience evaluations, and performance tests, are conducted. At the end of each testing process, a list of eligible candidates is created and provided to the departments for their selection.

Vacancy Announcement

The organization might already have a standard template for vacancy announcements; however, for higher-level positions, a special announcement might be necessary. Executive and non-civil-service announcements often resemble recruitment brochures and will include information such as community profile, job duties, dominant issues, salary, and benefits to generate greater interest in the position. It may also be beneficial to include a timeline of the recruitment process with legal requirements, the nature of the position, job competencies, and the period of time the vacancy will remain open. A position such as a health director with a medical degree requirement would normally take a great deal more time to fill than an administrative assistant position. For positions that are difficult to fill, the organization may elect to leave the closing date open to allow for a continuous flow of candidates until the position is filled.

Advertisement for non-civil-service vacancies generally goes beyond the organization's human resources web site to other media outlets such as trade magazines, external online recruitment sites, and other relevant publications. Advertising civil-service vacancies may become necessary if the hiring official cannot find a good candidate from the prequalified list.

Throughout the recruitment process, it is important to be open and honest about compensation for the position. If the candidate asks for a particular caveat, then the employer needs to provide a clear and immediate answer if the caveat is feasible. For most positions in public organizations, salary is a matter of public record. Hence, when advertising an open position, the announcement should include the salary or salary range or state that the salary is negotiable depending on qualifications. Additional incentives such as moving costs, accrual of vacation time, cell phone allowance, car allowance, temporary housing, scouting for permanent housing in the community, travel and training, memberships in organizations, and tenure appointment can also be mentioned and negotiated. If you do not clearly define the compensation for the position, you may receive applications from candidates who are currently compensated more than you can offer. Internal candidates who may be well compensated at their current jobs will need to know what their starting salary would be in the new position prior to applying for the job. If you have a stated pay plan that limits your ability to meet the demands of your top candidates, it is critical that you be forthcoming with such information early in the process. It is not necessary for the interviewer to divulge the salary of the current employee in the position or of the former employees that occupied the position. All pay issues must be finalized before selecting a candidate. Any compensation or additional benefits agreed upon during negotiation must be included in a written job offer.

Revealing the pay scale for a position will not necessarily dampen interest in the position because salary is only one factor that motivates people to apply for a job. Candidates may want to change careers, organizations, or be near family members or may be seeking a different climate or have various other personal reasons. Making candidate aware of the organization's pay plan, can minimize issues regarding pay scale parity, salary compression, or other pay distortions, while transparency about the position's compensation will restrict the candidate pool to those genuinely interested in the position.

Prescreening

The prescreening process may vary greatly by organization and recruitment method. It is important to establish clear and consistent guidelines for screening candidates that can include candidate ranking criteria and the development of any supplemental requests. For internal recruitment, applications may be reviewed only at the end of the recruitment period. However, senior and executive recruitment applications are usually screened upon receipt to determine if they meet the minimum qualifications set by the hiring official. Screening applications upon receipt allows both the organization and the recruiter to gauge the quality and quantity of responses to the advertisement throughout the recruitment process.

Typically, the organization will use a structured point system to evaluate applicants on educational attainment, experience, training, and additional certifications. The points then allow the officials to rank the applicants objectively based on their qualifications for the position. Individuals who meet the minimum qualifications may be asked to provide supplemental information via a questionnaire or a personality assessment. These supplemental evaluations can be used as the final criteria for determining which candidates to recommend to the hiring officials.

While candidates in the civil-service process have been prequalified and ranked, it may be necessary to customize the requirements for a particular position. Some positions may require foreign language proficiency, certifications such as certified public accountant or professional engineer, or statistical skills. If additional criteria or terms of measurement are utilized, they must be defined early in the process and applied consistently with all candidates.

Once the list of applicants is validated and ranked, the civil-service agency or the human resources agency transmits a list of qualified candidates to the hiring agency. With civil-service positions such as secretary, administrative assistant, police, or firefighter, priority is given to candidates on the prequalified list provided by the civil-service agency. Only after exhausting an existing list can a hiring official ask for a new or supplementary list of candidates. With civil-service positions, if the entire list of candidates is not used, then the hiring agency must document how the list was pared down.

Obtaining Applications and Resumes

Although specialized tests—for example, the federal civil-service exam—are used by certain organizations to select employees, the majority of public organizations rely heavily upon more familiar tools such as interviews, resumes, and applications. These time-tested methods are useful in triangulating an applicant's true personality, skill set, and experience. *Triangulation* is defined as using more than one data source to obtain accuracy on a research subject, and it is a concept that is applicable to the hiring process (Webb, Campbell, Schwartz, and Sechrest, 2000). With each new piece of information—a resume or curriculum vitae, an application, a test, an interview—a more complete image of the applicant begins to emerge.

Resumes and applications can be used in conjunction with interviews to verify knowledge, skills, experience, and abilities. Most public organizations at the minimum require an application. Although the information an application requires is similar to what is normally recorded in a resume, an application has the benefit of being standardized. This level of consistency makes an application an excellent form of official documentation about the hiring process. An application also provides the organization with a record that can be used for termination purposes if it is revealed that the applicant was hired under false credentials. Resumes allow the applicant to supplement basic job experience and education data with any other skills and traits the applicant might find useful. A resume is often accompanied by a cover letter and list of references.

Some public organizations use their human resources department to help them screen applicants for established criteria in resumes, applications, or curricula vitae. For example, if the position calls for an applicant to have a minimum of five years of experience, then human resources will automatically cull any applicant that does not meet the minimum threshold. The advantage to relying upon human resources personnel to sort applications is that they are familiar with job classifications and the knowledge, skills, and abilities (KSAs) required for the position and can save the hiring department time by removing unqualified applicants. The disadvantage to this process is that the hiring department may never see candidates who may have other strengths that, with training, can still make the applicant eligible for the position.

Interviewing

Transparency and accountability has opened the interview process up to public scrutiny, particularly in a climate of stiff competition for public service jobs and the suspicion of political motive and nepotism that still exists. In this environment, it is critical that the candidates experience a consistent evaluation process to ensure fairness, obtain a uniform base of information for evaluation, and prevent any possible legal challenges to the final selection.

Interviews can be scheduled either by the hiring official or, in the case of executive-level positions, by the external recruiting authority if one was used. In most cases the selecting official works with the recruiter to schedule and conduct interviews with the candidates. All the tests and questions used for the interviews need to be complete, pertain only to the duties and responsibilities of the job in question, be prepared in writing in advance, and if possible, be reviewed by a legal or ethics expert to avoid legal exposure from Equal Employment Opportunity protections. All participants in the process should receive copies of the tests, questions, and other interview exercises such as tours, in-box processes, and role play prior to beginning the process.

It is important to determine if one person will conduct the interview or if a panel or panels will be employed. The advantage of one-to-one interviews is that the applicant may be more relaxed interviewing in front of one person rather than a succession of employees or a panel of employees and may give more detailed answers to questions that are posed. However, on one-to-one interviews the hiring manager may not be consistent from applicant to applicant or may not ask questions that other employees would like the applicant to answer in order to evaluate the candidate's KSAs.

Panel interviews can assist an organization in obtaining greater insight via multiple perspectives into the candidate. The composition of the panel further supplements the process as it helps to validate the objectivity of the selection process. This can be achieved by either a single panel representing several aspects of your organization or by several panels representing different segments of your community. It is also desirable that the panel or panels be comprised of individuals with diverse ages, ethnic backgrounds, and culture and have a good mix of men and women so that each member of the panel can better detect the various traits and qualities that a candidate might possess. Greater diversity can also be achieved by bringing in people from outside the organization. Furthermore, diverse and balanced panels will demonstrate to the employees, the community, and the applicants that the process is equitable, open, and consistent, thus creating a more defensible hiring methodology. This becomes very important if the position in question requires a great deal of contact with the community or if the position is high profile. Do be aware that in some organizations the rank or position of a panelist within the organization can be a sensitive subject. It is possible that observers might question the qualifications of the individual to evaluate the candidate. However, the advantages of a "360-degree review" of a candidate can outweigh the perceived negatives.

In preparation for the interview process, the panel should be briefed on the manner in which applicants are going to be scored and what instruments will be used in the selection process. If more than one individual performs the interview, each interviewer's paper and materials must be clearly identified and recorded. Prior to the interview, a documented, preapproved scoring matrix should be distributed to all individuals involved in the interview process. A consensus should be reached as to how the merits of each candidate will be assessed and if any other elements will be used to evaluate the candidates. Sufficient time should be allocated during the process for all the interview questions and the other evaluation instruments to be completed. Enough time should be reserved to allow all candidates to ask questions and to make a closing statement about their qualifications and what makes them the best candidate for the position. No scores or ranks can be altered after the interview process is concluded and no interview instruments, notes, or forms can be destroyed. These documents are the basis for the final hiring decision and are subject to all future open records requests. In most states, almost all the information regarding the selection of employees, with the exception of Social Security numbers, is subject to Freedom of Information Act requests. The list of applicants, the interview list, resumes, applications, and other relevant data must be made available to media and the public upon request.

Questions asked during the interview and application process must pertain to the position. For example, a hiring manager may ask an applicant for an architect position if he has passed a professional certification exam. Another valid tactic is to provide software code to an applicant to decipher for a position that requires programming skill and the applicant lists that skill on her resume. Other common questions can include the following:

- How does the applicant work in a team environment?
- What is the applicant's greatest strength or greatest weakness?
- What professional certifications does the applicant have?

It is also important to ask questions that can be legally defended and not be of a questionable or personal nature. Some common questions that are illegal for a public organization to ask include the following:

- What does your spouse do for a living?
- How many children do you have?
- Where do you go to church?

There are some questions that can be personal and would be job related. The following questions, for example, can be asked of law enforcement candidates:

- Have you ever been convicted of domestic violence?
- Have you ever used marijuana?

Most of these types of questions relate to positions that involve public safety.

Following the completion of the interviewing process, the selection certificate should be returned to human resources for review and validation. Included with the selection certificate should be all documentation used during the interview process, including evaluation sheets and ranking documentation.

Validation of Qualifications

Reference and background checks are usually conducted either by a human resources employee or by an outside designee that confirms the candidates' references. Applicants are then notified of their status in regard to the position that is open. It is best to request from each applicant a wide range of references to include superiors, peers, employees, colleagues, and appointed and elected officials.

For critical positions, make sure that the person applying for the position has a long-term commitment to the organization and will not use the position as a "stepping stone" to something else. Job searches usually expend a great deal of time, money, and effort, and it would be a waste to conduct a search only to conduct the same search again a year later. The more critical the position, the longer it may normally take to learn the position and integrate with colleagues, the organization, and the community—yet another good reason to focus on candidates who have a serious commitment to the organization.

To avoid public embarrassment and to ensure that a public organization is not wasting money, conduct a background check prior to offering the position. This is to verify that the candidate meets all the requirements of the position and that there is nothing in the candidate's background that would disqualify the individual for the position or place the organization in a poor light. Semifinalists and finalist must be asked if any complaints have been filed against them by former employers or employees, if they have been sued in the discharge of their duties, or if they have sued any of their current or former employers. Questions asked during the interview can be validated using background tools such as Lexis-Nexis or Google. These services can provide great insight into the candidate and reveal any information that would be embarrassing or negative. All candidates should be asked to provide in writing a waiver to permit the conducting of a background check. Appropriate ways to conduct a background check include a reference check, criminal background check, driving record check, and financial credit check. Although getting a speeding ticket or having poor credit might not disqualify a candidate for some positions, for other positions, particularly those involving financial transactions (internal auditor, procurement manager) or public safety (police officer), these issues can disqualify the applicant from being hired. As long as transparency and consistency are maintained, these measures can potentially reveal more of the applicant's personality and style that may be helpful in the decision-making process and enable the organization to avoid potentially embarrassing or litigious issues.

Extension of Job Offer

Upon completion of all steps, it is the responsibility of human resources to extend a job offer to the selected candidate. Although a telephone call is sufficient for this task, official notification of the offer should be made in writing. In most public organizations, salary negotiations can only be done via the human resources office, although the hiring department may be consulted. A job offer can be contingent upon drug and alcohol tests or additional background checks. Depending on the tests or checks required, this step will take a variable amount of time. Once the candidate has passed all tests and checks, a firm job offer can be made and a start date arranged. After the candidate has signed an acceptance of the offer, all other interviewed candidates should be notified that the position has been filled.

Make sure that the offer given is for the same position for which the candidate interviewed originally. If it seems that the candidate would be a better fit in a different position, inform that person of the position and allow them to apply for it. It is important that the candidate follow the application process to ensure fairness and consistency in the hiring methodology.

Author's Experience

In 1994, Dr. Valcik underwent a physical agility test for a position with a small public safety department. The applicants were expected to perform the job responsibilities of a firefighter, police officer, and emergency medical technician and would have to train for three different professional certifications. The city was extremely small, covering three square miles, with approximately 8,000 residents. The physical agility test (in this case, the Cooper Test) required the applicant to run for 12 minutes and incorporated a sit-up test, a push-up test, a bench press test, a leg press test, a flexibility test, and a speed agility test with the applicant running through a set of cones.

While the test conditions were the same for all applicants, the passing requirements were not. Even though the position would involve the same job functions for anyone who was hired, the test results had lower or higher standards based on gender and age. For example, on the flexibility test, Valcik (who was 23 years old at the time) had to touch two inches past his toes but a 35-year-old male applicant was only required to touch below his kneecaps. This situation brings up two questions that can provide a legal challenge to the test. How useful is a test that accepts different results for different applicants if the position requires specific physical skills to execute the duties successfully? Second, how can a simple flexibility test, regardless of standards, prove that an applicant can perform the duties of the position successfully? Administrators should always keep these issues in mind when developing a physical agility test. A test that is developed that has different standards and has variables that cannot be tied to job responsibilities runs the risk of being legally challenged in court.

Final Notes

The hiring process should be about not only the knowledge, skills, and abilities that the applicant possesses, but also how the applicant's personality fits within the hiring department's culture. Personality testing can be an excellent tool to predict a candidate's success in the organization. The Myers-Briggs Type Indicator assessment, DISC, and other testing tools examine how the individual will relate to the people and culture of an organization. Organizations develop a culture, and certain personality types thrive in some organizational cultures but might be miserable in others. Failure to take personality into account can lead to tension, dysfunctional behavior, and workflow disruption. However, it is equally important to promote a diverse workplace with people who can enhance the organization with different work styles, skills, experiences, and perceptions. When faced with a challenge, an organization with a diverse group of employees is more likely to have that one person who finds a creative solution than a more homogeneous group whose members would all respond in a similar way. With some candidates, personality fit will not be obvious until the applicant has already been hired. This is why most organizations use a probationary period to promote the long-term health of the organization and to assess the proper fit and alignment of the applicant with the organization's culture and mission.

While most positions in public organizations fall under the jurisdiction of civil-service rules and regulations, there are employees who are employed at the will of the organization. These non-civil-service positions typically include the highest levels of an organization's administration and, conversely, entry-level positions. Entry-level positions usually include hourly workers who work directly for public officials (e.g., sheriff's deputies) or who work for lower pay than civil-service employees earn. Entry-level positions are reserved for people who have recently graduated from school or who require very little experience or training to perform the basic job functions required. These positions can also be used to evaluate a new employee's job performance to determine if that employee is capable of working in a more advanced, civil-service position. Because entry-level positions can be classified as non-civil service, this provides the organization more flexibility in terminating an underperforming employee. If an employee working in an entry-level position does not perform to expectations or does not demonstrate the ability to progress in the organization, the employee can be either be dismissed or kept in the entry-level position.

Important Points to Remember

1. Make sure that any test given to an applicant is applicable to the job that is being applied for.
2. If an applicant does not fit an organization's immediate needs, an administrator should consider future skill sets that the organization might need and ask if this applicant can meet the long-term needs of the organization.
3. Be flexible. An applicant may not be a perfect fit for a position, but this does not mean that he cannot be trained to become a perfect fit for the organization if he has the ability to learn on the job.
4. Personality and fit with other employees is important to make sure that an applicant can work well with employees who are already in the organization.
5. Have realistic expectations about an applicant. All applicants, regardless of skill and experience, will need a period of time to learn the way the organization conducts its work. This learning curve could take as little as a few weeks or as long as three months.
6. Utilize hiring processes that are in place with the organization and be consistent on how you evaluate the applicants.
7. Do not ask personal questions that can lead to litigation if the candidate does not receive a job offer (e.g., What religion are you? Are you married?).
8. Test applicants as thoroughly as possible on their knowledge, skills, and abilities if certain skills and traits are vital for the position. The last thing any organization wants is to hire an applicant who cannot perform the assigned tasks.

9. Have multiple employees review the applicants. Sometimes one employee may notice a quality about an applicant that another employee will not notice.

10. Understand that hiring new applicants is ultimately a long-term investment for the organization.

CASE STUDY 4.1
Hiring Practices

SITUATION FOR CASE STUDY 4.1

You are the director of the parks and recreation department for the City of Badlands, Texas, which is a large, established, and fairly wealthy suburb. Badlands has a reputation for maintaining a robust aquatics program during the summer, with five large outdoor city pools and two indoor pools owned by the school district. Your aquatics program staff is divided into a swim instruction program and a lifeguard component.

Justifying the budget for these programs has been relatively easy because the citizens want a high-quality parks and recreation program. The tax base is $75 million, $3 million of which was raised by your department. The parks and recreation department has a budget of $9 million; however, you know that there are still shortfalls in the type of rescue equipment needed and that the pools have antiquated pump systems that are difficult to maintain and operate. This is in addition to the cost of chemicals, water, salaries, and the liability insurance that the city must carry to enable patrons to use the municipal pools. High overhead costs prevent you from hiring well-qualified full-time pool managers over the pools, forcing you to continue to rely on high school or college students to fill the pool manager positions.* It is the pool staff that repaints, cleans, and makes minor repairs to the outdoor pools before summer starts. There is also no program budgeted to provide formal lifeguard training at Badland's pools.

You have two full-time employees in the aquatics program who work all year. Susan, who is an aquatics coordinator, is young and does not have much experience in managing personnel. Chuck is Susan's supervisor and is a retired schoolteacher.

The competitive salary requirement is $4.90 per hour for lifeguards and $8.50 per hour for water safety instructors (WSIs). These pay rates cannot be cut because neighboring communities pay their lifeguards and WSIs at a much higher pay scale, making recruitment efforts at Badlands very difficult. The neighboring City of Nemesis pays lifeguards $6.50 per hour and WSIs $8.50 an hour, plus has a teaching aide for every six children.† Furthermore, the City of Nemesis has a year-round swim program with all classes taught at indoor pools away from the blistering Texas sun.

---

* The city should have documented any training pool managers in human resources issues in regard to hiring processes. All positions in the Parks and Recreation department should have clear, documented job responsibilities and minimum qualifications for hiring personnel for a particular position.

† Salary equity compared with other organizations can lead to high turnover rates, continuing the hiring process, increases costs of hiring new employees, and affects compensation for existing staff members if salary rates are not comparable to other organizations.

Lifeguards by policy can only be allowed to sit in one position for 15 minutes at a time before rotating off for down time. In theory, the maximum amount that any one lifeguard has to sit for is one hour, plus 15 to 30 minutes manning the front desk and selling drinks as well as 15 minutes performing pool cleanup before any down time is given. Therefore, your lifeguard staffing requirements are very high because you have to hire a staff to account for the rotation requirements of eight lifeguards for three of your city pools: Cottonmouth Pool (four guard stations), Anaconda Pool (three guard stations) and Green Mamba Pool (four guard stations).

Cottonmouth Pool is difficult to guard because the main lap pool is separated from the diving board well by a concrete catwalk, which dictates that two lifeguards are in rotation at all times, even when there is low attendance.[*] City summer camp children attend Cottonmouth Pool and Green Mamba Pool, causing the facilities to frequently exceed the stated capacity and requiring more lifeguards to be called in from other pools or from a substitution roster. Cottonmouth Pool and Anaconda Pool are located in high-crime areas.[†] Cottonmouth, Green Mamba, and Anaconda have a morning lifeguard assigned to prepare the pools and a lifeguard over the swim lessons that are taught during the weekday.

The two largest pools, Cobra Pool (with five stations) and Adder Pool (five stations), require 10 lifeguards to comply with rotation requirements plus a lifeguard for morning setup and supervision over swim lessons. One lifeguard is designated as an assistant pool manager because Cobra and Adder require more management because of their size. These two pools have multiple diving boards and host multiple summer camps. Cobra Pool, which is located in the most affluent part of town, tends to attract younger children because the pool bottom is shallow.

You are required to provide two lifeguards and two WSIs for evening swim classes at two indoor pools that are on school district facilities. You also have an additional lifeguard and pool manager, known as the rover lifeguard and the rover manager, who rotate among the pools and fill in for employees on their days off. You maintain a substitution roster for times when your employees want a day off or when they are close to exceeding their 40 hours. You must budget for overtime pay for work on holidays and for guarding private pool parties that are held after normal work hours.[‡]

All lifeguards and WSIs must be American Red Cross certified, be certified in American Red Cross first aid, and be certified in CPR. Therefore, the pool of qualified employees is very competitive since other suburbs are hiring for the summer and annual swim programs. In total you will need 55 full-time lifeguards (which includes managers and assistant managers), 25 WSIs for instruction, and at least 20 substitute lifeguards and WSIs on roster for the next three months.[§]

---

[*] Physical requirements of the facilities can have a substantial impact upon staff requirements and staff schedules.

[†] It is not unusual for work environment staffing requirements to be impacted by externalities such as safety or neighborhood socioeconomic characteristics.

[‡] Operating hours and customized service provision often entail flexible staffing patterns and increase staffing needs.

[§] A cost–benefit analysis should be performed periodically to determine the viability and sustainability of enhanced services and programs.

Scenario One

It is May and you need to hire two new full-time lifeguards for the summer session. Most of your lifeguards from last summer will return for summer work, and the rest of the lifeguards will be placed on the substitution roster. You will also need to hire at least 10 new WSIs for summer classes.

Susan has announced tryouts and posted an advertisement in the paper for lifeguards only. Susan has not announced any tryouts for WSIs. More than 40 people show up for the lifeguard tryouts. There are three physical tests that all applicants are required to take. Despite the fact that lifeguard applicants must have a valid certification from the American Red Cross and should have certain skills that they are required to perform with and without rescue equipment, no tests or written exams for CPR or other pertinent skills are being required for the lifeguard position.* Your city does not have any safety equipment for the pools beyond a backboard for back and neck injuries. However, Susan is not testing lifeguards for knowledge of how to use the backboard. For the rescue test, Susan is pairing some smaller applicants with smaller victims while other applicants are paired with extremely large victims to rescue. Most of the applicants are high school students or college students who are home for the summer. However, Susan has not provided the managers with any guidelines on the hiring criteria for the lifeguards.†

How concerned are you about the lack of criteria and guidelines that Susan has given to the pool managers?

Are there any consequences that could occur from Susan's recruitment and hiring procedures?

How do you know if the best people were hired?

Do the three physical tests actually reflect the skills that are needed for the position of lifeguard, or are additional hiring tests required?

What other tests would you require for the lifeguard applicants when they apply for the position?

Scenario Two

Susan held the tryouts and allowed the pool managers or the assistant manager to select the new hires for the position. Tricia, the pool manager at Cottonmouth, is a recent college graduate working her last summer with Badlands. She is a mature young woman who takes her position seriously. Randy, the assistant manager at Green Mamba, is a high school student who does not take his responsibilities seriously at all. Both Tricia and Randy each hire an entry level lifeguard for their respective staff. Tricia chose Mike due to his exceptional performance on the lifeguard skills test, his mature attitude, and his previous work experience as a WSI for the City of Nemesis. Randy, at the urging of his lifeguard staff, chose Amanda,

---

* Test validation, recertification, and assurance of compliance with operating requirements are vital to smooth operations, risk avoidance, and litigation. An advisable action would be to have a risk manager do a regular review on testing procedures.

† Upper management should provide guidelines to subordinates for hiring procedures in order to avoid liability and have good results in the hiring procedure. Affirmative Action, Americans with Disabilities Act, and Equal Employment Opportunity statutes should be followed at all times in the hiring procedure.

an attractive high school student with no previous experience. Randy did not take her performance in the skills test into consideration when he hired her.

You compare the manner in which the new hires were selected and are concerned by how the lifeguard at Green Mamba was chosen. Neither Susan nor Chuck, Susan's supervisor, share your concerns; in fact, they promoted Randy to an assistant manager position because he had reported the previous pool manager and assistant pool manager at Green Mamba for embezzlement of funds. Your concern grows when you learn from other city workers that under Randy's management, hazing among lifeguards has become a frequent occurrence. When you confront Chuck about the allegations against Randy, Chuck tells you not to worry and that "boys will be boys." Randy continues to work as an assistant manager for now.

1. What concerns are raised in the manner that Green Mamba pool has hired their entry level lifeguard?
2. What concerns do you have over Randy being promoted as an assistant manager?
3. What can you do with the allegations of Randy allowing hazing at Green Mamba pool?

Scenario Three

Since there is no money in the parks and recreation budget for full-time city employees to clean and repaint the pools, you must have your lifeguards perform the work and have your pool managers supervise.*

1. What are the human resources issues that are raised with having the lifeguards perform tasks that they were not hired to do?
2. What are the risks of having workers perform work that they are not trained to do?

WHAT ACTUALLY HAPPENED IN CASE STUDY 4.1

The incidents in Case Study 4.1 took place a number of years ago, the severity of the scenario is lessened, and names and position titles have been changed to protect identities. The actual parks and recreation director and the two full-time employees were unaware of the incidents that occurred except where they were directly notified on a serious incident. The hazing issue was never addressed, and how much any of them knew at the time about the hazing incidents is debatable.

Today the City of Badlands issues the proper rescue equipment and has maintained it as standard equipment for at least 20 years. However, the person who presided over the tryouts (Scenario One) continues to be employed at the city, and numerous incidents have occurred to suggest that human resources issues have not been resolved. The lack of experience among the lifeguards has led to many problems. One of the pools was completely drained by an inexperienced

---

* In most organizations a human resources audit or investigation would be undertaken if such conditions were reported. In this case in particular, the employees were asked to take on additional responsibilities with no training, proper equipment, or compensation.

lifeguard and was closed for the day until the pool could be refilled. A fire was caused when another inexperienced lifeguard placed a trash bag next to the pump system generator, causing the bag to be sucked into the generator vents. This fire occurred in proximity to a vat of liquid chlorine, which, if it had ignited, could have endangered the staff and pool patrons. Fortunately, the fire was extinguished before it could ignite the chlorine. Good hiring practices that take experience and qualifications into account could have prevented these costly incidents.

KEY ISSUES RAISED IN CASE STUDY 4.1

The purpose of the selection process is to find the most qualified candidate based on performance, skills, and experience. The first lifeguard accomplished this objective, but the second lifeguard did not, electing to hire a person based on gender bias. This was allowed to happen because no hiring criteria were established or provided to the lifeguards or enforced by the lifeguards' supervisors. The consequences for having a poorly established selection process include injury or death to pool patrons due to the presence of a lifeguard with absent or inadequate skills, litigation as a result of injury or death, litigation from a rejected candidate who has successfully detected inconsistencies in the organization's selection process, and litigation from the unqualified employee if she should learn that she was hired because of her appearance.

Another key issue for the City of Badlands is the absence of a formalized training program. Not only does this create an unsafe environment for pool patrons and staff, but it is a huge liability for the city. Most suburban aquatic programs hire WSIs and lifeguards who have been trained through their city's American Red Cross certification program. Certification from an external agency recognized by many organizations as having sufficient standards of performance ensures that candidates who possess this certification come equipped with the skills necessary to perform the job.

The City of Badlands is experiencing a lack of proper internal and external controls. The embezzlement case is a clear sign that sufficient controls did not exist if both the pool manager and assistant pool manager *at the same pool* were able to take large amounts of money. The lack of audit procedures over the activities of the pool managers who were responsible for the pool's revenue should be a great concern for any organization that handles funds.

When conducting a physical agility test, it is important to ensure that all parts of the test are applicable to the position and that the test does not unduly discriminate against any individuals. While this case study pertains to a parks and recreation department, police and fire departments also face similar concerns that physical agility tests raise. Physical agility tests are perhaps the most commonly used construct validity test used by public organizations. However, the usefulness of physical agility tests, their applicability to the position, and their potential to discriminate against certain classes of applicants have been a matter of debate.

Some police departments do not use physical agility tests because of litigation issues and because they fail to prove that the scenarios they wish to test will be likely to occur on the job. For example, a police department cannot test an applicant on the ability to scale a six-foot wall if there are no six-foot walls in the patrol area. Such a test can discriminate against shorter applicants, which can include women and certain races whose members may typically be small framed such as some Asian Americans and Hispanics. Furthermore, if physical agility tests are not applied consistently with all candidates, they can open the department to litigation. The Cooper Test is an example of an agility test that evaluates applicants based on a matrix that calculates distance run within 12 minutes against age and gender of the runner. Another example is a police flexibility test that, based on a matrix similar to the Cooper Test, requires the department to pass a 35-year-old male who while bent at the waist can barely touch past his knees but fail a 23-year-old male who fails to touch two inches past his toes even though the younger candidate is applying for the same position.

Physical agility tests for lifeguards should include realistic situations that a lifeguard might have to face. If the scenario is to pull a victim from the water, all lifeguards must be able to pull the same victim regardless of the relative difference in height and weight between the candidate and the victim. In an actual situation, a small lifeguard might have no choice but to save a larger person who is in trouble. Thus, scaling a physical agility test so that small applicants are only required to save small victims does not reflect an actual situation and is neither useful as a test nor protective to the organization from legal action. The criteria on a physical agility test must be clear to the applicants and to the evaluators. Failure to clarify the criteria of physical agility can lead to litigation from failure to have consistent testing standards or because the evaluators did not conduct the test appropriately.

When a manager assumes that everyone in the organization is performing their jobs properly, that manager is displaying a logic of confidence. Without regular supervision, the manager becomes unaware of what is occurring with the employees, and the employees feel isolated and are much less likely to report issues that arise. This disconnect creates organizational drift, which can create a situation where operational ideals do not match operational reality. Employees stop reporting concerns to their supervisor when they believe their input will not stop the problem or if reporting will lead to retribution by other employees. In the case of the City of Badlands, retribution took the form of hazing.

WHAT COULD HAVE HAPPENED IN CASE STUDY 4.1

Several issues should have been resolved differently in this case study. First, adult full-time employees should have been managers of each pool and should have been operating under concise and consistent policies in regard to hiring employees for lifeguard work and swim instruction. This factor alone could have averted many of the problems that the parks and recreation department in the City of Badlands faced in their aquatics program. Since this did not occur, the director of the department should have taken more immediate action on the subordinates to ensure that legal statutes were not violated. Termination for Susan, Chuck, and the lifeguards who were involved in the hazing incident and the embezzlement is more than warranted in this situation and should have been carried out by the department director. Risk management and safety training should also have been carried out to protect employees as well as patrons, and proper rescue and safety equipment should have been supplied at every municipal pool.

Suggested Readings for Chapter 4

Herrenkohl, Eric, 2010. *How to hire A-players: Finding the top people for your team—even if you don't have a recruiting department.* ISBN: 978-0470562246. New York: Wiley.

Hunt, Steven, 2007. *Hiring success: The art and science of staffing assessment and employee selection.* ISBN: 978-0787996482. San Francisco, CA: Pfeiffer.

Yate, Martin, 2005. *Hiring the best: A manager's guide to effective interviewing and recruiting.* ISBN: 1593374038. Avan, MA: Adams Media.

Chapter 5

Performance Evaluations for Employees

Performance evaluations are part of the human resources experience for supervisors in nonprofit, medical, and public organizations. Although a performance evaluation is potentially a biased exercise and completing it takes time and can be tedious, it can also be an opportunity for a supervisor to assess employee strengths and weakness and to make adjustments that will benefit the organization. Performance evaluations, when conducted effectively, can aid an organization in retaining effective employees through merit-based salary increases and in providing constructive feedback, training, and counseling for employees who may be deficient in their work performance.

History of the Performance Evaluation

The beginning of modern performance evaluations can be traced to Frederick Taylor's theory of scientific management, a theory of management that analyzes workflow for the purpose of improving efficiency especially in labor productivity (Internet Center for Management and Business Administration, Inc., 2010). Scientific management introduced several new tactics to evaluate worker productivity in a factory setting. Among the most controversial of these new tools to evaluate worker productivity was the performance evaluation. Originally, the performance evaluation was based on tangible outputs, such as how many items were completed by one worker in an hour. The performance evaluation has changed since it was first used to evaluate factory workers and has now been adapted for the service industry. As stated by Vasu Stewart and Garson:

> Performance appraisal is a pivotal *management technique* with a number of purposes and dimensions. It involves a systematic evaluation of the employee by his or her supervisor or some other qualified person(s) who is familiar with the employee's performance on the job. (Vasu Michael L., Stewart, Debra W., and Garson, G. David, 1998, p. 347)

The purpose of the performance evaluation has therefore changed from a pure measurement of output to a mechanism managers and supervisors can use to evaluate their employees' knowledge, skills, and abilities as they pertain to the positions they hold. The theory of scientific management was based on the belief that machine-like efficiencies can be achieved by analyzing workflow and output and identifying areas in the assembly line where speed is reduced or quality compromised and repair the defect. It is now being applied toward analyzing the decision-making process, how workers interact with other workers and with customers, and identifying intangible qualities that impede or improve the delivery of services. Thus, performance evaluations have diverged significantly from their original purpose.

There are several benefits and disadvantages to using performance evaluations in public organizations. One benefit to using performance evaluations is that the instrument can provide constructive feedback to the organization's employees, which will allow them to focus on improving in different areas. Additionally, performance evaluations provide managers or supervisors an opportunity to interface with their employees and allow them the opportunity to provide positive reinforcement to the employee in areas in which they are currently excelling. By using positive reinforcement, the manager or supervisor has the potential to increase their employees' productivity (White, 2010). Another advantage for managers and supervisors is that the performance evaluation provides written documentation of an employee's performance, which can support decisions leading to merit increases or disciplinary action.

Performance evaluations have several shortcomings that need to be realized by managers and supervisors alike. In service industry positions in particular, the basis for evaluating an employee is subjective. This can create issues between management and employees if perceptions about an employee's performance are widely different. Secondly, if a performance evaluation instrument has a limited range or scale of assessment, the supervisor or manager will be unable to provide a nuanced and informative rating for the employee or may give the employee a higher rating or lower rating than the employee has earned. The performance evaluation also has the potential to be misused by managers or supervisors against employees who may have personal conflicts with supervisors, managers, or coworkers. The performance evaluation will only be effective if the organization uses the performance evaluation in an unbiased manner and takes the performance evaluations seriously.

Performance Evaluation Instrument

Evaluators need a valid and informative instrument to record performance evaluations properly. If the scale of the instrument is too restrictive, the lack of nuanced choices can skew the results. A performance evaluation instrument with a range of at least five values can allow the evaluator some degree of variability, and the assessment has a greater chance of reflecting the true value of the employees' abilities for that performance indicator category. A supervisor will have a more difficult time rating employees if a scale is based on a 1 to 3 rating system as opposed to a 1 to 5 rating system, where some variability exists. If faced with a 1 to 3 rating system, a supervisor is much more likely to weight the performance evaluations to one extreme or another since there is little room to rate employees as either 1 (*poor*), 2 (*acceptable*), or 3 (*exceptional*). Employees have a wide range of performance that falls between these ratings on a 1 to 3 scale in the example given.

A performance evaluation instrument must include different evaluations for different types of workers (e.g., administrative and professional versus classified employees). It is important that supervisors take performance evaluations seriously or run the risk that employees will consider evaluations as just another bureaucratic requirement of the organization. It is also essential that evaluations are free of bias. If a supervisor's performance evaluation is based on how their employees are rated, then the supervisor could be tempted to provide all employees with positive evaluations to ensure that their own evaluation will be positive.

Types of Evaluations

As stated earlier, a series of instruments should be used based on what the employee is expected to do in the organization. For example, technically skilled employees should have a different performance evaluation instrument than an administrative assistant, as these positions are very different and require different skill sets to be successful. While an administrative assistant may have to contend with the public and must have good oral communication skills, a computer programmer might only communicate with his or her direct supervisor; thus, oral communication skills may not be as critical to a programmer's success in the organization. A one-size-fits-all approach does not serve organizations well in regard to performance evaluations, and different performance evaluation instruments should be constructed to reflect the different types of positions that an organization may contain.

For executives or upper-level administrators in the organization, an effective performance evaluation could be tied to their departmental or organizational performance plan rather than to the performance of their subordinates. This will hold executives accountable for their assessment and implementation of the mission, goals, and priorities of their departments to the overall organizational goals.

Executive and upper-level administrators should have the knowledge, skills, and abilities to make their performance plan for their organization a reality if the performance plan is realistic in terms of the following three aspects:

- Are the resources available to ensure that the performance plan goals are possible?
- Does the performance plan effectively utilize the resources of the organization?
- Is the performance plan politically feasible for the organization to implement?

Based on these three factors a performance plan can be evaluated to assess whether or not there were resources available to execute the plan, the executive or upper administrator managed effectively, and the plan was workable from the beginning. If the upper-level administrators or executives fault the personnel for the failure of the performance plan to meet the objectives set forth, then the executives or administrators should be held accountable if they are responsible for recruiting, hiring, and evaluating personnel that work to accomplish the goals of the performance plan.

360-Degree Performance Evaluation

For supervisors in particular, using a 360-degree performance evaluation may be the best solution to getting an accurate assessment of how a supervisor or manager is performing. A 360-degree performance evaluation is a process where the employee is evaluated by upper management, the employee's peers, and the employee's subordinates. This type of performance evaluation allows for assessment to be given by two or three different layers of personnel that will provide data on the employee's performance from different viewpoints. The disadvantage of a 360-degree performance evaluation is that in smaller departments and organizations, subordinates may be more hesitant to give an accurate assessment of their superior due to fear of reprisals. Peers may also feel hesitant about giving an accurate assessment of a colleague's work since the peers will have to work with the employee in the future and the employee will be able to evaluate them in turn. Allowing the evaluator to be anonymous may alleviate the issue of reprisals.

The Role of Human Resources in Performance Evaluations

Human resources departments are essential to the performance evaluation process because they provide policies and procedures that allow organizations to recruit, hire, train, evaluate, discipline, and terminate employees through a variety of mechanisms (e.g., job pay scales). Without a human resources department, managers and supervisors would be left to their own devices to perform these tasks, which could lead to dire legal consequences if mistakes are made. In public organizations, the human resources department has additional responsibilities to ensure that all state and federal laws are followed and that all of the policies and procedures for employment are being followed by the organization. Where applicable, the human resources department ensures that all civil-service protocols are followed in the organization.

Human resources sets the tone for how performance evaluations will be administered by the organization. Human resources typically creates the evaluation process, constructs the evaluation instruments, and sets deadlines by which all evaluations must be completed. It is imperative that the department be proactive in distributing a viable performance evaluation instrument, making sure that the performance evaluations are being completed by the deadline, and ensuring that managers are giving good evaluations. If there are no consequences for exceeding evaluation deadlines, the evaluations will not be considered a priority by department managers. Organizations need to give human resources the tools to enforce deadlines for performance evaluations, which can include negative penalties such as withholding or decreasing merit increases for their department. Human resources will need to look for patterns with supervisors' evaluations (e.g., all negative or all positive reviews or reviews that are identical to previous years' reviews) and be prepared to audit the performance evaluations if these patterns persist.

Performance Evaluations Tied to Merit Increases

To ensure that performance evaluations are taken seriously, many organizations have tied increases in merit pay to performance evaluations as well as to work proficiency. When this practice becomes policy, two things can occur as a result: budget fattening and office tensions.

In many organizations, departments are given a merit pool for salary increases instead of a line-item increase in the budget to cover one employee's merit increase. These merit increases are often tied to the position rather than to the individual who holds the position. In an environment like that, it is possible that a supervisor might attempt to get a budget increase for his department by giving his entire staff excellent performance evaluations. If an employee leaves the organization, the vacant position will have additional salary money attached to it, thus giving the supervisor the option of hiring a new person at a more competitive salary, hiring a new person at a lower salary and using the balance for others in the department, or eliminating the position altogether and redistributing the salary money to others in the department.

On the other hand, a supervisor may not wish to give an employee a bad review because it might lead to confrontation or tension in the organization, which can hinder the organization's effectiveness. An administrator may also be disinclined to give an employee a bad review if the employee is being evaluated in a 360-degree performance evaluation.

Performance Evaluations Tied to Other Benefits

Positions such as police officers, firefighters, and medical personnel can have performance evaluations tied to future promotions or position classifications. With performance evaluations being tied to promotions, this essentially ties in benefits as well as salary issues for good or bad performance evaluations. For example, these benefits could include an increase in the number of days off per year that could be directly tied to a promotion or demotion. In essence, a performance evaluation may not impact an employee's salary, but it could impact the employee in other aspects of his or her employment with the organization, such as a change in an employee's shift time for an employee who works the first, second, or third shift as opposed to a traditional 40-hour workweek. Other actions that can be taken with performance evaluations would be to transfer employees to different positions in the department or to reclassify employees to positions that more closely fit their knowledge, skills, and experience.

Performance Evaluations of New Hires and the Use of Probation

Most new hires in an organization are put on probation for a set time, throughout which performance evaluations are given for the purpose of either verifying that the new hire is performing well or that corrections need to be made. If the performance evaluation of a new employee shows that corrections are needed, then the probationary status can be extended or a new hire can be terminated. The probationary status can be useful since new hires can potentially have issues that employers will be unaware of until a given time period reveals behavior traits that may or may not be able to be corrected. Also for more skilled positions, if new hires are not able to develop skills or their skills have been overrepresented during the hiring process, the new hire can be terminated during the probationary period.

Author's Experience

Performance evaluations can be useful if correctly administered. However, in Mr. Benavides's experience in city management, their implementation was uneven to say the least. While almost every public sector organization uses performance evaluations, the actual application and management of the evaluations is often burdensome and time consuming. It was not usual to learn late in the process how the evaluations were going to be designed, graded, and documented; how often the evaluations would be conducted; and who would conduct the evaluations. How far down the organizational chain these performance evaluations were used often changed with different leadership. Benavides once gave himself a poor performance evaluation because he did not complete many of his assignments within the fiscal year. After submitting the evaluation to his superior, he was instructed to redo the evaluation and give himself high marks even though the goals were not met.

Final Notes

In summary, performance evaluations can be a useful tool for public, nonprofit, and medical organizations. If performance evaluations of employees are seen as simply a bureaucratic requirement by supervisors, then the information that performance evaluations can provide the organization will never be captured on a yearly basis. Instead, what the organization will capture for data will be largely biased or self-serving data that will have little use to supervisors or upper administration. How would organizations know if they have the best employees or not if the information on the quality of their employees is never collected effectively in the first place?

In addition to using performance evaluations to effectively improve the employees of the organization and the organization itself, the performance evaluations can also be used to benchmark employee performance against other organizations, which can effectively help determine pay scale for employees who have certain knowledge, skills, and abilities. If a benchmark standard is not determined, then employees may be much harder to retain by upper administrators since the administration will be unable to effectively gauge the market value of their employees. At the other end of the spectrum, public, nonprofit, and medical organizations run the risk of overpaying employees in certain positions if an accurate benchmark is not established. Overpaying employees could cripple an organization that is on a tight budget or facing budget cuts.

During tough economic times, even public, nonprofit, and medical organizations are not immune from tight budgets and potential layoffs. When these tough times do arise, it is important to have an accurate assessment of personnel within the organization. When layoffs are required to realign an organization's budget, the process is better managed when supervisors are armed with objective performance evaluation information. Personnel identified as underperforming are least likely to impact the organization with their absence and most likely to impact the budget if they remain. Performance evaluations that most accurately represent employee knowledge, skills, and abilities are therefore the most useful toward achieving this goal. In medical organizations, accurate performance evaluation instruments serve the additional benefit of removing employees who could be a legal liability.

However, in public organizations seniority status can prove to be an immovable object for supervisors who need to lay off civil service employees. This is particularly true for educational institutions. Seniority forces supervisors to cut newly hired personnel and keep employees who have worked longer regardless of performance quality. University and college administrators who provide their faculty with tenure status are similarly constrained. Faculty members who hold tenure are extremely difficult to terminate even if their performance warrants termination. One way administrators can lay off tenured faculty is to eliminate academic programs that consistently have low enrollment and degree production. Faculty performance evaluations can be used to determine not only salary increases but other perks as well, such as promotion to a higher faculty rank or as head of a department, start-up money for research, larger laboratory space, additional student workers, and new equipment.

In short, performance evaluations can be used for a wide variety of purposes if the organization has accurate data and utilizes a good survey instrument. Using performance evaluations is more than simply having the performance evaluation instrument available. Success is also dependent upon the organization's ability to fully embrace the concept and use of such techniques and instruments to improve the organization.

Important Points to Remember

1. Performance measures are designed to accurately evaluate an employee's job performance.
2. Make sure that a performance evaluation accurately captures job performance for the job that is evaluated.
3. Be consistent on performance evaluations in how they are administered from employee to employee.
4. Make sure that performance evaluations have enough range that can be assigned to each item being measured by the evaluator. For example, it is harder to accurately assess an employee's performance if the scale on a given question is only 1 (*excellent*), 2 (*consistent*), or 3 (*below expectations*). Often, evaluators want to have more range than just a scale of three available answers.
5. A 360-degree performance evaluation can be useful if properly employed.
6. Any performance evaluation can be misused or employed to evaluate performance evaluations improperly. Keep in mind that a performance evaluation should provide useful feedback for the employee.
7. Performance evaluations are especially important to use properly for new employees that are on probation. If the employee's performance is far below expectations, a performance measure can be used to dismiss a new employee who is still on probation.

8. Performance evaluations can provide useful data to the organization so that promotions and salaries can be successfully tied to well-performing employees.
9. When evaluating employees, make sure that both the supervisor and employee agree on goals set forth for the upcoming year. Including an employee's input will more likely encourage the employee to improve.
10. If the organization puts no stock in the performance evaluations, then employees and managers will not take performance evaluations seriously.

CASE STUDY 5.1
Performance and Skills Not as Advertised

SITUATION FOR CASE STUDY 5.1

You are a director for a very small state agency that consists of 10 employees. In addition to your regular departmental duties, you are responsible for hiring, disciplining, training, and ensuring compliance of the employees who work for your department. Your previous experience has included being a director over several different departments, some small and some quite large, compared with the department you currently manage. The state agency you work for has over 1,000 employees and is responsible for a variety of tasks that support the local community. You now have a budget to hire a new certified public accountant (CPA) in your department and to advertise the position in the newspaper and with the state agency's web site. After interviewing several candidates, you have decided to hire Mr. Esined, who interviewed well and appears to have the correct skill sets you need for the operations of your department.

1. How many different ways can you test for the appropriate skills that were advertised for the position?
2. What types of questions should be asked of potential applicants to ensure that they are a good fit with the organization?
3. Should any other methods be used to determine whether or not an applicant will be able to perform the job as advertised or learn the skills on the job?

Mr. Esined countered the first offer with a request for more salary. You are convinced that this individual is the correct person for the position, and you are able to get an increase of salary in the job offer to Mr. Esined. Hiring this individual took more than two months of your time and considerable political resources to justify his salary to your superiors.

1. Should you have sought more money for the offer for Mr. Esined, or should you have kept the position open for another suitable applicant?
2. Can the director face political backlash for hiring an applicant who did not work out after using political means to find more salary?

Although Mr. Esined is a CPA and had the proper credentials on his resume, his performance on the job has been below the levels that you expected. In addition, there have been indications that Mr. Esined is causing difficulties with other staff members (rude comments about their intelligence, age, etc.). Mr. Esined has now been employed for more than four months and his probationary period will end in another two months, after which taking strong disciplinary action or terminating him will become a much more difficult and lengthy process.

1. What action do you take?
2. What consequences could this action result in?
3. How will your superiors react to your actions?
4. How will your staff react to your actions?

WHAT ACTUALLY HAPPENED IN CASE STUDY 5.1

Case Study 5.1 describes a situation that could have happened in either a private or public organization, although this particular incident occurred in a public organization. In most public organizations, a department head must obtain permission from his or her supervisor to request additional funds to give a desired candidate a higher salary than the minimum rate set for the position, which is what the director did in this case study. In the actual event, the director originally wanted to hire the two best applicants who applied for the position, even though he only had enough funding for one person. The director approached his supervisor to obtain funds to create a second position for the other candidate. However, after the first round of interviews, one applicant withdrew his application, which left only one applicant. The open position was offered to the remaining applicant, who then countered the salary offer. The director was eager to fill the empty position and justified the higher salary rate by pointing out the applicant's skills and qualifications. The applicant was given no skills test, and no additional interviews were conducted by other staff members in the department during the hiring process. The supervisor gave the director the additional funds.

Unfortunately, it soon became apparent that the applicant had overstated his expertise and skills. After two months on the job, and while he was still on probation, the employee began to belittle and sometimes yell at other employees. Over the ensuing four months, this aggressive behavior fostered an increasingly hostile work environment for the other employees in the department. The other employees informed the director of the situation, and the director spoke with the employee about his behavior. However, the employee became more belligerent, particularly to those who had lodged the initial complaints. The employee was retained after his probationary period, and the new employee's personality problems worsened with the other staff members. This employee did not improve his skill levels beyond what was minimally required on his performance evaluations. The combination of poor interpersonal relations and minimally useful skills harmed the department's efficiency and effectiveness.

KEY ISSUES RAISED IN CASE STUDY 5.1

The key issues raised in Case Study 5.1 were numerous. Some of the issues dealt with the hiring process for a public organization while other issues were related to performance evaluations and disciplinary actions. The initial hiring process, as discussed in some detail in Chapter 4, points out various issues that should have been detected in the applicant's skill levels before a job offer was made to the applicant. A skills test could have been given to all of the applicants to see which applicants indeed had the skills that were required for the position. In addition the applicants should have been interviewed by other staff members to see if any personality traits could have been detected during the interview process that could have potentially been detrimental to the department. Allowing only one person to interview candidates increases the potential for undesirable behavioral or personality qualities of the applicant to go unnoticed during the interviewing process.

In Case Study 5.1, the applicant countered the initial job offer for more money. At this point during the process, the director should have assessed whether or not additional funds should be collected for the departmental budget to hire the individual and whether or not the director should risk expending political capital for a hire that may or may not work out for the department and the organization. If the director decided that the applicant was not worth the political investment, then he should look for other applicants qualified for the position and willing to work for the salary listed. For some skilled positions, this approach is not viable if the salary level is too low for any applicant who would be qualified for the position. In situations where the salary level is significantly lower than for comparable positions in nearby public organizations or in private industry, the hiring director will have to request more funds to improve the competitiveness of the open position and attract qualified candidates.

The case study also explores how to evaluate the work performance of a new employee who is not meeting expectations. There were clear signs that the employee demonstrated a deficiency in performance as well as personality and behavioral problems during the first two months of employment. The director counseled the employee, but this did not rectify the deficiencies. Given that the problems were apparent during the probationary period, the director was within his right to terminate the employee at will and reopen the position. However, the director waited too late to address the growing performance problems, and the probationary period expired, thus making it much more difficult to terminate the employee. If a supervisor decides to retain a problem employee for reasons that do not pertain to job performance, the supervisor should be aware that the employee could destabilize the department. However, if the cost of restarting the recruiting and hiring process for the position is greater than the cost of counseling, additional oversight, and training of the troubled employee, then keeping the employee and working with him or her can have positive benefits.

The case study indicates that the employee was not performing up to an acceptable level of work. For supervisors it is very important to document any deficiencies in performance during the employee's annual performance review. For new employees, performance evaluations are usually held during the first three months of employment, at six months of employment (when the probationary period ends), and at a one-year interval for the annual performance evaluation.

While some supervisors have a jaded view on performance evaluations in public organizations, performance evaluations can prove to be quite useful to both supervisors and employees alike if the evaluations are used and completed objectively by supervisors. Performance evaluations will be useless if a supervisor merely completes the evaluation to fulfill a compliance requirement for a human resources directive or to justify more funding for certain positions in the department. If performance evaluations are used in an objective manner, the data that are compiled in an evaluation can be valuable feedback to the employee regarding areas in which the employee is doing well and areas that can be improved. Additionally, for supervisors, the performance evaluation is a useful tool that provides a skill set inventory of their employees and can provide data on how they are doing their jobs as supervisors.

WHAT COULD HAVE HAPPENED IN CASE STUDY 5.1

The director could not have known about the low skill level or behavioral problems that the employee would have until after the person was hired. However, the director could have terminated the person once these issues became known. The director probably kept the employee for fear of political fallout from the supervisor who granted the additional salary money to obtain the employee. The director had to weigh the efficiency costs to his department against personal political costs associated with terminating the employee. The director could have reconsidered hiring the employee before going to his supervisor to ask for additional salary money. The director could have weighed the cost of leaving a position open longer against the political costs of asking for more salary money to satisfy the counteroffer. The director could have informed the candidate that the original salary offer had to stand and gamble that the candidate would accept the position anyway.

CASE STUDY 5.2
Contending with Employee Reliability

SITUATION FOR CASE STUDY 5.2

You are the chief executive officer (CEO) of a county-owned hospital in Badlands, Texas, that has more than 1,000 employees, is designated as a trauma center, and includes an emergency room, a heart surgery center, and a neonatal unit. Your organization has been struggling with the results of medical accidents that have occurred during your watch. These incidents have damaged the reputation of the hospital and morale among the allied health staff, nurses, and doctors. Your employees work in shifts, and the hospital is struggling to keep its doors open.

One particular department maintains the minimum number of four employees for the second shift. Lately, two of the second shift employees have been arriving to work late and leaving work early. This leaves their shift understaffed during crucial turnover periods and reduces the effectiveness of the department. The manager who oversees this department has taken little or no corrective action, and the other employees are becoming despondent over the issue.

1. You are the CEO. What actions do you take?
2. What are the consequences of your actions?

You terminate one of the employees and counsel the other employee regarding what is acceptable behavior and performance on the job. However, you still have to deal with the department manager's inaction regarding this issue. The department manager, Mindy, typically does an exemplary job of keeping her department in compliance with the various regulations and has a great deal of experience. Mindy tends to stumble when she has to contend with difficult personnel matters and discipline issues.

1. How do you deal with Mindy?
2. What are the consequences or possible benefits from such actions?

Mindy has had additional issues with one employee, Halle. Halle was on the third shift; she arrived to work on time, performed her tasks well, and had little interaction with other people. After you terminated the troublesome employee, Mindy moved Halle to the second shift. Although Halle continued to perform her job well, she has become increasingly combative with other employees. In addition, you have learned that Halle is threatening to sue the hospital if disciplinary action is taken against her, claiming status under the Americans with Disabilities Act. Mindy has written warnings against Halle and has documented her behavior numerous times, but this action has had little effect.

1. As CEO, what actions should you take with regard to Mindy's management of the department?
2. What actions should you take against Halle at this point in time?
3. Is there any way you can protect the hospital against being sued and still take action against Halle?

The situation with Halle has reached a critical point. There are documented cases of Halle throwing items in the laboratory in a fit of rage and being verbally abusive to coworkers and to other technicians outside that department. Mindy wants to suspend Halle for a couple of days to make Halle "think about working here."

1. What are you going to do about Halle?
2. What are you going to do about Mindy?
3. Is a suspension enough discipline for a repeat violator of human resource policy?

Your best medical technologist, Sharon, worked on the second shift with Halle but has now resigned from the hospital to work elsewhere. Sharon was frustrated that Mindy would not transfer her to another shift. You have learned that Sharon repeatedly asked Mindy to take action against Halle, but Mindy did nothing.

1. What can you do to hire and retain a medical technologist on the second shift?
2. What will be your evaluation of Mindy's performance?

WHAT ACTUALLY HAPPENED IN CASE STUDY 5.2

The managers of this department did not take action on the employees, choosing instead to issue a general memo on proper employee conduct. No written documentation was compiled on any of the trouble employees. Later when the hospital was forced to conduct layoffs, one of the trouble employees was laid off along with another employee who was complaining of personality issues with other staff members. The remaining personnel who were doing their jobs well were expected to assume the work of the terminated employees with gaps in the four-person shift requirement filled by part-time workers. The unresolved personnel issues coupled with the increased workloads damaged morale among the good employees, causing many of them to seek employment elsewhere. The manager dealt with Halle's personality issue by using a rotation of part-time workers for the second shift. This decision had a long-term impact on the department; management saw that the part-time workers were a good budget solution and the department ultimately lost one full-time position.

KEY ISSUES RAISED IN CASE STUDY 5.2

This case study illustrates several areas related to performance on the job, retention of employees, and disciplinary actions on particular employees. The costs associated with failing to retain employees can be very detrimental to the health of a department or organization and can impact recruitment costs, hiring costs, and training costs as well as the loss of experience from employees who leave for other organizations. In this case study, the cost of retaining bad employees in the form of employee retention, performance inefficiencies, and a potential lawsuit outweighed the benefits of the work the bad employees performed. This case study also raises the issue of what happens when a manager fails to take effective disciplinary action against underperforming employees. How can a manager effectively evaluate annual performance when they fail to confront difficult employees in their department?

WHAT COULD HAVE HAPPENED IN CASE STUDY 5.2

Given that the hospital instituted layoffs anyway, the manager could have requested the terminations of the troublesome employees. However, the manager could not predict the upcoming layoffs. Terminating employees who generate a hostile work environment and threaten litigation on the basis of being a protected class can bring legal troubles to the department, particularly if the manager has not adequately documented the bad behavior and immediately followed each infraction with counseling or discipline. Ignoring the conflict among the employees fostered a hostile work environment and demoralized the effective employees. Since Halle did not cause trouble when she worked the third shift, another course of action would have been to restore Halle to the third shift and move an other employee to the second shift.

CASE STUDY 5.3
Work Not Completed

SITUATION FOR CASE STUDY 5.3

You are the city manager of Nemesis, Texas, a city of more than 100,000 people. You have been city manager for more than 10 years and have seen the changes that have resulted from a big population influx. The city is comprised of two distinct populations: a growing suburban culture and an older culture that wants things to stay as rural as possible. Currently your city has approximately 800 employees and has yearly expenditures of $140 million. The population in the newer section of Nemesis tends to be much more demanding of city government and have quite a bit more wealth than residents in the older, more rural part of the city. Your mayor and city council comprise new and old residents and are already questioning why the city is not more responsive to complaints.

It is Monday morning when you begin to receive several angry calls from citizens about the sanitation department failing to collect some or all of the refuse. The suburban citizens are particularly outraged because they are accustomed to having all refuse collected in a timely manner. Citizens are beginning to question why their taxes and fees are so high when their garbage is not being taken care of on a regular basis. Complaints such as these cause political pressure on the mayor and city council who in turn pressure you for quick results, particularly since some of the angry constituents are business owners who are heavily invested with the city. Elected officials have the ability to dismiss a city manager at will, so you take these complaints very seriously.

You summon the sanitation department supervisor to ask why the refuse is not being collected adequately in certain areas of the city. The supervisor tells you that two employees on this particular route have a history of not properly picking up refuse in their area. Both employees have been counseled before, but otherwise no action has been taken. The supervisor tells you that both employees are "good, honest, hard-working employees." However, the angry calls you have been receiving this morning contradict the supervisor's statement.

1. As city manager, what actions will you take to resolve the issue?
2. What is the responsibility of the supervisor over the two employees?
3. Should the supervisor have taken more action to ensure the smooth operation of the route in case of problems with the employees?
4. What human resource issues are involved?

WHAT ACTUALLY HAPPENED IN CASE STUDY 5.3

City managers hate to receive calls about sanitation issues. In this instance the Public Works director sent an employee to verify the residents' claims. One resident was found to have an unusual amount of debris left for pickup, and the employees had left some of the debris behind. Besides writing up the two employees, no other action was ever taken against them. On the next sanitation run, the sanitation director sent out additional workers to assist with the refuse pickup, incurring additional labor costs for the city.

The city eventually opted to outsource the entire sanitation effort to a third-party vendor, which resulted in even more complaints by the residents about the quality of service. The city manager's office conducted surveys in the downtown area to determine the magnitude of poor quality of service. However, the results were largely forgotten and no changes were ever implemented based on the survey results.

KEY ISSUES RAISED IN CASE STUDY 5.3

The city manager not only has to evaluate the two employees for the sanitation department but also has to evaluate the performance of their supervisors. In a large organization, should the city manager rely on subordinates to determine employee performance, or does the manager need to take an active role in gauging employee effectiveness? Did the disciplinary actions taken against the sanitation employees fit the employees' error and the costs to the city? This case study highlights the political pressure exerted by the citizens and elected officials, who expected a higher level of performance than had been expected of city employees in years past.

WHAT COULD HAVE HAPPENED IN CASE STUDY 5.3

The two sanitation workers could have received written reprimands and been placed on probation. Their immediate supervisor should have taken actions to provide more oversight to the employees as soon as the problem arose. This could have been accomplished by putting the employees on different routes with other sanitation workers who received good job performance reviews. Ignoring the problem cost the city more money because the city had to hire temporary workers to solve the problem.

While the sanitation workers need to be held accountable for their poor job performance, the supervisor should also be held accountable for the subordinates' actions since they had already been counseled once and the supervisor was well aware of the employees' issues. When services such as refuse collection are not conducted properly, elected officials can hold the city manager accountable for their subordinates' job performance and terminate the city manager. While this may be an extreme example of what can occur if basic services are interrupted, this case illustrates the potential danger of not contending with issues immediately when they occur.

Suggested Readings for Chapter 5

Hale, Judith A., 2002. *Performance based evaluation: Tools and techniques to measure the impact of training.* ISBN: 978-0787960353. San Francisco: Pfeiffer.

McDavid, James C., and Hawthorn, Laura R. L., 2006. *Program evaluation and performance measurement: An introduction to practice.* ISBN: 978-1412906685. Thousand Oaks, California: Sage Publications, Inc.

Merchant, Kenneth, and Van der Stede, Wim, 2007. *Management control systems: Performance measurement, evaluation and incentives.* ISBN: 978-0273708018. New Jersey: Prentice Hall.

Chapter 6

Rewarding and Disciplining Employees

Rewarding and disciplining employees are tightly interconnected. Public organizations in particular tend to develop reward systems that include competitive pay and benefits and nonsalary compensation strategies to attract, retain, and motivate employees to adhere to the organization's standards for job performance. For much of the 20th century and first decade of the 21st century, public organizations have strived to achieve comparable pay and benefits to that of the private sector. Most public sector organizations develop pay matrixes that set minimum and maximum pay levels for each position or pay grade within the organization. These pay matrixes are compared to their relevant public and private sector competitors.

Rewarding Employees

Pay Structures

The types of pay benefits organizations provide are also correlated to other governmental organizations with which they compete for labor. The majority of government organizations are much more likely to have defined benefit pension plans than their private sector counterparts, which have moved toward defined contribution plans. Most public sector organizations endeavor to provide pay and benefits that are competitive with their peer organizations. There are some organizations that attempt to be in the top quartile or even in the top tenth of pay structures for such positions as police officers where the competition for recruits is fierce. In addition to comparing their salaries to other jurisdictions in their labor market, most public sector employers attempt to maintain equity among positions with their own pay structures. Other public and nonprofit organizations will pay only up to a certain percentage of the going market value for positions. For example, a community college that has an open faculty position may only allot 80% of the current market value to hire a faculty member. Medical organizations are in a different situation. Often they have to use bonuses and competitive salaries to hire specialized positions that are in high demand, for example, registered nurses and medical technologists. A great deal of effort is spent determining if each job within the organization is valued appropriately when compared to all the other positions within the organization.

Determining Salary in Relation to the Marketplace

Organizations attempt to regularly adjust their pay and benefit structures so that they will not fall too far behind their competitors in the marketplace. Once an organization falls too far behind its competitors, it begins to experience competitive pressures such as increased turnover rates and morale issues. Public sector entities can check to see if their positions are competitive by conducting pay and benefits studies or by reviewing their turnover and other personnel statistics. However, this can lead to salary compression, a condition in which newly hired employees are paid at nearly the same rates as employees in the same or similar positions who have held those positions for a much longer time. It can be easier to provide competitive salaries for entry-level employees than to ask for pay increases for professional and managerial positions at higher grades because elected officials may be unwilling to ask the public, most of whom may not hold professional positions themselves, for higher salaries or more generous benefits. Therefore, it is not unusual for public sector organizations to experience difficulty hiring high-demand personnel such as engineers, nurses, and medical technicians because the organizations are trying to maintain pay and benefit structures that are politically efficacious or maintain harmony among less-skilled workers. In larger organizations and media markets, government agencies experience pressure to keep top management pay from reaching comparable market salaries, thus creating concerns that highly skilled individuals will stop applying for senior executive management positions in the public sector. Organizations that do not maintain competitive salary structures can fall victim to poaching from competitors. This phenomenon has been documented among public universities and colleges, particularly during state budget cuts or economic downturns. After repeated budget cuts at the University of Wisconsin system, other state institutions aggressively pursued Wisconsin's best faculty and researchers with offers of better pay and facilities. This tactic was successful, and the University of Wisconsin lost several top faculty to other universities, including private institutions (Foley, 2007).

Rewarding Employees through Nonsalary Means

In the past, public sector jobs were viewed as providing low pay but good benefits and job stability. However, the recent economic downtown has altered this perception. The Cato Institute published a report citing U.S. Bureau of Labor Statistics figures that showed public sector compensation averaged $39.66 per hour in 2009, 45% higher than the private sector average of $37.42 per hour for the same period (Edwards, 2010). The Cato Institute also found that state and local governments continue to cover a significantly higher share of health insurance, retirement benefits, life insurance, and paid sick leave (Edwards, 2010).

The continuing economic decline and evaporating tax bases for state and local governments is changing the stability equation of public sector jobs and their competitive pay and benefit structures. Public sector jobs are just as likely to be shed as private sector jobs. The recent federal stimulus plan attempted to preserve as many public sector jobs as possible such as police officers and teachers, to prevent the public sector from adding to the erosion of jobs that was occurring in the private sector. However, the slide in revenues and the mounting pressures from pension and health benefit obligations has forced many public organizations to make substantial reductions in public sector employment.

The public sector will have to exercise greater flexibility in setting future pay and benefits for its workforce. Future employees are more likely to favor higher pay and lower benefits in exchange for more work and life balance. Public sector organizations will have to incorporate more cross-training, greater use of temporary or contingent workers, and outsourcing to control salary and benefit costs and eliminate future obligations such as pension and health benefit costs. Public sector agencies would benefit from emulating private sector strategies, where employees are moved to defined contribution plans and the matching of employer contributions to employee plans depends on competitive labor market conditions and the fiscal health of the organization and the community. While it has always been important to have nonpay incentives to attract, retain, and reward public sector employees, the current economic environment is putting a premium on programs such as flexible hours, four-day workweeks, and wellness incentives to reduce health benefit costs. In a world where the mantra is "more with less," it is critical to compensate employees without breaking the budget.

Disciplining Employees

Discipline is a process to correct poor performance or in response to a violation of organizational work rules and policies. Discipline is also a process to maintain a proper work standard that is reinforced through daily communication. The type and severity of discipline applied to employees varies depending on the type of violation or misconduct. The best kind of discipline is applied on a timely basis and is appropriate to the scale of the misconduct. It is vital to document improper personnel conduct quickly and thoroughly.

Supervisory personnel must ensure that employees understand what is expected of them in terms of work performance and working relationships. When faced with improper actions or behavior by employees, it is incumbent on employers to use these opportunities to educate and provide training to employees on the organization's goals and objectives. This is particularity important during an employee's probationary period. Employees will assume that unacceptable working standards or behaviors are acceptable because they have not been challenged and corrected by a supervisor. Taking action early is an excellent strategy to set a positive tone and to prevent the need for stronger action at a later stage. If an employee's behavior is unsatisfactory during probation, it is probably a good indicator that future behavior will not be satisfactory either.

Employees who are performing their jobs well and meet all organizational requirements depend upon the supervisor to discipline employees who are not performing their jobs correctly. There is no quicker way to destroy morale and reduce productivity than to fail to address disciplinary issues quickly and appropriately. An administrator needs to provide all supervisors with training on how to administer appropriate discipline. In addition, each public agency needs to set up a system of providing human resources expertise and legal support to the supervisors and their departments on how to reward and discipline employees and the procedural processes necessary to implement effective disciplinary actions that are prompt, consistent, and appropriate.

Investigations

Before taking disciplinary action, it is necessary to prove that an employee did make an error and, if it did occur, to determine what action should be taken against the employee. One way to achieve this is to conduct a full, fair, and impartial investigation. Supervisors must obtain all the relevant information and documentation on each personnel matter under investigation. It is important to interview all the individuals who can provide information on the matter in an open process to obtain all points of view. An administrator must go to extensive lengths to ensure that the investigation is thorough and unbiased. It is sometimes necessary to have an external agent conduct an investigation to ensure impartially. While the investigation needs to be thorough, it is just as important to conduct the investigation in a timely manner. An administrator must be especially mindful of the organization's time frames for investigations, levying of charges, and appeal processes.

Process and Procedures in Place

An administrator will need to follow a defined process when levying discipline. Usually this requires putting the charges in writing and citing the appropriate human resources rules, procedures, or policies that have been violated. The charges must be clear and understandable by all parties involved in the personnel action. When outlining the charges, it is incumbent on the supervisor drafting the charges to review the employee's prior work history to see if this employee has any documented infractions. It is necessary to set the punishment in relation to the severity of the case and any relevant prior incidents. It is imperative that good documentation be produced along the entire disciplinary process in order to uphold the actions that were taken by the supervisors.

Establishing Expectations

For the orderly management of any public organization, it is essential for all members of the organization to know what is expected from them in the performance of their work duties. Discipline is not cruel but necessary to help employees comply with the organization's rules and goals and to provide timely and appropriate correction of improper behavior. Inappropriate employee behavior that is not corrected quickly usually leads to further and more severe violations in the future. Discipline must also be applied consistently. Employees need to understand that the organization will handle all personnel infractions in the same manner regardless of the employee's rank, job assignment, pay, race, gender, or any other characteristics. Disciplinary action must be well documented. In the event of future litigation, a successful case may hinge on how thorough disciplinary documentation was. Employees who earn multiple infractions will be eligible for harsher discipline, including termination. This means that discipline must be applied progressively. Initial or small violations can be addressed with verbal counseling or written reprimands. Subsequent or more serious violations can be managed with suspensions, transfers, or terminations. The more serious the discipline, the greater the need for precise documentation because this documentation will be needed if disciplinary actions are challenged by the employee, employee associations or other representatives, management, elected officials, citizens, or the media. Uniformed employee organizations like police and firefighters often codify types of discipline and severity of punishment in a standard operating procedures document.

Many public sector employees have the right to a hearing prior to termination so that they have an opportunity to respond to the reasons the employer has provided for terminating them from their positions. This right was established in the court case *Cleveland Board of Education v. Loudermill*, which established that certain public employees "have a property interest in their employment" and because of constitutional due process are entitled to a hearing or a written notice in which charges are described and the accused has a chance to defend themselves and to determine if errors were made by management or if management has reasonable cause to terminate the employee (United States Supreme Court, 1985). If reasonable cause for termination is confirmed, the employee is entitled to a written final termination notice.

The Finer Points of the Disciplinary Process

Organizations need to create a written process to allow employees to appeal most personnel actions and to file personnel grievances against rules, procedures, and policies that they feel are improper or in violation of the law. Some organizations do not permit appeals of some minor disciplinary actions such as verbal reprimands or demotions. While personnel rules and disciplinary procedures are very important, it is equally important to train all supervisory personnel to know the organization's personnel rules and to know how to identify and deal with violations. The organization must be supportive of supervisors who take appropriate actions when dealing with disciplinary matters. Effective disciplinary processes require an investment of time—time that may infringe on the supervisor's primary duties. Supervisors need to be given enough time to deal with discipline issues properly and not be pressured to hurry through the process.

An administrator needs to remember that under Weingarten rights, employees in unionized organizations are entitled to representation during an investigative interview that may lead to disciplinary action (United States Supreme Court, 1975). These rights were established in the court case *National Labor Relations Board (NLRB) v. J. Weingarten Inc.* In July 2000, President Clinton expanded these rights to nonunionized organizations, but this was reversed by President Bush in July 2004. The Supreme Court decision in *Garrity v. New Jersey* states that under the Fifth Amendment's protection against self-incrimination, public employees may not be compelled to make a choice between self-incrimination or job forfeiture (United States Supreme Court, 1967). While this ruling was a response to an incident involving law enforcement personnel, all public employees have the same rights under the Garrity ruling.

Training Supervisors

It is imperative that any employee with supervisory responsibilities be provided with training that includes handling discipline issues. This training is necessary to ensure that supervisors maintain the expected level of employee performance in the organization and that disciplinary actions will be timely, consistent, impartial, and appropriate. All levels of supervision, including top executives, must receive this training or must demonstrate an understanding of proper disciplinary procedures.

Managers at all levels need to be cognizant of disciplinary actions conducted within the organization that are not well documented or in accordance with the organization's rules and procedures and must take steps to review or stop the disciplinary process if mistakes have been made. If necessary, upper management may need to reverse lower-level personnel actions if they are not well grounded or are more stringent than the infraction warrants. It is better to correct inappropriate employee behavior at its early stages through lower levels of management to reduce costs and prevent inappropriate behavior from spreading to other personnel or departments. The best way management can control inappropriate behavior is to model the behavior desired by the organization.

Author's Experience

While it is important for public agencies to ensure that salaries and benefits are competitive with the private sector, it becomes problematic when salaries and benefits exceed those in the private sector. Mr. Benavides has learned from previous experience how critical citizens, elected officials, and the media become when public sector employees appear to or actually have better compensation packages than private sector employees. However, this criticism can be diminished if compensation is benchmarked to the area's market average and management can demonstrate their research to skeptical citizens. It is more difficult to achieve this goal with uniformed police and firefighters because there are few private sector analogies for salary audits; however, uniformed personnel's pay and benefits should at least be in line with other public sector employees. Then there are those times when public entities have to compete for employees in popular fields such as information technology, engineering, and medicine, where the level of pay would have to be very high to attract top candidates. In a situation like this, public agencies must acknowledge that they may not be able to provide rich compensation and should consider contracting employees or even outsourcing. Public agencies receive their hardest criticism during economic downturns because so many citizens are unemployed or underemployed while their taxes continue to pay for public employees' salaries and benefits at levels not seen in some areas of private industry.

Final Notes

Public organizations' human resource offices should provide supervisory training on how to deal with the appellate procedures of the organization and how to handle civil service or legal proceedings when disciplinary issues reach the later stages of the disciplinary process. Most supervisory personnel rarely have the kind of experience necessary to deal with disciplinary actions that reach civil-service board- or court-level adjudication and will need guidance to prevent making costly mistakes. Organizations need to be aware of media interest in high-profile disciplinary actions, especially those involving a great deal of expenditures due to adverse court rulings, large personal settlements, whistle-blower actions, or inappropriately harsh or lenient enforcement of personnel rules, and make plans to answer public concerns. When an employee is terminated, select a neutral site to inform the employee, keep the interview brief, have witnesses present at the termination, and record the procedure (Kulik). Take precautions in the event the person becomes violent by having security on standby, for example. Establish security mechanisms to enable terminated employees to gather their personal items and leave the building quietly and discretely.

Important Points to Remember

Because your employees are your most valuable asset, is important to reward and discipline them in a manner that keeps the organization focused on performance and alignment. The top rewarding and discipline points are as follows:

1. The pay structures that you design and implement need to be clear and create the type of environment that the organization desires.
2. The salary and benefit structure that is employed needs to be set in accordance with the policy of where the organization wants to be in relation to the market.
3. In addition, it is also important to create and use nonpay incentives and rewards to compensate your workforce or supplement your compensation systems.
4. The disciplinary process and procedures used must be clearly outlined and explained to the entire workforce so that the organization's expectations can be understood and how noncompliance with the organization's personnel rules will be administered.
5. The workforce must be given training on a continuing basis on how to administer the organization's pay and disciplinary systems so that they are fairly and equitability used.
6. It is important to treat everyone fairly in your organization.
7. Consistency in implementing the process of rewarding and disciplining your employees is key to avoiding problems in the areas of pay and discipline.
8. Let employees know how they are doing on a consistent and regular basis.
9. Respect and value your employees, and they will return the same to the organization.
10. Be sincere whenever giving feedback on performance, providing direction, or taking disciplinary actions.

CASE STUDY 6.1
Disaster at Municipality

SITUATION FOR CASE STUDY 6.1

You are a city manager for Hawk, Texas, and have been working for the city more than five years. Hawk has a population of around 8,000 inhabitants and consists largely of blue collar workers as well as farmers. The crime rate is fairly low, but the police department is small and the city has few resources to give the police department additional equipment or manpower. Geographically, the city is located next to a large body of water and has several inlets along the coastal areas.

On September 21, 2005, Galveston evacuated the city ahead of Hurricane Rita's landfall. Your city is in the path of the oncoming hurricane. On September 22, Texas Governor Rick Perry ordered the highway system to flow in one direction to accommodate the size of the en masse evacuation from the coastal areas. Larger metropolitan cities such as Houston began to evacuate their citizens as Hurricane Rita approached.

On September 23, Hurricane Rita struck your city and inflicted a massive amount of destruction to houses, businesses, and infrastructure. You are missing two of your police officers, who are critical for your first-responder capability. After searching for your two missing officers, you discovered that they literally walked off the job. You now have a crisis on your hands as you try to get more first responders to assist people who could be injured. Your police department is responsible for protecting the city from looters. The department, which is now comprised of 18 on-duty officers, is stretched thin.

Your city sustained severe infrastructure damage, and you need help getting electrical, gas, and water systems back in operation. You have some mutual aid agreements with other municipalities, but you realize that those municipalities may be in the same situation as you are and that they will address their own emergencies before sending any aid to Hawk. You face the prospect of enlisting volunteers to assist in the repair work to relieve your remaining city employees who are now getting exhausted. The National Guard has been activated to assist with the crisis, but they are nowhere near your city to offer immediate assistance.

1. How do you recruit personnel for first responders?
2. What is the responsibility of public officials to the public in times of crisis?
3. How will you get volunteers for infrastructure repair?
4. How will you prioritize your city's needs vis-à-vis the needs of your city employees?

WHAT ACTUALLY HAPPENED IN CASE STUDY 6.1

Evacuation of the city was ordered by city officials. The city's first responders were charged with assisting motorists along the evacuation routes. The hurricane caused a huge influx of people from outside the city who had to travel through the area to reach safety. Cities such as Houston evacuated early, which caused significant traffic congestion on all of the roads. City officials were literally handing out water and food to motorists as they drove through Hawk. The horrible traffic conditions also meant that Hawk's residents left later than they had planned. The traffic and need for evacuation flow control strained local police resources.

The city manager ordered all citizens to evacuate the city and made a statement that residents were on their own if they chose to ignore the order. This was in large part due to the fact that the city manager would not risk first-responder lives on residents who essentially placed themselves in potential danger voluntarily. Hurricane Rita did hit the city and cause damage to the community. The two first responders who abandoned their posts and left the city during the time of the natural disaster have not been rehired by the city (2010). The city manager of the city stated that he "would never rehire those individuals again."

KEY ISSUES RAISED IN CASE STUDY 6.1

Abandonment of a civil-service post or an at-will employment situation (which was the employment agreement for the police officers of the City of Hawk) during times of crisis raises several issues. Certainly there were many cases in New Orleans during Hurricane Katrina where first responders left the city and did not return (Coral Springs, 2007). During Hurricane Rita, several first responders also left the cities that were in the hurricane's path. First responders take an oath to defend, protect, and serve the public. All first responders understand when they are hired that emergency situations can arise not only from criminal and terrorist threats but also from natural disasters. First responders are necessary to ensure the public is safe from harm and to ensure public order is kept by preventing rioting and looting.

First-responder employment comes with the understanding that their services will be required in times of crisis regardless of any personal concerns or dangers the first responders must face. While it is the duty of the organization to ensure all steps are taken to protect first responders from harm, it is the duty of first responders to act when required in the appropriate manner in the way that their job responsibilities and training mandate. Upon abandonment of one's job, an organization is not legally required to retain that employee. In the case of Hawk, the two officers left voluntarily, thus vacating the positions.

WHAT COULD HAVE HAPPENED IN CASE STUDY 6.1

If possible, Hawk should develop a reserve force of volunteer police officers to deploy in times of crisis. In regard to the two police officers who abandoned their posts, the municipality should never rehire these two first responders since the public cannot rely on them to perform their duties during times of crisis. The municipality should begin to search for their replacements immediately.

CASE STUDY 6.2
Dealing with Abusive Coworkers

SITUATION FOR CASE STUDY 6.2

You are an employee in a medical unit at a maximum-security state prison. The prison has a warden who is in charge of security and who oversees a diverse staff of prison guards and staff support. The prison houses around 1,500 inmates and provides a large medical unit that supports an entire region for the state prison system. You are a medical doctor who has worked for the state prison system for a number of years. A 63-year-old fellow medical employee named Nats is often abusive to other employees in your department. Nats is frequently absent from work and often arrives late. The only supervisor over your department is located 600 miles away and has limited oversight of any of the prison medical units. The situation is getting worse, and now junior members of the staff are turning to you for some type of leadership and stability.

1. What are you going to do about Nats?
2. What do you expect will happen when you take action?

You have contacted your supervisor about the situation with Nats. The supervisor's solution is to install you as the manager for your department and grant you the authority to take any necessary human resources action against Nats. It has now come to your attention that Nats will attempt to litigate if any action is taken against him. However, you refuse to allow Nats to continue to abuse the junior members in your department. You are now attempting to use the human resource policies to gain leverage over Nats.

1. How do you proceed with Nats?
2. What consequences do your actions have?

Over the course of a year you have documented every infraction committed by Nats, including when he was late to work, when he left work early, disruptive actions, security policy violations (which have now come to the attention of the prison warden), and Nats's insubordination to you at every turn.

1. Will the effort to document Nats's actions benefit you in the long run?
2. Will the action steps that you have taken lessen the disruption Nats has caused to your staff?
3. How serious is the issue of Nats infringing upon the warden's security policies?

Prison security issues cannot be ignored or violated, particularly since this prison has experienced riots in the past. You decide that you now have enough documentation to justify terminating Nats from his position at the medical unit. Nats promptly sues you and the state in civil court and files a grievance against you with the state medical board. Due to your meticulous documentation, both of Nats's efforts fail.

After contending with Nats and enduring a long commute every week, you decide to transfer to a prison closer to where you live. You are put into a managerial leadership position over the medical unit upon arrival. One day you and the warden have an argument over whether a prisoner should be transferred outside the prison for medical care. Since the medical unit has authorization to do the transfer of the prisoner, the warden expects you to comply with their wishes. You do not grant the authorization for the transfer since you believe there is no basis for the transfer on medical grounds.

The next day you are summoned to see two prisoners in the isolation wing. When you arrive, you notice that the guards usually posted are missing and doors that are supposed to be locked are open. After seeing the two prisoners, you decide to report this odd situation to your overall supervisor, who is based hundreds of miles away in the main state prison hospital. The supervisor informs you that similar situations have occurred before with other medical personnel who had disagreements over security issues, and that some medical personnel have been injured in these types of situations.

1. What is your interpretation of the situation?
2. What actions do you take?

WHAT ACTUALLY HAPPENED IN CASE STUDY 6.2

Ultimately, the manager transferred to another maximum security unit closer to home after his previous experience with Nats. After his confrontation with the warden and then being left alone with two prisoners without proper security, he consulted his supervisor. His supervisor told him these incidents in which medical personnel who had quarreled with the warden were placed in situations that exposed them to injury had occurred before. The supervisor understood that the manager would be in danger if he remained at that unit and offered the manager a transfer to a medical unit hundreds of miles away. Although the manager was not in a position to relocate his family, he decided that the environment was too dangerous, and 24 hours later he resigned from his position. It is unknown whether this incident was ever investigated by the proper authorities.

KEY ISSUES RAISED IN CASE STUDY 6.2

How do you discipline a highly skilled employee who works in a dangerous and stressful environment and would be difficult to replace? Unfortunately, organizations that have dangerous work environments—and have a difficult time filling vacant positions—are more likely to tolerate trouble employees unless they begin to further disrupt the environment or the employee begins to destabilize the safety and security of the environment. The doctor addressed the situation of the violent employee by contacting his superior to ask for guidance. Once he was granted managerial authority, he began to document policy violations by the employee. Although it took a year, the documentation effort proved to be very successful and essentially paved the way for the employee's termination. The documentation protected the doctor and the state later when the terminated employee filed a grievance and a civil suit, both of which were overturned based on the completeness and strength of the documentation.

The issue of the doctor's safety in the second prison brings up several key human resource issues. How do you protect skilled professionals who work in a dangerous environment? Since security was under the warden's purview, the warden was responsible for the medical staff's protection. However, it could not be proven if the warden orchestrated the doctor's dangerous situation because of a disagreement. At best, a lack of protection in an isolation ward points to failures in security or incompetence rather than violent intent. The prison itself could have been held liable if any injury occurred to the medical doctor in that situation. There could have been legal judgments against the state as well.

WHAT COULD HAVE HAPPENED IN CASE STUDY 6.2

Although the manager was correct in documenting Nats's behavior, the documentation process was lengthy and enabled Nats to continue to disrupt the department. Documentation protects the organization and the manager from legal reprisals but does not alleviate other employees' misery from working with a dysfunctional employee. Documenting poor behavior is a passive response to poor behavior; it must be supplemented with direct and immediate responses that include private consultation, consultation with witnesses, reassignment to other projects, written reprimands that are placed in the employee's personnel file, and poor performance evaluations. Safety violations should be immediately reported to upper administration for an investigation.

CASE STUDY 6.3
Smoking Policy

SITUATION FOR CASE STUDY 6.3

You are the fire chief for the City of Rags, Texas. The city currently has 120,000 residents and is growing at a rapid pace. You are responsible for not only the inhabited areas of the city but also large tracts of rural farmland that has not yet been developed. The firefighting staff has been severely underfunded for years, and as a result you only have half the firefighters that you need for a city this size. This situation is not likely to change since firefighters are both expensive to hire and retain and in short supply in the first place. If firefighters are hired, they usually have to go to an academy (which is also expensive) and are unavailable to work while they attend the academy. There is also the cost of supervising the new firefighters during their probationary period.

The city manager's office has decided that it is time to upgrade their risk management policies. The current risk management policies are out of date, insufficient, and not recorded digitally because the last time they were updated it was done on a typewriter. The current risk management policies do not address any issues for employees wearing protective gear, for example, using steel-toed boots for construction work. Risk management policies are necessary to protect the city from liability and to protect employees from risk and are used to reduce or cut costs for organizations in respect to employees taking sick time or being off the job for injury-related reasons.

The new risk management policies propose a strict antismoking policy that prohibits smoking within 25 feet of any municipal facility or inside municipal vehicles. The city manager's office is eager to pass the new antismoking policies to prevent employees from smoking inside municipal vehicles. Also, it is possible that by having an antismoking policy in place, health care costs for the city could be reduced when the municipality negotiates health care coverage. You know that more than half of your seasoned firefighters, many of whom are otherwise very good at their jobs, are heavy smokers and would potentially violate these new policies or go to work somewhere else that did not have a no-smoking policy.

The city manager's office succeeds in implementing the new risk management policies, including the antismoking policy. You have already given verbal warnings to employees who are violating the new policies, and yet the violations continue. In your opinion, firefighters are expensive to train, and it is extremely hard to recruit good personnel for those positions. You would hate to lose any of the firefighters you already have on staff.

1. What is your response to the current situation?
2. What is the consequence to the actions that you take?
3. Is the city justified in putting in place new antismoking policies?
4. Will the new antismoking policy reduce costs to the city?
5. How will the new antismoking policy impact recruiting for the fire department?

WHAT ACTUALLY HAPPENED IN CASE STUDY 6.3

This situation occurred at a municipality that was in the process of rewriting its risk management policies. The smoking clause was eventually removed from the risk management policies because the fire chief pointed out that his firefighters were already restricted to smoking in the firehouse garage and felt that his firefighters would not support a more restrictive clause. The fire chief also mentioned to the assistant city manager that the firefighters had made progress in their efforts to reduce smoking. In the end, the assistant city manager relented and took the proposed smoking restriction clause out of the risk management policies.

KEY ISSUES RAISED IN CASE STUDY 6.3

Smoking ban statutes are fairly new with public organizations, although such bans have been instituted around the country since the early 1970s. At some public organizations, for example, the University of Texas Southwestern Medical School, smoking is banned on the entire campus. Health care institutions tend to be much more stringent about antismoking clauses than other organizations because their patients can be sensitive to second-hand smoke. At many places, designated smoking areas are located far away from the general areas to limit smoke exposure to bystanders. Smoking can increase health problems and in turn increases the costs of medical insurance and the number of sick days taken by employees who suffer health problems resulting from smoking. Therefore, many organizations offer incentives to stop smoking or seek applicants who do not appear to smoke, although excluding applicants who appear to smoke may cause legal problems for the organization.

WHAT COULD HAVE HAPPENED IN CASE STUDY 6.3

The assistant city manager created an environment resistant to the proposed risk management plans by failing to communicate with the department heads prior to introducing the plans at the departmental meeting. The department heads felt that they were being ordered to accept the new plans rather than being consulted for their professional opinions. The assistant city manager could have sent a rough draft of the policies and requested input prior to introducing the plans at the departmental meeting. The assistant city manager could have considered incentives to encourage employees to quit smoking. Incentives are sometimes received more positively by employees than punishments, although compliance might be less universal. Other cities' policies could have been reviewed and those municipal leaders contacted to determine how their antismoking policies have impacted their organizations. A return on investment study could have been initiated to see if offering incentives would actually lower the costs of health insurance as well as improving effectiveness and efficiency of workers who quit smoking.

CASE STUDY 6.4
Unauthorized Pay Increases

SITUATION FOR CASE STUDY 6.4

You are the city manager of a large metropolitan city with a population of more than half a million people. This city is run by a council-manager form of government. The city council was faced with the option of enabling two executive officers, who had been selected and was supervised by the city council, to grant or refuse pay raises to their employees without the express consent of the city council. The city council had voted to allow only police officers and firefighters to receive across-the-board pay raises and to continue to receive incremental pay raises while civilian employees would only receive pay adjustments through promotions. Recently, the city attorney and the city auditor—both of whom are direct reports to the council—granted merit pay adjustments to 14 employees in the attorney's office and 2 employees in the auditor's office. These merit pay adjustments were done without the approval of the city council. You learned of the merit pay adjustments when the human resources director, who reports directly to you, informed you that paperwork had been submitted to payroll for processing. None of these employees had been granted promotions.

You contact the city auditor, who is not only a colleague but a good friend, to discuss the merit pay adjustments she granted to her two employees. You remind the city auditor of the council's directive that no civilian employees can be awarded pay adjustments except for promotions and that the auditor's request was not in compliance with council policy. However, the auditor still intended to proceed with the pay adjustments. The human resources director will not process the pay adjustments unless directly ordered by you to proceed. You now have to decide whether to support the human resources director's decision to deny the pay adjustment requests or to authorize the pay adjustments in contradiction to the city council's policy. After giving the problem some thought, you decide to allow the pay adjustments to be processed. You inform the human resources director to draft a memorandum authorizing the adjustments and placing responsibility for the decision on you. The human resources director wrote the memo and then processed the pay adjustments.

1. What should the human resources director have done in this matter?
2. How should the city manager have handled this matter?
3. What was the city manager's obligation to the city council?

WHAT ACTUALLY HAPPENED IN CASE STUDY 6.4

The city manager never informed the council of the unauthorized pay adjustments by the city attorney and city auditor. Since the city manager did not have a good relationship with the attorney, he did not speak with him about the pay adjustments. Furthermore, the attorney had the support of the mayor and the majority of the city council, while the city manager's own standing with the mayor and the council was less secure. Later, the council asked the city manager if he had ever awarded any unauthorized pay raises to civilian employees. The city manager confessed that he had processed several pay raises for the city attorney and city auditor. The council became angry at the city manager for not stopping the unauthorized pay raises. The council then asked if the city manager had authorized any pay adjustments for his own staff, to which he responded that he had not. When the council asked why the city manager had not informed the council about the unauthorized pay raises nor tried to stop them, the city manager said that he was not in a position to stop the adjustments because the city attorney and the city auditor did not report to him. The city council demanded that the city attorney and the city auditor justify their unauthorized actions in a public meeting. Both city officials provided written and verbal explanations for their actions. They were verbally reprimanded by the city council for their actions, but the unauthorized pay adjustments were not rescinded.

KEY ISSUES RAISED IN CASE STUDY 6.4

The key issue raised in this case study involves organizational structure and responsibility. While the city manager is directly responsible for human resources and payroll issues, he was not the direct supervisor of the city auditor, who was a personal friend, or the city attorney, who had strong political support from the mayor and council. If these requests had been made by any other supervisor, the city manager would have likely rejected them. The city manager did not apply policy evenly to all pay adjustment requests. He based his decision on political considerations. Were politics also at play when the city council issued only mild reprimands to the attorney and the auditor and did not rescind the pay adjustments? The city manager had approached the auditor about her pay adjustment request but did not speak with the attorney about his pay adjustment request. Did this uneven treatment affect the council's decision regarding the reprimands?

WHAT COULD HAVE HAPPENED IN CASE STUDY 6.4

When the human resources director informed the city manager of the impending pay actions by the city attorney and the city auditor, she could have informed the city manager that she would not process the unauthorized pay actions. In addition, she could have refused to process the pay actions even after the city manager had authorized her to do so, requiring the approval of the city council for the pay adjustments. If the city attorney and the city auditor refused to ask the city council for authorization, then the city manager could have placed an item on the council's executive session agenda. Aggressive action like this can be necessary for self-preservation; the city council could have reprimanded the city manager for not following council policy and for being an accessory to the city attorney's and city auditor's illegal actions.

Suggested Readings for Chapter 6

Beam, George, 2001. *Public management: What it is and how it can be improved and advanced.* ISBN: 0-8304-1569-6. Chicago: Burnbum Inc.

Mader-Clark, Margaret, and Guerin, Lisa, 2007. *The progressive discipline handbook: Smart strategies for coaching employees.* ISBN: 141330561X. Berkeley, California: NOLO.

Mitchell, Olivia, and Anderson, Gary, 2009. *The future of public employee retirement systems.* ISBN: 978-0-19-957334-9. New York: Oxford University Press.

Randall, Harvey, and Randall, Eric D., 2009. *The discipline book.* ISBN: 9781601458001. Bangor, Maine: Booklocker.com., Inc.

Redeker, James R., 1989. *Employee discipline: Policies and practices.* ISBN: 0871795957. Bethasda, Maryland: Bureau of National Affairs Books.

Wise, David (Editor), 1987. *Public sector payrolls.* ISBN: 9780226902913. Chicago: The University of Chicago Press.

Chapter 7

Retention and Separation of Employees

Employee retention and separation strategies need to be closely aligned as part of an overall organizational strategy to have the best workforce possible. Employee turnover is a great concern for most public organizations because recruitment and training of new employees can be time consuming and costly. Although it is impossible to eliminate all turnovers, public organizations should endeavor to keep the turnover rates as low as possible because they usually do not have the resources to compete effectively with the private sector for skilled workers, especially during prosperous economic times. A wide range of strategies, including competitive pay and benefits, liberal time off, family-friendly policies, mentoring, training, good working conditions, clear career ladders, open and fair promotional practices, challenging and fulfilling work, and excellent leadership, can be used to retain talented and experienced public employees. In some circumstances employees must be separated from the organization because of budgetary conditions or performance issues. The processes by which employees are separated from an organization are as critical as those concerning recruitment and retention. This chapter will explore how to accomplish retention and separation successfully and thereby enable the organization to achieve its goals.

Evaluation of Employee Knowledge, Skills, and Abilities

Successful organizations constantly evaluate the knowledge, skills, and abilities (KSA) of their employees to determine who should be retained, who requires further training, and who could be replaced by a better-performing individual. The evaluation process is a continual one. As the organization evolves, employees who were once competitive might require training to keep their skills current, while weaker employees might improve considerably over time. All employees must have technical and functional experience, have an understanding of the public service area they are working in, and maintain a results-oriented attitude. As public service employees advance in their careers, they need to understand the importance of soft skills such as teamwork, communication skills, relationship skills, effectiveness, and leadership abilities. As they advance to higher-level positions, the vast majority of employees are less likely to use the technical skills that originally earned them employment and their early promotions. While they must maintain some of those technical skills, they must supplement those skills with soft management skills such as listening, consensus building, cooperation, speaking, writing, and leadership.

Generational Values in Relation to Employment

It is important to be sensitive to the differences among the different generations that comprise the workforce. It is also important to keep in mind that while each generation exhibits certain characteristics and holds distinct values, not all individuals fit into their generation's "profile." The smallest and oldest generation in the workforce was born prior to 1945. Known as the "greatest generation" and the "silent generation," these employees typically have vast work experience, appreciate common goals, and can make excellent mentors. Baby boomers are workers who were born roughly between 1946 and 1964. Baby boomers are dedicated, are committed, and consider themselves to be a special generation unlike any other before or after them. They are also known as the "sandwich generation" because they are caring for their aged parents while trying to raise and educate their children. This generation needs flexibility to deal with their personal responsibilities. Generation X, also known as Gen Xers, consists of employees who were born approximately between 1965 and 1976. They "work to live" not "live to work." Gen Xers believe a balance between life and work is essential for a good workplace environment and consider flexible work schedules to be the norm, not an exception. Gen Xers are not necessarily loyal to any organization and will frequently switch jobs. Some Gen Xers have found a near-perfect environment in colleges and universities as these institutions value flexible work schedules and the wide use of contract or contingent workers. The latest generation to enter the workforce is comprised of those born after 1977. Known variously as Gen Y, millennials, or echo boomers because they are the children of the baby boomers, these employees have high standards and expectations, a sense of entitlement, are responsive to recognition and praise, are civic minded, and are tolerant of diversity. They are also the best-educated group in history and are the most comfortable with technology.

It is important to recognize that different generations interact not only with each other but with their employers. The employer should remember that cultural, social, and ethnic factors can influence how employees work and how supervisors work with them. Taking these factors into account can help administrators as they build and manage their departments.

How Retention Impacts an Organization

High turnover rates can be financially costly to a department. For many public agencies, the size of the organization directly impacts its ability to deliver high-quality service. As governmental organizations grow, they require long-term employees that administrators can trust to be reliable and hard working. High turnover is disruptive and can result in service interruption and an increase in errors as new people learn on the job. Supervisors can foster an environment that motivates employees by making an effort to get to know their employees and by asking what is important to their employees, what they want to accomplish, and what their goals are. It is also important to review your organizational practices to see if you are meeting the expectations of your employees. Ensure that the organization creates job descriptions with clearly defined duties, interacts with employees instead of dictating to them, asks employees for their ideas, eliminates favoritism, refrains from using employees for tasks they were not hired to do, and aligns responsibility with authority.

Strategies for Improving Retention

An organization that treats its employees with respect and provides them with challenging and meaningful work is much more likely to retain its best performers even when those employees are offered higher wages at a competing organization. Good employees will want opportunities to train and upgrade their own skills, so provide your employees with training as your budget allows. Employees are more likely to continue their employment at an organization where they can communicate openly and freely with all levels of management. This benefits not only the employee but also the organization. The organization will receive valuable, truthful input from their employees on how work is progressing and where problems are occurring. Administrators must be willing to solicit and accept feedback from employees, no matter how unpleasant the information might be.

Administrators should provide employees with opportunities for personal growth within the organization and make employees feel like an important part of the team. Ensure employees who are loyal, maintain positive attitudes, and provide good work have opportunities for career advancement within the organization. Other incentives can include educational programs, tuition reimbursement benefits, and sabbaticals. The pay and benefits system must be competitive, provide fair pay practices, and compensate employees for learning new skills. Conflict resolution through the establishment of a timely and fair grievance process can improve working relationships among employees.

Balance is the key to good supervision and contented employees. While most supervisors want employees who can be flexible with their working schedules to fill in for absent coworkers or to deal with an emergency situation, supervisors must also understand that employees have personal responsibilities—families, homes, community involvement—and depend on their supervisors' flexibility in this area. A supervisor who allows a working mother to go to a parent-teacher conference during a slow time, for example, can more likely count on her to work extra hours on a time-sensitive project, or at least have the moral authority to ask for those extra hours. It is equally important for supervisors to maintain just enough personal distance to prevent favoritism and to enable them to apply discipline when necessary. As the nature of work has changed from the output of product into using special skills and knowledge to provide service, employees are no longer just workers but colleagues.

Sometimes termination can improve retention. The termination of an employee should only occur when it is clear that the employee is not meeting the basic standards of the organization. Employees who do not adhere to policies about proper conduct or who do not complete their tasks generate conflict among employees who are compliant and productive. The continued employment of poor performers undermines the other employees' motivation to work hard because they see no repercussions for poor performance. Poor performance in one employee can also undo the excellent work of others or cause other employees to forgo their duties to take on the underachiever's work load. It is better to remove the poor performer before the good employees find work elsewhere.

All organizations deal with turnover. The rate of turnover varies from job to job and from one public entity to another. Organizations that do not have competitive pay and benefit structures, are not supportive of their employees, or are structurally unstable are more likely to have high turnover rates. However, positions that are very demanding, stressful, or dangerous can also contribute to high turnover rates regardless of how well the organization is managed. If an organization experiences high turnover, the causes must be determined. Sometimes people leave for reasons that administrations cannot control, such as retirement or relocation due to family needs. Sometimes employees leave because they are offered salaries that your organization is unwilling or unable to match. However, turnover due to poor working conditions, poor leadership, an unstable organization setting, uncompetitive pay and benefits, or lack of challenging work is within a supervisor's power to correct.

Organizational Assessment

To determine if turnover is due to specific workplace issues, it is necessary to incorporate some kind of exit survey into the job separation process. This survey can be a few questions regarding overall job satisfaction, empowerment, fulfillment, salary, satisfaction with work groups, security, training, and quality of benefits. The survey can be completed in the human resources office or some other neutral place and should not be mandatory. Data from these surveys, no matter how painful or unfair the answers might seem, can provide important information on the effectiveness of an organization's retention strategies and policies.

Another feedback tool is the job satisfaction survey of all current employees. To ensure that data from job satisfaction surveys are unbiased and honest, the survey must be absolutely anonymous. If employees believe that their responses can be traced back to them, they will not answer the survey honestly, if at all. Information derived from the satisfaction survey must be acted upon in a positive manner and must generate real change within the organization. Otherwise, it is an empty gesture that employees will disregard in the future.

Another way to retain employees is through engagement with the organization. Effective engagement occurs when employees are given critical information that helps them to understand the organization's goals, needs, and methods. A common mechanism for delivering this information is the new employees' orientation. Another mechanism is targeted training and development that strengthens employees' skills in their field, for example, Microsoft Word and Excel training for administrative assistants. Providing career planning for entry-level employees is another way to engage and motivate employees. Employees who believe that the organization values their contributions and that it cares about their well-being will more likely feel a greater sense of commitment to the organization and will strive to help it succeed.

An employee who cannot or will not perform his or her job duties and does not contribute to the organization's performance goals must be dismissed. As budget shortfalls become the norm, organizations can no longer afford to keep unproductive employees by shifting them into nonessential positions. There are no nonessential positions anymore. The recruitment process has become a vital tool in identifying the best potential employees and eliminating the wasted resources that are expended when dealing with poor hires. Replacing poorly performing employees with new employees who bring improved skills and knowledge will keep the organization in the forefront of the public service arena and enable it to perform quality services that the public demands.

Layoffs

Layoffs, or terminations due to budgetary constraints, are unrelated to employee performance. Occasionally, organizations are required to reduce personnel to cope with economic conditions or to streamline operations to provide public services in the most efficient manner. Layoffs must be executed with care, and the process needs to be transparent to all employees.

Every effort should be made to minimize the negative effects of layoffs. Formulate a communication plan that includes why the layoff is necessary and how many employees and in which areas the layoff is most likely to impact. The communication plan must include the public, the media, and elected officials. To secure sufficient support for the layoff, it may be necessary to inform elected officials before any other groups, including employees, are informed. The organization's legal department needs to be fully engaged in the planning and implementation phases to minimize the risk of lawsuits and to ensure that no one group (race, age, etc.) is overrepresented. Conduct an assessment of how employees are likely to react to the layoff announcement, taking the organization's culture into consideration. Rumors need to be acknowledged and addressed promptly with facts. A completely transparent process is essential to preserve the organization's credibility with the workforce.

Employees involved in the layoff process deserve to be treated fairly. The layoff process should be handled privately and face-to-face with supervisors properly prepared to deliver the information accurately and in a sensitive manner. Remember to thank the employees for their service. Shake their hands. These tokens of respect are very important to employees, will lessen the pain of separation, and will leave a lasting, positive image of the organization with the departing employees. Provide a transition out of the organization with outplacement assistance that includes resume writing, interview training, and job placement within other departments in the organization, with other government agencies, or with the private sector. In many public organizations, layoffs are regulated by civil service processes that take into account labor contract requirements and seniority rules.

After the layoffs occur, care must be taken with the remaining employees. Some may feel that they do not deserve to be saved from the layoff process. The layoff could engender a feeling of job insecurity. Employees may find their job duties and assignments altered or increased as work is distributed to the remaining employees without additional compensation. Be prepared to provide counseling to assist employees through the transition.

There are several alternatives to layoffs that reduce costs and make the organization leaner and more efficient. Many organizations have used financial incentives to induce employees to retire early. If time allows, the use of hiring freezes will slowly reduce the workforce as workers quit or retire. Eliminating overtime work is another method to reduce staffing costs. Offering employees the opportunity to share jobs and work fewer hours can avert a layoff. Another tactic is *in-sourcing*, where job functions that contractors had normally provided can be added to the list of tasks performed by permanent employees, thus cutting costs. Examples of this include light janitorial work and small maintenance jobs. Regardless of what tactics are used to cut costs, human resources will need to be engaged with management to determine the minimum number of employees necessary to fulfill the mission of the organization.

Author's Experience

Mr. Benavides hired the first African American police chief in the history of the city in 1999. Although he considered him to be an excellent person for police chief, the chief started having problems with the media, the police department workforce, and the public. However, Benavides did not document the police chief's managerial shortcomings because all personnel files were subject to open records requests. All job reviews were conducted verbally, and no documentation was generated. This caused problems for him later during the litigation over his termination. The police chief never received adequate feedback on his job performance. Therefore, his job performance continued to deteriorate. After four years, Benavides had no choice but to fire the police chief and replace him. The police chief sued Benavides personally for $50 million for allegedly exceeding his authority under the city charter and sued the city as well. Although the termination decision was upheld, the police chief appealed. During the next seven years, the city and Benavides appeared in the federal district court twice, the federal appeals courts twice, and then finally the Supreme Court, which upheld the termination when it refused to hear the police chief's appeal and let the federal appeals court ruling stand. The incident with the police chief was a painful object lesson on how not to retain and separate someone from a public organization.

Final Notes

Keeping the best employees is one of the most important things that management can do to keep its public organization running efficiently and effectively. While good pay and benefits are important for retention, other factors like employee involvement in the organization's decision-making process, providing challenging tasks, and a feeling of being valued and trusted keeps employees engaged and committed to the organization. Management needs to be vigilant in assessing the job satisfaction, attitudes, talents, and performance of its employees to encourage strong employees and identify weaker workers. Employers must be willing to remove employees not aligned with the goals and objectives of the organization. Sometimes this means finding duties or positions better suited to the interests and skills of the employees, and at other times this means eliminating these employees from the organization.

Retention and separation are difficult to accomplish in any organization, move so in public organizations. If the economy is good or the public organization is located in a well-paying, high-tech region, then retention will be very difficult for public organizations because of the intense local competition for top employees. Certain positions will experience higher turnover due to the stress level and workload associated with the job functions. In those cases, public organizations will need to assess how they can make employees' responsibilities and job functions less stressful and attempt to lighten workload through additional employees or through automating certain processes pertaining to that job function.

Higher education institutions have certain advantages for faculty retention that other public organizations do not provide. For example, a university can offer tenure and tenure track positions that essentially guarantee employment until they retire, barring any violation of policy or law. Furthermore, many higher education institutions allow employees to benefit from intellectual property rights, for example, publications, copyrights, and patents, thus ensuring that employees can receive at least some of the profits generated from their inventions. Outside most private technology companies and research organizations, this kind of financial arrangement is rare and can work as a financial inducement for highly skilled and well-trained employees to stay with the organization.

To retain good employees, public organizations must rely on their strengths over private industry. Public organizations have generally better benefits, offer more vacation and sick leave, enforce a 40-hour workweek, and do not engage in frequent layoffs or outsourcing. However, private industry can offer higher salaries, bonuses, stock options, and access to the latest equipment and nicer facilities than public organizations. Large private organizations can also offer quick career advancement for talented employees. Public organizations will need to find creative solutions to retain employees while being able to operate within legal statutes and constrained budgets.

Separation of employees can occur when the employee takes a position elsewhere, goes on permanent disability, or retires, or when the organization decides to lay off or terminate an employee. While layoffs are not common in public organizations, they do sometimes occur. In the public sector, layoffs occur when collected taxes in a municipality are below expectation, when patient load in a hospital is lower than expected, or enrollment in higher education institutions has declined.

When an employee is terminated, it is important for administrators to make sure that documentation is in order and that all the proper procedures have been followed according to organizational guidelines. Terminations should be done in a neutral location, and conversation during termination should be kept very brief (Kulik, 2004). Administrators need to be sensitive to the employee's feelings and attempt to keep emotions from both parties as calm as possible. In spite of all precautions, some terminated employees can exhibit frustration, anger, and even threatening behavior that administrators should take very seriously. If the situation warrants, the employee should be escorted out of the organization's facilities and the employee's property brought to them outside the building. In the case of the U.S. Army officer who was charged in the 2010 Fort Hood massacre, it was alleged that the officer's superiors were aware of difficulties that he was experiencing. Rather than deal with the personnel issues, his superiors promoted the officer and arranged for his transfer to another unit that was unaware of his behavioral issues. It is critical that organizations not ignore signals being given by their employees and forthrightly address personnel issues before they escalate in severity.

Important Points to Remember

1. Every organization needs to have a well-documented process for separating employees from the organization.
2. There must be regular evaluations of the employees. Feedback should be given frequently and not just at the annual evaluation. Treat every employee with respect.
3. Openly praise employees for good performance and behavior, but criticize in private. Every employee must be offered an opportunity to respond to evaluation and be provided written explanations of discipline or separation.
4. The organization should have a written strategy for retaining and attracting excellent employees.
5. Clearly communicate the organization's responsibilities and expectations and explain how noncompliance with those expectations will be handled.
6. Involving employees in the organization's plans and decisions through an orientation process ensures that everyone will be informed of organizational goals and priorities and will work toward achieving those objectives.
7. Improve the workplace by creating opportunities for employees to learn and grow.
8. Management should "walk the talk" and be examples of good behavior. Employees are always watching what management does as well as what it says.
9. Challenge your employees to always do their best.
10. When underperforming employees are identified, attempt to correct their behavior, but be ready to replace them with stronger employees if necessary.

CASE STUDY 7.1
Budget Shortfall

SITUATION FOR CASE STUDY 7.1

As a city manager of Badlands, Texas, you have learned that your city will have a huge budget shortfall. You feel that the best solution is to cut resources to services that are currently provided to the public. However, the city council wants no services reduced or stopped but has not provided any realistic alternatives since the residents would be opposed to tax increases. Your budget director has recommended targeted layoffs, and your assistant city manager has recommended a selective reduction of services. These recommendations will not be well received by the city council, but you see no other alternatives with the exception of raising property taxes, which would be even more unpopular. These selective service cuts will impact only part-time, seasonal employees and will not cause the layoffs of any full-time employees. You close down some of the city pools that are older and have less patronage.

1. As the city manager what is your plan going to be?
2. How will your plan affect your employees?
3. How will your plan affect the citizens of Badlands?
4. If you lay off city employees, what human resource issues will you need to be aware of?

Lately, being the city manager of Badlands has not been a very enjoyable experience. The public and the elected officials are outraged over your plan to close some city pools. The city council has now decided that the police chief has not been doing a good job lately and wants him terminated. You are reluctant to terminate the police chief because he has been employed by the city for more than 30 years and is nearing retirement. However, if you do not comply with the council's wishes, you could be the one looking for a new job. You decide to give the police chief one year to improve his job performance.

1. As city manager what other actions will you take?
2. What will be the consequences of your actions?

WHAT ACTUALLY HAPPENED IN CASE STUDY 7.1

This scenario is actually taken from several different situations. Ultimately, most of the organizations that provided the inspiration for Case Study 7.1 did everything possible before layoffs occurred, including the elimination of services. One city closed local community pools to meet it budget restrictions. The assistant city manager of that particular municipality received many complaints for closing the pools, but as the budget director said, sometimes it is necessary to make difficult choices when working for public organizations. Some people even harassed the assistant city manager's family when they ran errands or went to restaurants. Given that the city was racially divided, a great deal of care had to be taken in deciding which city pools to close to avoid inflammatory political backlash.

In the case of the police chief, the city manager gave the police chief a timetable for improving the department before the city manager terminated him. The police chief did demonstrate improvement within the timeframe allotted and then retired. However, the fact that the city manager did not terminate the police chief when the city council ordered him to placed the city manager at odds with the council, who in turn forced the city manager to resign from his position.

KEY ISSUES RAISED IN CASE STUDY 7.1

How do you retain key personnel during a budget shortfall? In this case study, the city manager chose to cut nonessential city services, like the swimming pools, and terminate part-time workers (mostly teenagers) who worked at the city pools rather than to lay off full-time employees. This allowed the city to retain highly trained staff who provided crucial support to a wide range of more essential city services. The fallout from this decision was public harassment of the city manager's family for decisions that the city manager made to address the budget shortfall.

In the situation with the police chief, the city manager felt obligated to give the police chief a chance to improve the organization before he was terminated. As the city manager stated to one of the authors, "You just don't treat a 30-year civil servant who has served the community for so long by firing him without a chance to turn things around." However, because he defied the city council's wishes, the city manager was told to resign from his position. The key issue raised is this: does a public official want to face consequences for making decisions that are unpopular with elected officials and the public?

WHAT COULD HAVE HAPPENED IN CASE STUDY 7.1

Although the city council should not have forced the city manager to resign, elected officials are not trained administrators and do not have to follow civil-service procedures when terminating a city manager. From the city manager's standpoint, there were only two options: terminate the police chief or give the police chief a second chance. While it was courageous for the city manager to give the police chief a chance to vindicate himself before retiring, ultimately, both the city manager and the police chief lost their positions. Furthermore, the city was responsible for providing retirement services to the police chief, which could have been avoided if the chief had been terminated. Likewise, the other city manager had two difficult choices to make: either terminate essential, full-time employees or close nonessential services, like the swimming pools. Terminating full-time employees might have been more popular among tax-paying citizens and their elected officials but would have made it more difficult for the organization to deliver crucial city services.

CASE STUDY 7.2
Employee with DWI

SITUATION FOR CASE STUDY 7.2

As city manager of Nemesis, Texas, you have enacted a tough new policy against employees who are convicted of driving while intoxicated (DWI). The mayor and the city council are both concerned about how enforceable the new policy is since it also covers an employee's personal time. However, some of your employees, like the police and some directors, have take-home privileges with their city-owned vehicles.

Weeks later, you receive a call at 2:00 a.m. that one of your directors was in a car accident as he was driving home. No one was hurt in the accident, but as a precaution, the director was taken to the hospital for overnight observation. The director was driving a city-owned vehicle that had been issued to him. The vehicle was completely totaled. Your police department did not cite the director and obviously could not perform field sobriety tests since the director was being taken to the hospital. Something about the accident makes you suspicious. What if the director was intoxicated while he was driving the vehicle?

1. What is your first action?
2. What are the consequences of that action?

You have asked your director to turn over all blood test results from the hospital laboratory. The director has refused your request on the grounds of medical privacy laws. Other than the blood work taken by the hospital, you have no other evidence that could indicate whether the director was intoxicated while driving a city-owned vehicle. Your DWI policy indicates that the director could be fired for drinking while driving and criminal charges could also be brought against the director. You are faced with a quandary: do you take action to obtain the laboratory results from the night of the accident, do you take disciplinary action against the director without the laboratory results, or do you let the whole matter drop even though you are convinced the director was drinking?

1. Are you in violation of patient privacy policies for asking the director for his blood test results?
2. What course of action can be taken for the director's refusal to provide this information?
3. What are the repercussions for not taking action against the director?
4. Can the director take action against the city if he is disciplined for DWI without evidence to support the allegation?

WHAT ACTUALLY HAPPENED IN CASE STUDY 7.2

The actual incident occurred as described above except the city director did not get a blood test performed at the hospital. Since there was no blood test, there was no evidence to suggest that the director was actually intoxicated at the time of the accident. The director retained his position and no disciplinary action was taken.

KEY ISSUES RAISED IN CASE STUDY 7.2

The first issue raised in this case study is the potential violation of city policy by an upper-level administrator. Should an upper-level administrator be held to those policies, and if so, what punishment should be levied on someone that high in the administration? If one employee is not held to the same standards as the others, this sends a dangerous message throughout the organization that there are two different standards for accountability. Allowing a double standard also presents a potential legal problem if one employee is punished for breaking the rules while another employee is not held accountable at all.

Since the director agreed to abide by city policies as a condition of employment, it would seem reasonable that he release his laboratory results. When using a municipality-owned vehicle, even after hours, the employee is operating as a municipal employee. What would have been the protocol if the director had the accident during work hours?

Another issue is the right to privacy. Can a public organization force an employee to turn over medical records if the organization suspects that the employee has violated policy? While the organization may not be able to force the employee to relinquish medical records, the organization can terminate an employee if the medical records are critical to proving whether an employee has violated the organization's policies. In this case, the employee was also driving a publicly owned vehicle, which was destroyed. This leads to another issue: how enforceable is a policy that covers an employee on personal time. If the employee was not driving a city-owned vehicle, would the policy apply?

WHAT COULD HAVE HAPPENED IN CASE STUDY 7.2

This case study presents several problems for a municipality. Since DWI is a criminal offense, an employee who is successfully convicted could be terminated, transferred, demoted, or have vehicle privileges revoked under city policies. If the employee's license is revoked, the city would need to determine if the employee should be retained and in what capacity the employee could operate without a driver's license. A successful conviction in this case study will be difficult to obtain because the city had no evidence. However, the director prevented city officials from obtaining evidence and could be terminated for failing to comply with city policies. The fact that the violation occurred after hours is irrelevant since the director was driving a municipality-owned vehicle.

CASE STUDY 7.3
Nightmare Employee

SITUATION FOR CASE STUDY 7.3

You are an assistant director for a federal agency. You manage a department with 50 employees. One of your employees, Fred, has worked for you for two years. You are beginning to hear stories that Fred has been physically threatening employees in other departments. After talking with other employees and confronting Fred, you learn that this story is accurate. Fred threatened one director in particular with physical violence. You meet with this director to apologize for the incident.

1. What are you going to do about Fred's behavior?
2. What policies is Fred violating?
3. Should you be worried about Fred threatening other employees?

You privately counsel Fred about his inappropriate behavior. Fred tells you that he understands he cannot behave this way and will control his temper in the future. A few months later an audit reveals that Fred has been embezzling from the department for months. In addition, you discover that Fred has been intimidating other personnel outside your department, downloading pornography onto his computer, and sexually harassing a couple of female employees.

1. What actions and procedures should be taken against Fred?
2. What safeguards should be in place to handle Fred?
3. What are the human resources issues?
4. What are the consequences or benefits of your actions?

You now have more than enough documentation to take disciplinary measures against Fred. You decide to terminate Fred immediately and ask for criminal charges to be filed since you have turned over the results of your investigation to law enforcement officials. However, Fred planted a time-delayed loop program on his computer that requires his password every week or else his hard drive and the department's network drive will be erased. You learn of this malicious code when your department's network drive is erased and no one can access Fred's terminal. The data erased from the network drive has crippled your department, and there is little hope that all of it will be restored from the backups.

1. What should have been done with Fred?
2. What should you as the assistant director do as a follow-up action to Fred's destructive behavior?
3. Can you hold Fred liable for the damage he has caused on public property?

WHAT ACTUALLY HAPPENED IN CASE STUDY 7.3

Fred's many violations were drawn from an actual event. The director that Fred physically threatened suggested to Fred's supervisor that he should be counseled and mentored in correct behavior. Furthermore, the director did not file a complaint against Fred. When Fred was terminated, he was not immediately escorted from the building and was allowed to retain computer access just long enough for him to delete documents from his computer and the network drive. Fred was eventually convicted of theft of funds and sent to prison.

KEY ISSUES RAISED IN CASE STUDY 7.3

The key issues raised in this case study contend with threatening acts, sexual harassment, destruction of public property, accessing pornographic material through public information resources, and embezzlement. Were there any steps that the assistant director could have taken once Fred's behavior was noticed? Were there any safeguards that should have been put into place to ensure embezzlement could have been prevented, limited, or caught sooner? Were there any steps that could have been taken to detect that Fred was accessing and downloading pornographic material? Besides the criminal charge of embezzlement, what other criminal charges could have been brought against Fred?

This case study contends directly with directors putting safeguards in place to detect behavior that is not only against policy but also criminal in nature. In addition the director should have taken proactive measures against the employee sooner to safeguard other employees from potential physical harm as well as sexual harassment. If Fred had injured any of these employees or any of the sexual harassment victims brought suit against the organization, the organization would stand to lose a substantial amount of money in civil litigation. Even though the organization may be successful in winning the case, the amount of money in defending against a suit (or multiple suits) could be sizable.

WHAT COULD HAVE HAPPENED IN CASE STUDY 7.3

Not only are Fred's acts a violation of organizational policy, but these acts can also be classified as criminal acts and should be treated as such by the supervisors. When an employee begins to act suspiciously and is threatening other employees with physical violence, an administrator should intervene to stop such behavior. If the employee's behavior continues, the administrator should go through all of the steps for termination and, if the situation warrants, have the employee escorted out of the building.

In the modern age of computing, it is easy for an employee to create turmoil and damage to the organization by damaging the information systems. This case in particular illustrates why an organization should invest in a backup system to protect data that are critical to the organization's operations. Furthermore, the organization should invest in software to recover data once it has been maliciously deleted. Software also exists that can block access to pornography sites.

Suggested Readings for Chapter 7

Ahlrichs, Nancy, 2001. *Competing for talent: Key recruitment and retention strategies for becoming an employer of choice.* ISBN: 0-89106-148-7. Mountain View, California: Davies-Black Publishing.

Denton, D. Keith, 1992. *Recruitment, retention, and employee relations: Field tested strategies for the '90's.* ISBN: 0899306616. Westport, Connecticut: Quorum Books.

Fields, Martha R. A., 2001. *Indispensable employees: How to hire them, how to keep them.* ISBN: 1-56414-516-6. Franklin Lakes, New Jersey: The Career Press, Inc.

Sandler, Corey, and Keefe, Janice, 2008. *Fails to meet expectations: Performance review strategies for underperforming employees.* ISBN: 1598691457. Avon, Massachusetts: Adams Business.

Walsh, James, 2004. *Rightful termination.* ISBN: 1-56343-067-3. Santa Monica, California: Merritt Publishing.

Chapter 8

Violence in the Workplace and Hostile Workplace Issues

Numerous books have been written on the subject of violence in the workplace, hostile work environments, and mentally ill employees. In this chapter we have chosen to focus on how administrators can deal with violence, hostility, and mental illness within nonprofit, public, and medical organizations. Any organization is vulnerable to health and safety risks in the workplace. While some dangers may be beyond an organization's control, other risk factors can be anticipated and steps can be taken to prevent or mitigate the dangers. *Workplace violence* in the context of this chapter is any action of a criminal nature that results in death or injury to employees. Violent acts can include assault, battery, attempted murder, rape, and homicide.

In some ways public organizations tend to be more vulnerable to workplace violence than private industry counterparts due to the issue of civil service. While civil-service rules and regulations are excellent for protecting the employment status of state and federal employees, these regulations can inadvertently provide protection to employees with violent tendencies or mental health issues. While private organizations tend to have more flexibility in dismissing troubled employees, public organizations have certain procedures that must be followed under civil-service rules and regulations before employees can be put on probation or dismissed.

The Vulnerability of Public Organizations

Many large, private-industry firms and public organizations have the resources and mandates to operate a robust security infrastructure. Such security infrastructure can include security guards, outside perimeter gates, metal detectors, security cameras, and electronic card reader access. Increased security does not necessarily mean that violence in that organization's workplace will not occur. There have been times in the past when violence has occurred outside of an organization's building since these areas are frequently in public domain and not controlled by the organizations themselves, for example, the Central Intelligence Agency (CIA) shooting in 1993 (CNN, 1997).

In the recent past, there have been a number of shootings in schools and courthouses. Schools and courthouses are similar in that they are open and accessible to the general public, making them *soft targets* for individuals with violent tendencies. As a result, courthouses and schools have installed metal detectors and hired additional security personnel to better protect those who work and visit at these places (Copeland, 2005). Government buildings are also considered soft targets for violence. In 1998, a lone gunman, Russell Weston, attempted to breach security in the U.S. Capitol building and was stopped by Capitol police after killing Detective John Gibson and Officer Jacob Chestnut (*Washington Post*, 1998). Without the security in the Capitol, the number of injured and dead could have been much higher. However, many public organizations simply do not have the resources to install metal detectors or hire more security. Sometimes, all the security one can buy cannot prevent the unforeseen. Some acts of violence in organizations have been carried out by the very force that is sworn to serve and protect the public. An example of this situation occurred in Farmersville, Texas, in 1997 when a Farmersville police officer shot and injured the police chief (McCracken, 1997).

Higher education institutions, by mission and functionality, traditionally maintain open campuses, which makes it very difficult to safeguard the organization from external threats or from internal threats posed by disgruntled students, staff, and faculty. As seen in Figure 8.1, there have been several deaths from shootings and violence since 1966 (Murchison, 2010).

One classic example of an external threat to a college campus continues to resonate: the attack by Charles Whitman at the University of Texas at Austin in 1966, which resulted in the death of 16 people (Macleod, 2010). Internal threats can be just as deadly. In 2007, Virginia Tech students were attacked by a mentally imbalanced student, resulting in the deaths of 33 people (MSNBC.com, 2007). In 2010 at the University of Alabama—Huntsville, 6 people were allegedly shot by a faculty member (Genomeweb LLC, 2010).

Sustaining Your Workforce during Long-Term Disasters

It has become vitally important to plan for sustaining your workforce's ability to remain engaged and effective during a long-term natural or man-made disaster.

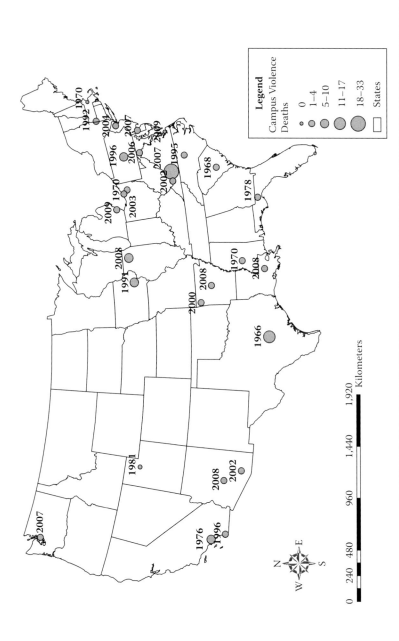

Figure 8.1 Institutional deaths caused by shootings and violence by year.

Disasters are often of an extended duration, and disaster plans need the involvement of human resources personnel to ensure that the organization can continue to provide public services over a long period of time until the situation can return to normal. Situations that are extended in duration will require an organization to plan for the utilization of their entire workforce and the development of processes and procedures to assist the workforce with personal issues such as shelter, utilities, and care of loved ones while they are providing services to the public. By addressing the employees' personal matters and assuring them that their loved ones are taken care of and their personal matters are in good hands, they can perform the vital public services that citizens require during a disaster. Furthermore, long-term disaster plans must address the issue that employees at all levels and in all types of positions may be required to perform duties not normally assigned to them.

To manage employees during a long-term disaster, the organization must maintain current employee records that include emergency contact information, addresses, telephone numbers, and e-mail addresses. Several methods for coordinating public employees and helping them maintain contact with their families include prearranged meeting places, web sites, blogs, and other media services. Arrangements must be communicated well in advance of any emergency. Policies and procedures need to be regularly updated and distributed. Employees should be encouraged to compile their own emergency records, which can include medications and financial records.

The New Specter of Terrorism

Terrorism on U.S. soil is a fairly new threat to public organizations. However, terrorism has been a consistent problem for years internationally. Terrorist groups such as the Irish Republican Army, al-Qaeda, and Chechen separatists have all been responsible for a number of attacks that have claimed lives in public facilities (BBC News, 2004; Kimery, 2007; Williams, 2004). U.S. federal agencies such as the Environmental Protection Agency (EPA) and the Internal Revenue Service (IRS) have offices in large office buildings, which makes those organizations vulnerable to attacks. The Oklahoma City bombing on the Alfred P. Murrah building in 1995 is an example of workplace violence that goes far beyond a single person with a handgun (Oklahoma City National Memorial and Museum, 2010). The Oklahoma City bombing consisted of a domestic terrorist attack that was aimed at destroying an entire building along with several government agencies. Another example is the 2010 attack on the IRS building in Austin, Texas, by a disgruntled suicidal taxpayer flying a single-engine plane into the building, which caused the death of one IRS employee (WEBCPA, 2010). No measures could be taken to prevent this person from flying his plane into that building.

Mitigation and Prevention

If organizations take certain steps, there is a good possibility they can mitigate or prevent workplace violence. For public organizations that have a history of violence in the workplace due to the nature of the job (e.g., the U.S. Postal Service) or for public organizations that are unpopular with certain factions of the public (e.g., the IRS), added security infrastructure should be seriously considered to mitigate any violence that may occur. If the public organization has the resources, modernization of the building itself or construction of a new building may be warranted to reduce potential death and destruction (e.g., the Pentagon in the 9/11 attacks). If the use of security cameras is possible, organizations should not only have the cameras inside the buildings but also have security cameras installed to view the surrounding external area such as parking lots and nearby to deter violence and other criminal acts. For medical organizations or other organizations where employees work in shifts, it is important to have security in parking lots (e.g., security guards and security cameras) so that employees feel that they are protected coming in and going out of the workplace. A public organization's employees need to feel safe and secure to work productively.

Guns at the Workplace

The issue of employees being allowed to carry firearms to and from work if the employee has a concealed handgun license (CHL) has become increasingly controversial in the last few years. Recently there have been political movements that would allow more guns in public facilities (and thus in the workplace) by introducing legislation that would permit persons with a CHL to carry handguns in certain public facilities. In the State of Texas a bill was introduced, but not passed, that would have allowed employees with a CHL to carry their weapons onto public higher education campuses. The State of Utah has already passed a provision allowing the right to carry on their public higher education institutions. There are both advantages and disadvantages for legal statutes that deal with right to carry.

In the ideal world, anyone who has a CHL would be trained to use their weapon responsibly for self-protection. However, that is not always going to be the case, and unfortunately accidents can occur even under the best circumstances. Where large groups of people are gathered, even a trained person could accidentally injure an innocent bystander if a bullet ricocheted or if a bullet passed through the target and struck a bystander. An employee with a handgun could inadvertently interfere with security forces during an emergency situation by getting in their way, by accidentally shooting security personnel, or by being mistaken for an assailant. Liability issues raised by an armed employee with a CHL could outweigh the benefits of the protection such an employee could offer the organization. The advantage of allowing guns carried by CHL persons would be to provide additional protection in case an attacker did begin a killing spree in the workplace. A gun used for self-defense in this particular situation could potentially save lives. College campuses are typically spread out over several acres of ground but generally maintain relatively small security forces whose reaction time to a crisis might be too long, particularly if a gunman is firing on bystanders. Allowing staff or faculty to carry weapons could make the difference between life and death.

As an alternative to permitting concealed weapons, some organizations have opted to train their employees in self-defense, relying on hand-to-hand combat skills rather than weapons to defuse a violent situation. There are several organizations that can be brought in to train employees in self-defense, such as Executive Defense, which specializes in teaching self-defense to company executives and employees (Webb, 2010). Another option is to provide office furniture equipped with barriers, such as bulletproof glass, or raised desks that make it more difficult for someone to reach over and grab an employee. Furniture arrangement can provide distance between the attacker and an intended victim or can prevent an attacker from escaping easily. Silent alarm buttons, used for years by banks, can notify first responders of an emergency situation in progress. As one of the case studies will demonstrate, a normal desk does not offer an employee much protection from an irate customer.

Hostile Work Environment Issues

A hostile work environment is one in which an individual feels threatened, either mentally or physically, by one or more individuals within the department. Hostile work environments can be caused by intimidation, verbal or physical threats, or sexual harassment. A newer form of harassment in the workplace is cyber-stalking, also known as cyber-bullying or cyber-terrorism. This type of harassment utilizes electronic means to harass the victim through e-mails, text messaging, and phone calls. Whitty and Carr describe cyber-harassment in the following manner:

> Electronic communication can be used to harass in both similar and new ways to offline traditional harassment. Before exploring how cyber-harassment might take place in our places of work, this paper outlines two severe forms of cyber-harassment: cyber-stalking and cyber-terrorism. (2005, p. 249)

Many states in the United States have stalking laws that criminalize cyber-stalking and cyber-bullying (Valcik and Lavin-Loucks, 2006). If the harassment is serious enough, a criminal charge can be filed by the organization against the offending employee. In the State of Texas, for example, *sexual assault* as defined by the Texas Penal Code is a person receiving an unwanted sexual advance by another person (State of Texas, 2010). Clearly, having criminal charges filed should be used as a last resort and should not be used as a substitute for sound human resources policies and procedures. A hostile work environment also includes bullying. As stated by Einarsen, Hoel, Zapf, and Cooper (2005, p. 230):

Bullying at work may be defined as repeated actions and practices that are directed at one or more workers, which may be done deliberately or unconsciously, but are unwanted by the victim, and that may interfere with job performance and/or cause an unpleasant working environment (Einarsen and Raknes 1997).

For nonprofit, public, and medical organizations, a set of policies and procedures must be in place to prevent or mitigate a hostile work environment. Not only does an organization need to have policies and procedures in place, but the organization also must have administrators who will not tolerate such behavior occurring in the organization. A culture must be established and maintained in the organization that will show a zero tolerance for harassment and bullying in the workplace. It is imperative that when inappropriate behavior and harassment occurs, administrators take action immediately to stop unwanted actions from occurring.

Sexual Harassment

In 1998 the Supreme Court ruled on two sexual harassment cases, *Faragher v. City of Boca Raton* and *Burlington Industries Inc. v. Ellerth* (United States Supreme Court—No. 97-282, 1997), (United States Supreme Court—No. 97-549, 1997). In these cases, the Supreme Court basically stated that the employer is responsible for the actions of the supervisor, even when the employer is unaware of the supervisor's behavior. Employers can no longer claim that they did not know about the sexual harassment because the employee did not inform them, nor can they claim that they were unaware of the supervisor's behavior.

The Supreme Court also stated that the court will no longer heavily rely on the two different forms of sexual harassment: *quid pro quo* and hostile environment (United States Supreme Court—No. 97-544, 1997). The Court called these two forms of sexual harassment of "limited utility" in assessing employer liability (United States Supreme Court—No. 97-549, 1997). As a result, an employee who refuses the unwelcome sexual harassment of a supervisor, and who suffers no adverse job consequences, can still bring a sexual harassment lawsuit against their employer if the employee can show they were the victim of discrimination through sexual content. The employee will not necessarily be required to show a loss of advancement, retaliation, loss of income, or stress as they once did under *quid pro quo* and hostile environment. They will need to show that the nature of the sexual content they experienced caused them to feel discriminated against.

Therefore, even though the employer has a policy against sexual harassment and even when sexual harassment training is provided to supervisors, the employer still can be held vicariously liable in cases where a supervisor uses sexual content to discriminate against an employee. The courts are now looking at what a "reasonable person" would determine to be sexual content used for discrimination versus the old standards of *quid pro quo* and hostile environment. The Supreme Court did not throw out the old standards but will not rely on them as courts have in the past. The Supreme Court created a two-part test to be used by employers in defending themselves against a sexual harassment lawsuit:

1. The employer needs to show that they took reasonable care to prevent and correct any sexual harassment behavior within their workplace.
2. The employee unreasonably failed to take advantage of any preventive or corrective opportunities provided by the employer.

Even lower courts have applied vicarious liability and the two-part test to determine employer responsibility in cases involving other forms of protected discrimination under Title VII (*Deffenbaugh-Williams v. Wal-Mart Stores Inc.* and *Fierro v. Saks Fifth Avenue*) (United States Court of Appeals for the 5th Circuit, 1988) (United States District Court for the Southern District of New York, 1998).

In this legal environment, it is necessary for employers to change how they deal with sexual harassment in their organizations. Currently at least 40% of all women report being sexually harassed at some point in their career, and men currently account for 11.6% of all sexual harassment cases filed with the Equal Employment Opportunity Commission (EEOC). Therefore, the chances of an organization needing to respond to a sexual harassment concern are great. Good preparation can help companies deal with a sexual harassment complaint successfully (employer-employee.com, 2010):

1. If the company does not have a sexual harassment/discrimination policy, get one fast! The policy should communicate that the company takes a "zero tolerance" approach toward sexual harassment. Have an attorney review it, and make sure it is distributed to all employees either through the employee handbook or in memo form. Have the employees sign it acknowledging that they received and read the policy. The policy should be communicated to all new employees and posted in the workplace. If there are employees whose primary language is not English, have the sexual harassment policy translated or communicated to them in their primary language.
2. Provide different routes that employees can take to file complaints; e.g., calling a hotline, contacting the human resources department, or contacting their supervisor. The employee should have the option of talking with either a male or a female company representative.
3. Conduct sexual harassment training, even if it is only composed of reading material or watching a video.
4. Conduct yearly meetings with supervisors to review the sexual harassment policy and to make sure that they understand that retribution for employees who file a sexual harassment claim will not be tolerated. Inform the supervisors that even mild sexual jokes or statements can create an atmosphere of hostility that will make some employees uncomfortable and can create an

environment where sexual discrimination could develop. Supervisors should be directed to inform upper management of any sexual harassment complaints they receive. Supervisors should never promise confidentiality to an employee when the information relates to sexual harassment.

5. Conduct a yearly sexual harassment survey among the employees. The survey should be conducted anonymously and distributed with a copy of the company's sexual harassment policy. The survey can simply ask the employees (male and female) if they have experienced any form of sexual harassment during the past year. The results of the survey will demonstrate to a court of law that the company is actively engaged in preventing and correcting sexual harassment.

6. Conduct investigations promptly and thoroughly. After the dispute is resolved, a follow-up should be done with the employee to ensure that no one has suffered retaliation. Make sure the sexual harassment policy spells out clearly that retaliation against an employee filing a sexual harassment complaint is illegal and will not be tolerated.

7. Same-sex harassment and a man's reporting of harassment should be treated the same way as a woman's report of sexual harassment by a male supervisor or colleague.

8. Always document the results of any sexual harassment complaint or investigation. Include any corrective action that the employee or supervisor was asked to take. Follow up on any corrective action to determine if the employee fails to take advantage of the company's polices/procedures or if the corrective action successfully prevents sexual harassment from occurring again.

9. Inform all employees that it is their obligation to report sexual harassment that they either experience or witness.

Passive-Aggressive Employees

Passive-aggressive employees are an administrator's nightmare. As described by Laurence Miller (2008, p. 95):

> Unlike the brash, confrontational challenges to managerial authority that may characterize the antisocial, narcissistic, borderline, or paranoid personality, the passive-aggressive personality's sniping is almost always indirect and under the table. Indeed the very term *passive-aggressive* denotes the intention to do ill while appearing good.

A passive-aggressive employee will perform the minimum amount of work required by the administrator or will do a task so poorly that he or she will not be asked to perform the task again or will not be asked to do additional work in the future. Passive-aggressive employees construct so many barriers to task completion that they, in effect, sabotage any effort to improve the organization. Work assigned to a passive-aggressive employee will rarely launch and will likely fail due to the constant struggle to obtain progress and due to the discord this type of employee causes among other employees. Other characteristics of a passive-aggressive employee include being very vocal during meetings, behaving in an obstinate manner to other employees and supervisors, being defensive in the face of constructive criticism, and being combative when forced to perform the task.

If this type of employee is involved in a project, a few options can be used to nullify the problem. The first step is to document the employee's behavior and why it appears that this person is purposely attempting to sabotage or cause problems with a project. Next is to discuss the issue with the employee's superior to make them aware of the situation. Allow time for the supervisor to contend with the problem successfully. If the supervisor has failed to rectify the issue, request that the employee be removed from the assignment. If you ask for the employee's removal, make sure to have documentation supporting your stance on this issue.

A supervisor who has a passive-aggressive employee must make sure to provide the employee with well-defined instructions and be prepared to provide a high degree of oversight (Miller, 2008). Given the civil-service laws, documentation is essential if terminating an employee is warranted. For medical organizations, a passive-aggressive employee can lead to untold litigation woes if sabotage occurs. This will require medical organizations to act more quickly because patients' lives could be impacted negatively, which could lead to lawsuits stemming from patient care issues.

Guerilla Employees

A new study by Rosemary O'Leary discusses a category of employee that exists in every public, nonprofit, and medical organization: the guerrilla employee. O'Leary describes the guerrilla employee:

> "Guerilla government" is … the term for the actions of career public servants who work against the wishes—either implicitly or explicitly communicated—of their superiors. (O'Leary, 2010, p. 8)

Guerilla employees tend to have a great deal of training and expertise in their field and are motivated to work against their supervisor due to a belief that they are being proactive or have the best interests of the organization in mind. With guerilla employees, the conflict is generally political rather than operational. A guerilla employee is willing to take a calculated risk by acting against a superior's policies. If the guerilla employee is wrong, he or she loses credibility with peers and with superiors. If the employee is successful, resulting in positive outcomes for the organization, the supervisor's authority over other employees will have been undermined. When this occurs, the guerilla employee risks retribution from his or her supervisor. The line between guerilla employees and passive-aggressive employees is thin. The difference between the two lies in intent and outcome. The guerilla employee sabotages the supervisor's authority but has the organization's best interests at heart. A passive-aggressive employee works to sabotage the organization but does not necessarily target the supervisor.

Mental Illness

Employees can have mental health issues ranging from small anxieties and depression to more severe forms of mental illness that can include manic depression and schizophrenia. Most people with mental health issues are able to function well in work environments. A manager who suspects that an employee may cause harm to himself or others should contact local law enforcement. Law enforcement then has the option to remand the individual over to mental health officials for observation (Texas Mental Health Code, 2010). Laws governing how law enforcement can contend with such individuals will vary by country, state, and local statutes. For situations that are less serious, public organizations may have a clause in their policies regarding fitness for duty, which will allow a manager to send an employee home if the employee's behavior warrants such an edict. If a manager has a suspicion that an employee's behavior may in fact lead to the employee harming him or herself, the manager is often limited since an intervention by a manager could lead to liability to the manager or the organization. In some public organizations, counseling services may be offered to employees. However, employees may be very hesitant or resistant to using such services due to a perceived stigma that the employee may feel is attached to using such services.

However, some employees must be under constant medical care in order to remain functional in society, let alone in a workplace environment. When these employees do not utilize medical assistance or have lost their medical health care coverage, they can become unpredictable, aggressive, disruptive, and potentially dangerous to themselves and to others. Administrators should be aware of employees who can potentially cause human resource issues and prepare to deal with those employees proactively rather than reactively. Administrators should always maintain confidentiality when discussing any personnel issue with employees and understand that medical issues in particular should be safeguarded from being accessed by unauthorized personnel. If administrators find that a particular employee is being disruptive, they should have a conference with the employee as soon as possible. During one of these conferences, the administrator should remain very calm and discuss the issue with the employee in a clear, even tone. After the conference, the administrator should document what was discussed in the meeting and date the document. Such documents should be kept under lock and key. If a mental health issue begins to impact an organization, the administrator should consult with the human resources department to see what other options may be available to assist the employee with mental health issues. This could range from personal counseling or group therapy with a social worker or psychiatrist to medical intervention.

With some employees, mental health issues might prove to be insurmountable in their current position. There might be too much stress within the department, or the other employees might be inadvertently aggravating the problem. In situations like these, an administrator may want to transfer the employee to another position within the organization. The administrator should work closely with human resources, who would then work with any potential supervisor to make sure they understand the employee's issues and can work with them. This allows the employee in question to get a fresh start and a chance to improve his or her productivity.

If an employee begins to exhibit erratic or troubling behavior, the administrator should call the employee in immediately for a meeting or, if the situation warrants, call discretely for security. For organizations in which employees interface with patients on a regular basis, special attention should be given to any alarming behaviors that are being exhibited by a caregiver. As stated by Hockley:

> Fortunately it is accepted by the public that most health professionals are non-violent and caring. Unfortunately, there is a small element within the healthcare industry that exhibits violent acts towards those they care for. Furthermore, many of these acts are so horrendous, not only because of their effects, but also because they target some of the most vulnerable people in our society and because the perpetrator is a repeat offender. (2005, p. 93)

Organizations that have a great deal of contact with patients should review areas where a mentally disturbed employee can cause the most amount of damage or have the least amount of oversight and take steps to establish a system of checks and balances to ensure, for example, that no one employee can obtain, use, and discard medicines or controlled substances without another employee documenting the transactions or that no employee can be alone with a patient for long periods of time unsupervised. Large hospitals and emergency rooms are highly vulnerable to the actions of a mentally disturbed employee who can move through large facilities unsupervised or do something while others are distracted, and to the litigation that could result from their actions.

Author's Experience

When Dr. Valcik was a young man, he worked as a lifeguard for a municipal pool. During his employment, there were several hostile work environment situations and potentially dangerous incidents that occurred at the pool. The pool was located near an impoverished, high-crime area. In one incident, the pool's office was robbed at night after the pool had closed for the evening. The manager of the pool was always at risk of being robbed because she carried the day's cash receipts to her personal vehicle.

A second incident occurred when a gang came to the pool entrance and demanded entry into the facility. The lifeguard stationed at the cashier desk told them that they would have to pay to enter the facility. The leader of the gang then pulled a knife on the lifeguard and threatened to kill him and his whole family if he did not let them pass. The gang members then entered the facility, where the pool staff called the police, who then arrested the gang members. Unknown to the police and other lifeguards, the assistant pool manager on duty had just purchased a brand new 9-millimeter Ruger handgun and 1,000 rounds of ammunition, which were in the trunk of his car. However, when the gang members were at the pool, the assistant pool manager was in the pump room performing maintenance. The issue of having a gun accessible to a public employee at a dangerous location should concern public managers for three reasons. The liability of having a weapon which could have been accesible during a potential violent crime, the gun was illegal, kept in a vehicle which was on city property (1992) and the potential for violence to have been escalated if the gun had been accessed by the assistant pool manager.

A third incident occurred when Valcik ordered a swimmer to stop jumping off the high dive while his friend was under him in the diving tank. The two swimmers did not speak English, and no rules were posted at the pool area. The horseplay ceased and Valcik resumed his lifeguarding duties, although he noticed another lifeguard near his area. When Valcik climbed down from the lifeguard stand and spoke with the other lifeguard, he learned that the two swimmers were heard debating with each other whether to attack Valcik by climbing up the back of the lifeguard stand. Despite these incidents and others that are not recorded here, the city did not provide additional security for the pool staff.

Final Notes

As the reader can infer, many factors can contribute to violence in the workplace and to a hostile work environment. This chapter covers only a few of the issues that administrators will be faced with in the workplace and intends to provide only general guidelines that administrators will need to consider when addressing any of these topics. Many of these issues, such as terrorism or guns in the workplace, are fairly new in the United States. In some cases administrators can merely mitigate a dangerous situation since many of the examples referenced in the text could not have been prevented. However, administrators can learn from these instances in history and better prepare their organizations to lessen the impact of violence in the future.

Other issues, such as cyber-stalking and guerilla employees, are not new concepts in the workplace but are being researched in more detail than in the past. Employees who have mental health issues will need to be dealt with carefully and consistently. Failure to do so risks violation of the Americans with Disabilities Act. Therefore an administrator must have thorough documentation if action against a mentally ill employee is to be taken. An employee with health issues, including mental health, has the option of using the Family Medical Leave Act to recuperate. An administrator must be aware that this option exists for employees and understand that the organization is legally bound to allow the employee time off according to the federal statute.

The goal of any administrator should be to reduce the risk and liability to the organization from violence or harassment. If an act of violence does occur, it is imperative to have policies and procedures in place that can mitigate the impact upon the employees and organization. With some positions, such as police officers and firefighters, risk will be more inherent to the tasks assigned. For these types of positions, organizations will need to put forth additional resources to ensure the safety and security of personnel, for example, by providing an allowance for police officers to buy new bulletproof vests every three years. It is also important for organizations to have up-to-date and effective risk management policies in place. Not only will these types of actions improve the well-being of the employees, but they will also reduce the costs to the organization in the long term. Keeping employees healthy and secure should be a priority for any organization. Finally, on the importance of prevention, Miller states:

> For virtually no other type of major tragedy are education, training, and preparation so important in foreseeing and planning for emergencies as in the area of workplace aggression and violence. In many cases, you can see this one coming. Consequently, special attention is given to what companies can do ahead of time to reduce the risk of this kind of tragedy. (2008, p. 182).

Important Points to Remember

1. Violence can occur anywhere and at any time, so organizations should have an emergency action plan.
2. Organizations should have policies and procedures in place to ensure the safety and security of employees and organizational assets.
3. If safety and security equipment is owned by the organization, make sure the equipment is well maintained and that those assets are being utilized properly.
4. Managers should know and understand local and state laws on harassment in order to recognize violations of the law when they occur in the workplace.
5. An organization should have yearly training for their employees on the organization's sexual harassment policies.
6. Administrators should take action quickly against employees who violate organization guidelines. If an incident is serious enough, an administrator should report the employee to human resources as soon as possible.
7. Administrators should document any incidents regarding violent behavior and sexual harassment in the workplace. Lack of proper documentation can hamper actions taken by human resources.

8. An organization should evaluate if any security measures can be put into place when remodeling occurs or when a new building is constructed. Many effective safety and security measures can be put into place that may be affordable during the construction or remodeling phase.

9. It is better for an organization to think in terms of prevention in regard to safety and security. Failure to do so could be very costly to an organization.

10. There are many different ways to increase safety and security. Do the research and find innovative and creative security ideas that fit your organization.

CASE STUDY 8.1
Employee Gets Aggressive with Coworker

SITUATION FOR CASE STUDY 8.1

You are a school district superintendent. You have a regularly scheduled meeting with one of your principals when she mentions a personnel issue that she is having difficulty resolving. Karen, a special education coordinator, has been using forceful tactics to gather coworkers' personal information. Karen has asked coworkers' friends personal questions in an attempt to gather information on specific employees. Karen has also been requesting home addresses of coworkers from the administrative assistant who works at the elementary school. When the administrative assistant refused to give her the information, Karen resorted to asking coworkers directly for that type of information. Karen claims that she wants to know so that she can send cards and gifts to her coworkers. Until now, the principal tolerated the disruption because she has valuable skill sets. Karen appears to have a particular issue with Mandy. Karen has e-mailed Mandy for her home address, and when that failed, Karen asked the administrative assistant for Mandy's home address. The administrative assistant refused to provide that information to Karen. One day, Mandy is walking down the hallway to do an errand for her supervisor when Karen suddenly grabs Mandy's arm and asks for her home address.

1. What course of action should you take?
2. What will be the consequences and benefits of the actions you take?
3. What are the human resource issues that are involved with this situation?

WHAT ACTUALLY HAPPENED IN CASE STUDY 8.1

It is unknown whether the supervisor was aware of Karen's attempts to collect information on her coworkers. When this incident occurred, Mandy calmly pulled her arm away from Karen and stated that she did not give out her personal information to people she does not know very well. Furthermore, Mandy stated that anything that Karen wished to give her could be given to her at work. Since there was no eyewitness to the incident, Mandy decided not to file a complaint with human resources. After this incident, Karen did not pursue Mandy's personal information. Mandy did inform her supervisor at a much later date but did not expect any action be taken. Karen was known, however, to obtain other coworkers' personal information and either call them at home or simply show up at their house after hours.

KEY ISSUES RAISED IN CASE STUDY 8.1

Depending on the situation, touching or grabbing an employee could be considered assault, which is a criminal offense. Mandy attempted to defuse the situation by staying calm and by not attempting to escalate the incident further, which could have led to a more violent reaction from Karen. The other issue that should be asked is what is Mandy's right to self-defense in this situation? If Mandy had used self-defense techniques and injured Karen, what would have been the consequences to Mandy both criminally and in civil litigation terms? Could the principal have taken any steps to prevent what happened to Mandy? Should the principal be held responsible for not attempting to stop Karen's activities? What should Mandy have done differently if anything? If these activities were reported to the human resources department, what could that department have done to alleviate the problem?

Karen seems to have control issues. She attempts to control other employees by owning personal information and even using physical restraint. What personnel acted appropriately in this case study? Would you consider Karen a stalker by her actions and behavior? Does your organization currently have policies and procedures in place to contend with behaviors displayed by Karen? When Karen attempted to intimidate Mandy, Karen created a hostile work environment. The most serious and frustrating issue for supervisors is when employees stalk their coworkers after hours. If the activity occurs off site, there is little that supervisors can do. It is up to the employees who are being harassed to report the incidents to law enforcement.

WHAT COULD HAVE HAPPENED IN CASE STUDY 8.1

It can be difficult for a supervisor to determine if an employee will become violent toward other employees. Some signs might include unusual behavior and wild mood swings, for example. When an employee behaves unusually, supervisors should take action quickly to counsel their employee, document the behaviors, and attempt to get the employee assistance in resolving whatever issues may exist. In Case Study 8.1, Karen's supervisor should have been alerted to the fact that she was controlling and at the very least disruptive to the department. However, there is very little that coworkers can do other than file a complaint with human resources.

CASE STUDY 8.2
Sexual Assault of a Minor

SITUATION FOR CASE STUDY 8.2

You are the director of an after-school program with the school district. The after-school program has several locations within a wealthy suburb and employs more than 50 employees who work for you throughout the school year. Employee ages range from 13 to more than 65 because most of your employees are local middle or high school students and retirees. The employees are paid hourly, and each location has an assistant director who is responsible for overseeing the welfare of the children and employees.

An assistant director has just reported that one of his female employees, who is a minor, has complained that a male employee, James, who is about 25, has been touching her inappropriately. You are horrified and hope for the organization's sake that the allegation is unfounded. You immediately investigate the alleged incident. During your investigation you collect names and eyewitness accounts and interview a wide range of individuals, including James and the alleged victim.

After your documentation of the incident, you have verified that these actions have in fact occurred and that James was known by several of his coworkers to have made sexual advances on other female employees in your after-school program. Many of his older female coworkers ignored his sexual advances and simply told James to "get lost" rather than file a complaint. This is a criminal offense under state statutes and is a violation of organizational policy.

1. What is the course of action that should be taken?
2. What will be the consequences and benefits of the actions you take?
3. What are the human resource issues that are involved with this situation?

WHAT ACTUALLY HAPPENED IN CASE STUDY 8.2

The organization had no employee orientation on sexual harassment, which would have defined unacceptable behaviors in the workplace. Whether or not this would have changed any of James's actions is purely speculative. However, by not having an orientation for employees on this subject matter, the organization made itself vulnerable to civil lawsuits if sexual harassment or sexual assault took place. After the incident occurred, James's supervisor gave him a verbal warning, told him to stay away from female employees, and reassigned James to another location. However, he was permitted to continue working at the after-school program. No law enforcement officials were ever contacted, and the employee was not written up for his actions. Information about the incident leaked throughout the organization. James's new coworkers learned of the incident at the old location and became uncomfortable around him. The young female employee quit the after-school program after the incident occurred.

KEY ISSUES RAISED IN CASE STUDY 8.2

When serious criminal actions, like sexual assault and physical violence, are reported, the supervisor is obligated to report the incident to the human resources department. The fact that this individual was known by coworkers to make unwanted sexual advances on other female employees should have led to his termination from the after-school program after the investigation was concluded. The organization failed to provide policies and employee orientations to inform employees about proper behavior and the consequences of illegal activity. Another issue is confidentiality by the supervisors during an investigation. Until an investigation comes back with a finding, a supervisor should keep all information about the investigation confidential to keep all witnesses as unbiased as possible.

Law enforcement officials should be notified immediately to begin an investigation. While an employee is under investigation, organizations have the option to remove the employee from the workplace by suspension with pay, suspension without pay, or termination. However, if the organization suspends an employee without pay or terminates him and the employee is found innocent of the allegation, the organization could be found liable for taking illegitimate actions against the employee. An organization must be very sure that organizational policies have been violated if an employee is suspended without pay or terminated. The organization needs to document the incident thoroughly as well as any investigation that the organization has conducted to provide to law enforcement officials and to protect itself from civil litigation.

WHAT COULD HAVE HAPPENED IN CASE STUDY 8.2

The supervisor should have documented the actions of the employee and notified human resources immediately as well as local law enforcement to begin an investigation. By not taking action against James, the supervisor has opened the door for James to sexually assault other coworkers or even children who are in the after-school program. The lack of action could result in a liability lawsuit if anything were to happen to an employee or child. The employee should have been suspended with pay until the investigations from both human resources and law enforcement were completed. The organization was very fortunate that the victim did not press for a civil lawsuit against the organization.

CASE STUDY 8.3
Threatened Employees

SITUATION FOR CASE STUDY 8.3

You are a testing coordinator at a community college in Badlands, Texas. The community college serves a large county and has students ranging from high school students to retirees. The college serves a very diverse socioeconomic group that comes from a variety of cultures and backgrounds. Your administrative assistant is the gatekeeper to your office and has been working for the college for more than seven years. One of the administrative assistant's main responsibility is to prevent stuffor faculty from walking into your office without an appointment. The administrative assistant often contends with a variety of employees and students in the course of carrying out her responsibilities. Your administrative assistant is in her 60s and is very mild mannered and polite.

An incident occurred yesterday with a disgruntled student, who demanded to see you, stating that he had an appointment. When the administrative assistant said that no such appointment was on the calendar, the student smashed the glass top of a display case with his fist and threatened to kill your administrative assistant by "slitting her throat." Your administrative assistant sits at a standard desk that has no physical barrier between her and the student. Although the administrative assistant is upset and intimidated, she will not let the student into your office until you are ready to see him. The noise from the smashed display case brings you out of your office but you are not aware of the verbal threat or what precisely happened to the display case. There has been no screaming, and everyone seems calm.

You speak with the student about academic matters but the student seems unsatisfied and leaves your office. As the student is walking away, one of your other staff members informs you about the student threatening the administrative assistant's life. You follow the student to confront him about the threat, but the student keeps walking and never looks back at you. Your administrative assistant is extremely upset and you are not happy about the situation.

1. What course of action should be taken?
2. What are the human resource issues that are involved with this situation?
3. Have criminal offenses by the student occurred?
4. Could this situation be considered a hostile work environment by the administrative assistant?

WHAT ACTUALLY HAPPENED IN CASE STUDY 8.3

The administrative assistant called the police department and gave a statement. An administrator from the student's program of study apologized for the student's actions and assured the administrative assistant that the student would be reprimanded on this issue. The administrative assistant made a point to tell the administrator that she wanted the student to understand the seriousness of his actions.

The administrator in charge of student disciplinary actions, however, was dismissive of the incident and would not pursue disciplinary action even though the student's behavior warranted disciplinary measures. The administrator stated that "the student probably had a bad day." A staff member from the testing coordinator's office then pointed out that the student threatened the administrative assistant's life, which was a criminal offense. Under state law, it could even be considered a terrorist threat. The student later apologized to the administrative assistant. The administrative assistant decided not to press criminal charges, and no disciplinary action was taken by the school toward the student.

KEY ISSUES RAISED IN CASE STUDY 8.3

One issue raised in this case study is how to contend with someone who verbally threatens an employee. Secondly, the student violated the college's policies on student behavior. Although permitting threatening behavior sends the wrong message to the community, by letting a violent student walk away instead of confronting the student, the testing coordinator permitted the situation to defuse. Confronting violent people is a job best left to law enforcement officers who are trained to deal with these situations.

Another issue raised in this case study is protecting employees in the workplace. In this case study, it would have been difficult to provide any physical protection since the administrative assistant's job responsibilities include being a receptionist for the testing coordinator. Since the college is an open access institution, it is difficult to secure a particular facility or office that interfaces with students, staff, faculty, and the public on a regular basis. It is possible to put a silent alarm system in place which contacts the campus police immediately if an incident occurs. Another option is to provide the administrative assistant with a desk that has a physical barrier built into it.

WHAT COULD HAVE HAPPENED IN CASE STUDY 8.3

The initial responses taken by the supervisor and the administrative assistant were the correct actions. The police and the college administrator who oversees student behavior were contacted. The police were more than willing to press charges against the student; however, the administrator charged with enforcing the campus policies on student behavior dismissed pressing charges as an option. The rationale behind this decision was that it seemed an excessive response to this student's behavior, and it would have consumed a great deal of time and effort from the testing coordinator's administrative assistant and anyone on the staff involved in the incident. Therefore, disciplining the student would have been much more preferable and cost effective than pressing criminal charges.

CASE STUDY 8.4

Employees Making Racially Charged Comments

SITUATION FOR CASE STUDY 8.4

You have just been hired as the director of public works for Hurricane Alley, Texas, a large suburban city outside a large metropolitan area whose residents range from the very wealthy to deeply impoverished individuals. This is a big step in your career because you are now at a growing city and are going to have a much larger budget to work with every year. Your previous place of employment in the City of Cactus was a rural town whose chief economic output was agriculture. The move to a new city will likely bring bigger and more complex challenges because you are managing a larger workforce. At Hurricane Alley, the public works department has more than 50 employees, mostly blue collar and middle aged. In your previous position you managed 15 employees who were nearly all white and worked well together. At Hurricane Alley, your workforce is much more diverse, with half of the employees Hispanic, and there have been no previous racial issues in the department. Lately, you have been hiring more women into the department to fill roles such as dispatchers, clerks, and secretaries.

You have been working as the director for more than a year when one of your female employees comes into your office and makes a statement about three white male employees who work on the street construction crew. Apparently these three employees have been making racially inflammatory and sexist comments on their morning coffee breaks. Other employees have overheard these comments and are very upset that three city employees would make such comments. You know you have to act quickly to defuse the situation. When you confront the employees, they are offended that you would discuss the issue with them and do not see anything wrong with the remarks that were made. You now know that these employees are creating a bigger issue in your department and that your response will need to be very forceful. You are concerned that if you do not act aggressively on this issue, the situation may create more tension in your department. You are also concerned that the racial and gender divisions may be much more widespread than you had previously thought. The first step you take is to contact the human resources director to gain insight on how to best proceed with the situation.

1. What actions should be taken?
2. What are the potential consequences of not taking action?
3. What leadership qualities should the director exhibit in contending with this situation?

WHAT ACTUALLY HAPPENED IN CASE STUDY 8.4

The human resources director was contacted and asked for guidance on the issue by the public works director. While the public works director wished to take very stern action against the three employees, the human resources director wanted to give them the minimum disciplinary action possible. The human resources director realized that there was no proof the alleged comments were made; the report consisted mostly of hearsay. Therefore the workers were verbally warned against making bigoted statements at the workplace. No further disciplinary action was taken. While the organization had policies in place and the human resources office had the authority to carry out more stringent disciplinary action, they opted for a more passive approach to contend with the issue. Furthermore, although written policies regarding inappropriate language were in place, the human resources department had never conducted formal employee orientations on inappropriate language and behavior. Because of this oversight, the employees could legally claim they were not properly instructed on the organization's discrimination policies regarding improper language.

KEY ISSUES RAISED IN CASE STUDY 8.4

Contending with a hostile work environment as a manager is the key issue raised in this case study. Not only do other employees feel uncomfortable working in a hostile work environment, but this can hurt the organization when recruiting and retaining employees if the organization is seen as tolerant of unprofessional behavior and language from its employees. Furthermore, these cases can result in EEOC investigations and civil lawsuits, which, if made public, can hurt the organization's reputation and again impact recruitment and retention. The case study also demonstrates why it is so important to have an effective human resources department that can provide support to managers.

WHAT COULD HAVE HAPPENED IN CASE STUDY 8.4

In this case study, the human resources department did not provide the support that the manager needed to successfully contend with the problem inside his department. If the human resources department had been more proactive with discrimination training, some of these issues may have been prevented, or at the very least the manager could have taken more appropriate action against the three employees. Additionally, the human resources department could have asked the city manager for an investigation to determine how widespread racial and gender tension may be throughout the city staff. If the problem was widespread, programs could be put in place by the human resources department to educate personnel about the city policies and reinforce the fact that derogatory comments will not be tolerated. The three employees should have been written up for making such comments in the workplace. The fact that the comments were made and overheard by other employees in the organization gave that particular department (and supervisor) a reputation for tolerating those types of comments in the workplace.

CASE STUDY 8.5
Hostile Work Environment

SITUATION FOR CASE STUDY 8.5

You are a director of a municipal budgeting office that has seven employees. The budget office is very important to the city, and the employees who work in your office have a reputation for having strong skills and a good work ethic. Most of your employees are women in their 20s. With the exception of one employee, a middle-aged man, your department works well together. You hope that adding another person to your department who can work with your problem employee will improve that person's behavior.

You have received authorization for a new position. From the applicant pool you decide to hire an accountant, Vernon, who is an older male employee who has an advanced degree and an impressive resume. Unfortunately, Vernon demonstrated in the first few days of employment that he does not have the skill sets that he stated on his resume. Vernon is resistant to budget processes that are different from what he has always used in the past. The problem is that Vernon's way of doing things is slow, antiquated, and prone to errors. Additionally, Vernon has been asking the female staff odd questions like, "Why don't you wear a dress?" (because they all wear pantsuits) and, "Where's the coffee?" (because they all buy or brew their own). Your female employees are getting annoyed.

1. What should you do about Vernon?
2. Which human resource issues are of concern, and how do you address those issues?
3. How should you approach the situation with your female employees?

Because Vernon gets along well with your problem employee, you decide to ignore Vernon's shortcomings and keep him past his probationary period. You hope that in time Vernon will learn the updated budget processes and get along with the other staff members. Recently, you have learned of another of Vernon's shortcomings. He has been heard yelling at one of his female subordinates, Julie. Another female employee from a different department has complained to you that Vernon was rude to her when she requested data from him. It appears that Vernon's work process is still slow and error-prone and that he has trouble effectively utilizing the two employees who work for him. Vernon tends to micromanage every project. When Julie or the other employee disagrees with Vernon on best practices, Vernon ignores them, citing their "obvious lack of experience," and continues his work using the same methodology he has always used. Everyone else in the department works with Vernon if they must, but generally they avoid him if they can because he is difficult to work with.

1. Since you did not take action on Vernon during his probationary period, what do you do about Vernon now?
2. What are the primary issues involved?
3. What other human resource factors should you take into account?
4. Are the age differences in your department creating tension among the employees?

WHAT ACTUALLY HAPPENED IN CASE STUDY 8.5

The hope of improving the work output of the difficult employee was never realized, and that employee left the organization soon after Vernon was hired to work with them. Vernon's female coworkers patiently explained to him that they found pantsuits to be more comfortable and practical and that fetching or brewing coffee was not part of their job descriptions as budget analysts. As the questions persisted, they informed him that his hands seemed to be in good working order and capable of making coffee without female assistance. Vernon would not adapt to the newer methods or technology that was available to him and tended to micromanage his projects, thus missing important deadlines. Vernon would not consider alternative solutions presented by his subordinates, even if those solutions were more efficient and effective than the methods he was employing.

Vernon seemed to resent his coworkers due to their youth, gender, and skills and the positions they held in the department. Vernon's resentment led him to accuse coworkers of making changes to projects without his approval and to suggest to the director that other people in the office were inept. Vernon eventually quit the organization.

KEY ISSUES RAISED IN CASE STUDY 8.5

From a human resources standpoint, it is difficult to deal with employees like Vernon. Case Study 8.5 demonstrates subtle forms of age and sex discrimination by an employee. The remarks made to the female employees regarding coffee making and their attire could be construed as honest questions due to generational differences or be interpreted as sexist remarks. Given that Vernon persisted in asking the coffee question, the intention seemed to be less inquisitive and much more hostile. There is also the issue of an employee who has become inefficient, rude, and difficult to work with.

A manager will not always be able to determine if an applicant has been truthful about his or her skill levels until the individual has been hired into the position and demonstrated those skills. A bigger concern to managers should be how the employee behaves toward other coworkers or subordinates. While technical deficiencies can be overcome, behavioral issues are more difficult to address. Hardened attitudes and deficient personality traits can be very disruptive and hinder the work output of the department.

WHAT COULD HAVE HAPPENED IN CASE STUDY 8.5

The supervisor should have made Vernon aware that sexist remarks, being abusive to subordinates, and being rude to organizational employees is totally unacceptable. If Vernon chose to keep acting in the same inappropriate manner, the supervisor should have begun documenting such actions and at some point written Vernon up for that type of behavior. In addition the supervisor needed to address the fact that Vernon's job performance was also below acceptable standards, which could be addressed by attempting to retrain Vernon or, if that action failed, by putting Vernon on probation.

CASE STUDY 8.6
Stalking Incident

SITUATION FOR CASE STUDY 8.6

You are a department head of a public relations department in a state agency. You have been in charge of the department for more than 20 years and have seen several trends throughout the years in regard to hiring employees in your organization. The city where your agency is located is a rural college town. Therefore, your agency tends to hire many of the local college graduates because they can utilize newer technology faster and better than the older workers. You currently have four employees in your department who work more than 50 hours per week and are efficient and effective. However, the drawback with recent college graduates is that they sometimes have unstable personal lives that affect their professional life.

One of your employees, Mary Beth, has recently ended her relationship with her boyfriend, Mike. Ever since she left Mike, Mary Beth has been jumpy and unfocused. Mike calls Mary Beth at home and at work and has been seen loitering outside the office building. Apparently, Mary Beth's parents are worried about her safety and have told Mike a number of times to quit contacting Mary Beth. Yesterday, Mike stormed into your building, knocking furniture over and screaming at Mary Beth. You called the police and interceded in the situation. You ordered Mike to leave and never return. Mike left before the police arrived.

1. What steps should you take to protect Mary Beth?
2. What steps can and should you take as a manager to protect the other employees?
3. What are the human resource issues involved?
4. What are the criminal issues involved?

WHAT ACTUALLY HAPPENED IN CASE STUDY 8.6

As stated in the case study, the police were called, but Mike was gone by the time they arrived. Because neither the director nor Mary Beth filed charges, the police could not pursue Mike or attempt to arrest him. Mary Beth did not wish to file a restraining order against Mike and made a mistake by not completely severing communication with Mike even after the incident.

Mike continued to stalk Mary Beth at home as well as work even after the incident occurred. During this time, Mike continued to cause problems in the community and had a couple of encounters with law enforcement on other issues. These encounters were not followed with arrests because the infractions were viewed by law enforcement as minor. Unfortunately for Mary Beth, there were no safety precautions or security enhancements at the workplace. The office where Mary Beth was employed remained a fairly open atmosphere for people to come and go through the facility as they liked. The stalking only stopped when Mike moved away.

KEY ISSUES RAISED IN CASE STUDY 8.6

The case study illustrates the problem with stalking offenders in general. It is difficult to protect an employee from a significant other when the employee is vulnerable to harassment through electronic communications (e.g., telephone and e-mail) and when they have to interface with clients through such communication. Most states now have stalking laws that contend with people who actively stalk their victims through physical proximity or by electronic means.

Anyone can be stalked by a person who is either obsessed with them or has had prior contact with them. There are a number of legal mechanisms that can be used against stalkers. One mechanism is through the criminal justice system by leveraging antistalking laws against an aggressor. A second mechanism can be utilized through the civil courts in the form of a restraining order, which legally prevents an aggressor from contacting the victim through any type of communications and limits the person from coming within a set distance of a person physically. Any violation of a restraining order can result in the person being arrested.

Employers can take certain measures to keep their employees safe. One option is to use security cameras both inside and outside their place of employment. Security cameras may potentially deter people from committing criminal actions if they fear being caught after they commit an offense. Security alarms are also a good mechanism for making a facility safer since police or first responders can be summoned quickly if an incident occurs. If the organization can afford the expense, uniformed security guards or police officers can provide immediate on-site response to incidents.

WHAT COULD HAVE HAPPENED IN CASE STUDY 8.6

Employers have a wide range of options available to them to protect an employee if they are aware of a potentially dangerous situation. To stop electronic harassment, an employer can have the employee's calls screened by another employee. The organization can keep copies of offending e-mails to turn over to law enforcement. For organizations that have the resources, security cameras and door card keys at the entrances can assist prosecutors in charging suspects with stalking or harassment violations. These measures can also protect the organization itself if it is singled out for harassment by disgruntled individuals. Having a strong security presence at a facility location can enhance the overall safety of employees working for an organization.

Suggested Readings for Chapter 8

Bowie, Vaughan, Fisher, Bonnie S., and Cooper, Cary L., 2005. *Workplace violence: Issues, trends, strategies*. ISBN: 1-84392-134-0. London, England: Willan Publishing.

Falkenrath, Richard A., Newman, Robert D., and Thayer, Bradley A., 1998. *America's Achilles' heel: Nuclear, biological, and chemical terrorism and covert attack*. ISBN: 0-262-56118-2. Cambridge, Massachusetts: Belfer Center for Science and International Affairs, John F. Kennedy School of Government, Harvard University.

Lesser, Ian O., Hoffman, Bruce, Arquilla, John, Ronfeldt, David, and Zanini, Michelle, 1999. *Countering the new terrorism*. ISBN: 0-8330-2667-4. Washington D.C.: Rand, Project Air Force.

Ricks, Truett A., Tillett, Bill G., and Van Meter, Clifford, 1994. *Principles of security. Third edition*. ISBN: 0-87084-746-5. Cincinnati, Ohio: Anderson Publishing Company.

Chapter 9

Employee Benefits

To remain competitive when recruiting and retaining personnel, public entities must provide benefits for employees and their families. The types of nonwage benefits vary among public organizations but usually consist of retirement plans, medical insurance, dental and vision plans, disability insurance, life insurance, paid time off, worker compensation programs, and domestic partner benefits. Fringe benefits can include tuition assistance, flexible medical or child care benefits, and performance pay.

Medical Insurance

Medical insurance covers the costs of physician and surgeon fees, hospital rooms, and prescription drugs. Dental and optical care might also be offered as part of an overall package, as separate benefits, or not covered at all. Coverage can sometimes include the employee's dependents.

Medical coverage is generally provided through managed health care plans. The most common types of managed health care plans are health maintenance organizations (HMOs) and preferred provider organizations (PPOs). Managed health care plans enter into contracts with doctors, hospitals, clinics, and other health care providers such as pharmacies, labs, x-ray centers, and medical equipment vendors. This group of contracted health care providers is known as the health plan's network. In some types of managed health care plans, an employee may be required to receive all health care services from a network provider. In other managed health care plans, an employee may be able to receive care from providers who are not part of the network but will pay a larger share of the cost to receive these services. In an HMO, employees and their dependents receive most or all health care from a network provider. HMOs require that the employee selects one primary care physician who is responsible for managing and coordinating all of their health care. If the employee needs care from a physician specialist in the network or a diagnostic service such as a lab test, the primary care physician will have to provide a referral. PPOs, on the other hand, contract with a network of preferred providers from which an employee can choose. If employees receive care from any doctor in the preferred network, they will only be responsible for the annual deductible and co-payment for the visit.

Disability Insurance

Disability insurance replaces all or part of the income that is lost when a worker is unable to perform his or her job because of illness or injury. This benefit is not commonly offered. There are two main types of disability insurance: short-term and long-term. Short-term disability insurance begins right away or within a few weeks of an accident, illness, or some other disability. Long-term disability insurance provides benefits to employees when a long-term or permanent illness, injury, or disability renders them unable to perform their job duties.

Life Insurance

Life insurance protects an employee's family in the event of the employee's death by providing money to pay for the family's expenses. Insurance benefits are paid all at once to the designated beneficiaries of the policy, usually a spouse or child. You can get insurance through an employer if they sponsor a group plan. Public agencies usually sponsor life insurance plans that are standard for their full-time employees up to a certain amount, for example, $15,000 to $20,000. Most public agencies allow their employees to purchase additional insurance coverage at the employee's expense.

Retirement Benefits

Retirement benefits are funds set aside to provide employees with an income or pension when they end their career. Retirement plans fit into two general categories: defined benefit plans and defined contribution plans. In defined benefit plans, the benefit amount is predetermined on the basis of salary and years of service. The employer pays a pension to the retired employee for the remainder of the employee's life, however long it may be. In these plans, the employer pays the benefit and bears the risk of the investment. In defined contribution plans, employer and employee contributions are specified. However, the benefit amount is usually tied to the performance of the investment and to the level of employee contribution toward the investment. Risk is placed on the employee rather than the employer. These plans are set up under federal regulations known as 401k, 403b, and 457 plans. The vast majority of public sector pension plans are still defined benefit plans, but pressure is increasing due to financial market returns and budget constraints for public sector employees to be placed in defined contribution plans.

Fringe Benefits

A variety of noncash payments are increasingly being used to attract and retain talented employees. These are referred to as fringe benefits and can include tuition assistance, flexible medical or child care spending accounts, and other child care benefits. A flexible spending account allows employees to contribute to a fund in pretax dollars, and then use that money to pay nonreimbursed medical expenses. Expenses such as co-pays and medication costs can be offset by this fund.

Paid Leave

Vacation days, sick days, and paid time off plans are another common feature of employee benefit programs. Paid holidays are usually included in this type of benefit as well. Most public agencies allow employees to accumulate vacation days throughout the year and give more vacation and sick leave days with tenure.

Financial Impact of Benefit Plans

The cost of providing health and pensions benefits for public sector employees is becoming an increasing challenge to policy and managerial leadership. Currently, the gap between public and private sector benefits is quite substantial. The average public employee earned $4.45 worth of health benefits per hour compared with $2.01 in the private sector (Barro, 2010). In general, public sector employees have more generous health plans and pay a smaller portion of their insurance premiums. Retirement costs are another area where there is a wide gap between the public and private sectors. The average cost is $0.92 per hour in private sector retirement benefits against $3.19 per hour for state and local government employees (Barro, 2010).

One of the recent actions by the Government Accounting Standards Board is GASB Statement 45, which requires more complete, reliable, and analytical financial reporting on the costs and financial obligations that governments incur when they provide postemployment benefits (PEB) other than pensions. Postemployment health care benefits, the most common form of PEB, are a significant financial commitment for many governments. Prior to Statement 45, governments typically followed a "pay as you go" accounting approach in which the cost of benefits was not reported until after employees retired. The new approach requires an accounting of all costs and future obligations incurred by governments for promised future benefit payments to employees. This new disclosure requirement forces governmental entities to change their commitment to pay for future employee benefits or fund these future benefit obligations in a systematic process.

The recent health reform act passed by Congress will also have impact on public agencies in the provision of medical health benefits. Public agencies are in the process of assessing the impact of the new health reform act. The short-term impact will be on group health plan mandates, eligibility rules, administrative requirements, account-based health plans, new fees, and retiree health plans. In the long term, the act will have additional administrative requirements, Medicaid expansions, free-rider penalties, free-choice vouchers, exchanges and subsidies, excise tax, and tax changes.

Author's Experience

Public service management over medical and retirement benefits provides some of the most challenging financial situations and has immense impact on employee pocketbooks and morale. The first crisis that Mr. Benavides faced was an unfunded pension obligation in a civilian employee pension fund. After the 9/11 attack, the market value of the pension fund dropped from $2.0 billion to $1.4 billion. A very sobering actuarial analysis determined that the pension fund could not earn its way to fiscal health. The fund growth assumptions were too aggressive, and the underestimation of the impact of a new plan allowed employees to retire at ages earlier than those in the previous pension plan. After a blue ribbon committee reviewed the situation, some key decisions were made to correct the funding shortfall. Some minor adjustments were made to the pension plan, but the primary solution to the underfunding was to increase employer and employee pension contributions and to issue $600 billion in pension obligation bonds to fully fund the pension benefit obligations. The new contribution rates were raised to 28% of pay. It was not clear that the new employer and employee contribution amounts were sustainable. Furthermore, the city did not require that new employees be switched to a defined contribution plan.

The second issue that weighed on the institution was the shifting of all health benefit increases to the employees to lessen the impact of funding future health benefit obligations promised to employees. These changes were made in a fiscal year when the local economy was in a difficult situation and budget reductions were feasible. The changes to the city's pension plan and the health benefit plans created a great deal of resentment within the workforce and created some long-term morale problems.

Final Notes

Providing balanced employee benefit plans that are competitive but fiscally responsible can be a challenge. It seems that many public agencies must constantly relearn the lesson of not providing employee benefits that are too generous only to be retracted or reduced during difficult economic times. Public sector leaders are almost always facing the need to balance their budgets either by cutting government services that are popular with their elected leaders and the public or by reducing the pay and benefit packages of their workforce. Public employees look to their managers to preserve their benefits against budget cuts. However, these managers are usually in the position of explaining to their workforce why they must shoulder the brunt of the budget cuts to limit the impact of scarce revenues upon the citizens whom they serve.

Important Points to Remember

1. The provision of health benefit plans for employees and their dependents and for retired employees is no longer a given.
2. The provision of health benefits impacts how public agencies balance the needs of their citizens and those of their workforce.
3. Fringe benefits that are provided by public sector agencies must be constantly compared with the market and with other employers to adjust to economic and competitive forces.
4. The new Governmental Accounting Standards Board requirements necessitate regular financial analysis of the type and scope of health benefits offered to the workforce.
5. Analysis of what competing employers offer in terms of health and other fringe benefits should be done regularly.
6. Organizations need to regularly review their health and other benefits to ensure the financial affordability and suitability of their offerings while remaining competitive.
7. It is important to structure paid leave offerings in a manner to provide employee flexibility while ensuring that the organization can always have enough employees to provide needed services.
8. Public organizations must provide employee assistance plans to help their workforce cope with the pace and stress of the workplace and life.
9. An atmosphere must be created that allows employees to ask for help and to know that it will be provided without stigma.
10. Every organization must be vigilant for employees that are having trouble dealing with the stress of work and life and be ready to intervene with assistance.

CASE STUDY 9.1
The Health Benefit Fund Surplus Cash Transfer

SITUATION FOR CASE STUDY 9.1

The city auditor is required to conduct audits of city operations that their risk analysis indicates would make the city vulnerable to fraud and high financial exposure if funds were not handled properly. One of the areas that the city auditor's risk analysis identified was $100 million that was funneled through the city's health benefit fund annually. This fund financed several hundred vendors that needed to be checked to ensure proper billing and to determine that the services were rendered to the employees and the city. This fund was of particular interest to the city auditor because he once worked in the health benefit division that was responsible for management of the funds. During the financial and performance audit, the city auditor determined that the fund had a surplus of $9 million that needed to be returned to the general fund and the enterprise funds that originally contributed the majority of income stream to the health benefit fund.

At the time of the audit, the city was experiencing a budget shortfall. Many strategies were being employed by mangers to balance the city's budget. One favorite strategy was to identify surplus funds in different governmental funds. During such a search, the employee health benefit division's financial personnel had discovered the $9 million surplus in the health benefit fund that the city auditor had identified. The city's employee benefit consulting firm and the employee benefit division financial staff planned to keep city and employee contribution levels to the health benefit fund in line with the previous year's costs. Therefore, the $9 million surplus could be used to balance the city's general fund and enterprise fund budgets in the upcoming fiscal year without damage to the fiscal health of the fund. The city auditor agreed with this assessment, believing that the surplus was created by contributions from the general fund and the enterprise funds and not from employee contributions. The city manager's staff did not verify the city auditor's assertion but proceeded with the transfer.

WHAT ACTUALLY HAPPENED IN CASE STUDY 9.1

Management decided to transfer the surplus funds to the appropriate contributing funds based on the number of employees that each of the contributing funds had on the respective payrolls. This decision was based on the city auditor's findings. Management did not inform the employees, the elected board officials, and the citizens that the surplus funds were being transferred out of the employee health benefit fund. The recommendation for the transfer was in the city auditor's final report to the city council, but it did not receive any attention from the employees, the employee groups, the citizens, the city council, or the media.

The cost containment strategies implemented for the health benefit plan succeeded, and the rates for the city departments and the employees were not changed. The employees did not receive a pay raise that fiscal year due to budget constraints caused by the economic downturn. However, after the employees and the employee groups discovered that the city had transferred the health benefit funds back to the contributing funds, they demanded to see the evidence that none of the surplus funds came from employee contributions. The city council demanded that the city auditor and city manager verify their financial analysis, but they were not able to do so with complete certainty. The employee groups lost trust in the city organization over the transfer of the surplus funds. To restore trust, the city manager returned the entire $9 million to the employee health benefit fund the next fiscal year. After this incident the employee groups demanded to have an advisory committee made of employees from all the city employee groups to supervise the operations of the employee health benefit fund, to select vendors, and to have input on future audits. This episode forever limited the city manager's ability to transfer funds without a great deal of scrutiny. Later, when substantial changes had to be made to the operation of the health benefit fund, it took extended periods of time to achieve any changes. Health benefit costs started to rise faster than inflation.

KEY ISSUES RAISED IN CASE STUDY 9.1

City management should have disclosed the transfer of the surplus funds to the employees, elected officials, and citizens more explicitly in the city's budget document. The management team's actuarial analysis showing that the surplus money could be used to balance the budget was correct. However, the city manager and his staff should have verified the city auditor's analysis that the surplus money in the health benefit fund was only from contributions, the general fund, and the enterprise funds and that the surplus did not contain any employee contributions.

WHAT COULD HAVE HAPPENED IN CASE STUDY 9.1

The management team could have shown their data to the employee groups to prove that the surplus money in the health benefit fund was only derived from contributions by the city and not from any employee contributions. The management team should have clearly documented the transfer of surplus funds to the general fund and the enterprise funds to address the budget shortfall. The lack of transparency resulted in a loss of trust with the employees, the city's employee organizations, the elected board, the citizens, and the local media. The following year, the elected board insisted that the city auditor conduct an audit of the health benefit fund. The city council also ordered an investigation to determine if any wrongdoing had been committed by the management team, the human resources department, and the health benefit division. The investigation did not find any evidence of wrongdoing by city staff, but several careers were ruined over this incident. Future budget reviews of the health benefit fund were problematic because of the perception of the improper transfer of funds held by the city employees.

CASE STUDY 9.2
Selection of New Hospital Network for the City

SITUATION FOR CASE STUDY 9.2

The city had a five-year contract with a hospital network which included a PPO and two HMOs to provide medical services for the city's workforce. The city issued a new request for proposals in an attempt to reduce the city's health benefit costs, which were running just over $100 million per year. The city council and the workforce were notified at the beginning of the fiscal year that the city would be soliciting bids for a new hospital network.

The city hired a consulting firm to draft new bid specifications for the city's hospital network. The human resources department solicited employee representatives from all employee groups to review all of the hospital network bids and to help select a new hospital network provider. The employee committee received training in what its duties would be from the consultant. However, the consultant took longer than expected to draft the new bid documents. This reduced the time the staff had allocated to analyze the bid document, review all the bids, and select the winning bidder.

The assistant city manager assigned to supervise the human resources department and the selection of the hospital network provider did not supervise the processes as closely as this complex process required. The city hoped to identify a new hospital network provider with a more extensive network that could reduce the city's existing costs, provide savings to the general fund and the enterprise funds, provide budgetary relief during a time of great fiscal stress in the local economy, and provide equal or better health benefits to the city employee. The consultant assured the city that the new specifications would generate costs savings and improve coverage for the city's employees by securing additional bids with hospitals in the suburbs where many of the city's employees resided.

WHAT ACTUALLY HAPPENED IN CASE STUDY 9.2

The city received five bids for the hospital network proposal. The bids were all opened six months prior to the adoption of the new city budget so that the bids could be evaluated and the new hospital network provider be incorporated into the city's health benefit budget for the upcoming fiscal year. However, this schedule shortened the time available to draft and approve the contract for the new hospital network. The lateness of the bid completion and the short bidding process caused trouble for the bid review and evaluation process. Management and the employee committee quickly reviewed the five bids within the truncated time frame. Three of the bids were declared to be nonresponsive. This left the existing hospital network provider and a new out-of-state firm as the only responsive bidders in the process.

The new provider was declared the lowest cost bidder. The staff responsible for evaluating the bids and bringing them forward to the city council convinced city management that the new bidder could provide the services required with higher quality than the other two bidders. Upon learning that they lost their contract, the existing hospital network provider chose to go political to keep their contract. They lobbied the city council and the workforce that the winning bidder, who was not a local firm, did not have a sufficient number of hospitals to serve the entire city and all the employees that lived outside the city. In addition, only about half of the doctors in the current network had a relationship with the new hospital network. In fact, one of the city council members was a doctor who was not in the proposed hospital network.

A majority of the city council appealed to city management to withdraw the new bid or prove that the new network hospital provider was really the best deal for the city. The human resources department and the assistant city manager were not able to convince the city council that the new network hospital provider was a viable bidder. The management team decided to pull the award from the new hospital network provider, even though that meant losing a lower cost provider and losing the budgetary relief in the upcoming fiscal year. City management then recommended a one year extension of the existing hospital provider and to forgo the savings. The city council was delighted to avoid voting on such a difficult issue, the employees were relieved, and the existing network provider performed the following year satisfactorily.

KEY ISSUES RAISED IN CASE STUDY 9.2

The staff assigned to select a new network provider did not fully evaluate all the issues related to selecting a new hospital network, nor did they keep the city's employees fully informed on the ramifications of the bid process. Although the employee representatives were appointed by the employee groups, they were not granted any authority to make decisions for their employee groups. City management did not provide sufficient time in the bid schedule to allow all the vendors to submit responsive bids. The specifications did not provide sufficient safeguards to ensure that the winning provider could fulfill all the requirements of the city's management and workforce.

WHAT COULD HAVE HAPPENED IN CASE STUDY 9.2

The staff assigned to handle the selection of a new hospital network should have known that a contract of this size and complexity required a much longer lead time to be executed correctly. Given the importance of health services to the workforce, they were deeply concerned as to which vendor would provide the best level of service to them and their families. The assistant city manager and the human resources department should have been reprimanded for the way they mishandled this contract process. However, they were not disciplined in any manner, much to the consternation of the workforce, the existing hospital network provider, and the losing hospital network provider. The only action that was taken was that the assistant city manager supervising the human resources department was given a new assignment.

Suggested Readings for Chapter 9

Maiden, R. P., Herlihy, Patricia, and Attridge, Mark, 2005. *Integration of employee assistance, work/life, and wellness services.* ISBN: 0784030632. New York: The Haworth Press, Inc.

Miller, Laurence, 2008. *From difficult to disturbed: Understanding and managing dysfunctional employees.* ISBN: 0-8144-0922-9. New York: AMACOM, American Management Association.

Reddick, Christopher, and Coggburn, Jerrell, 2008. *Handbook of employee benefits and administration,* ISBN: 9781420051926, CRC Press, Boca Raton, Florida.

Van den Bergh, Nan, 2000. *Emerging trends for EAPs in the 21st century.* First edition. ISBN: 0-7890-1019-4. Binghamton, New York: Haworth Press.

Chapter 10

Mentoring Employees in the Workplace

Mentoring is vital to building a strong and flexible public workforce. A mentoring program strives to identify those employees who are best and brightest in the organization and provide them with the resources to succeed and advance in the organization. Mentoring is done to develop a deep and well-rounded workforce and to groom and promote the future leaders of the workplace at all levels of the organization. To succeed, a mentoring program needs a well-defined plan, a strong list of objectives, a process for assessing the program on a regular basis, consistency of purpose, and the resources and leadership to keep the program on track and relevant to the organization.

Essential Aspects of a Mentoring Program

A clear set of goals and objectives and a means for measuring progress are essential for a successful mentoring program. The support of top management is also crucial for all mentoring programs. Management's involvement shows that the organization is serious about the initiative. Mentoring must be integrated into the very fabric and culture of the organization. Without the active incorporation of the mentoring program into the organization's culture, there is little hope for its success and continuance. Mentoring programs need a solid commitment of staff support and financial backing to launch and sustain the program. Management not only has to actively support the program but also must allocate the most precious resource that any executive team has—which is their time. The task of sustaining the mentoring program cannot be delegated to the human resources function of the organization.

Management's Participation and Mentoring Program Guidelines

While human resources should handle all the logistics and day-to-day management of the mentoring program, they can never be expected to carry the program on their shoulders. The vision for the program has to come from the top. Management must be actively involved in the program and consider it a top priority of the organization. Effective mentoring has to be more than just matching experienced employees with new or inexperienced employees. Quality mentoring programs need to be carefully conceived and structured with clear and comprehensive program guidelines. A mentoring program will not be successful if it begins with little structure and guidelines and parameters are added after the program starts. The mentors and mentees are going to expect clear and concise rules of engagement for the mentoring program. For the program to operate properly sufficient funding is vital, as well as other resources, including staff members to actively manage the mentoring program.

An organization might want to start a pilot program to work the kinks out of the mentoring program until the organization has a good understanding of how the program will work. This will also give the organization time to adjust the program to align it with the organization's culture. Management must be mindful that they should not make unrealistic expectations for the program. The management team must also decide if mentors are going to be allowed to have more than one mentee and how the program managers will assess the effectiveness of mentors who have more than one mentee. It is vital that the organization determine how many mentor–mentee matches are going to be allowed, as the size of the group will dictate how big the training and mentoring program needs to be to ensure its success. Trying to run and manage the program by assigning it to existing staff who have other job duties will likely bring difficulties if the size of the mentoring program is too large.

Recruiting Employees into a Mentoring Program

When employees and mentors are identified to participate in the program, time has to be allotted to sustain the program. Managers should look for talented employees who have the ability to rise through the ranks of the organization. It is critical that the most promising employees are selected to be in the mentoring program to ensure the greatest return on investment. Management will need to promote the program through seminars, webinars, networking events, podcasts, question and answer sessions, guest speakers, participant surveys, and focus groups. It is easier to start with a small program to verify program costs, manageability, how it fits into the organizational culture, and strengths and weaknesses. If the small program yields a definitive return on investment, the program can be expanded. If the program does not work at all, it can be dropped with little lost investment. By evaluating the strengths and weaknesses of the program in its early stages, management can modify the structures and processes that will ensure the success, viability, and continuance of the program even with a change in leadership.

The Selection Process for Matching Mentors and Mentees

Pairing of mentors to employees is critical to the success of the program and can be accomplished in a variety of ways. Although it is a challenge to determine who is a good fit, match mentors and mentees based on similar work styles and competencies or by matching mentors who possess strengths in areas where a mentee is weakest. Because matching is so important to the success of the mentoring program, a climate must be created and maintained where the mentors and mentees feel free to dissolve a match if it is not productive without repercussions to either party. It is necessary to make it simple to dissolve a match for other reasons, which can include changing job assignments, transfers, or other events that require a new mentor–mentee match.

The first thing required of mentors is a strong commitment of time and availability to the mentee. The mentors will need to observe the mentees to determine what other issues may need to be addressed to ensure the mentees' success. To derive benefit from the relationship, the mentees must show interest and be willing to invest the time necessary to achieve their goals. The mentees need to clarify their goals and outline how they will work with their mentors to achieve their goals.

Benefits to the Mentor

The mentor can also learn a great deal from the mentoring relationship. Mentors can learn new technological skills, social networking techniques, different perspectives on issues, and how to improve their ability to impart knowledge. Both individuals will expand their professional networks; enhance their time management skills; and improve their relationship, communication, and persuasion skills. Both parties must be willing to find different venues inside and outside work to exchange information and provide counsel and direction when necessary or desired by the mentee. Since everyone has preferred methods of interacting, coaching, and learning, it is necessary for the mentor and mentee to learn each other's style and preferences.

Maintaining the Mentoring Program

The mentoring program should be regularly evaluated to see how the relationships are working and to determine if the organizational goals of the mentoring program are being achieved. The organization will need to establish a framework for administering and supervising the program. Monitoring will allow the organization and the participants in the mentoring program to refine the program to ensure it is being managed and implemented properly. An education program should be developed to increase awareness of the program and how to participate in it, how the individuals will be selected, how the program fits into the strategic plan of the organization, and what the goals of the program are. After the process for selecting the mentors and mentees is established, it is important to develop a training program for the mentors and mentees. The mentors and mentees will need direction in understanding the goals of the program, their role in the program, and how best to relate to the other individual in the mentoring relationship. No one should be allowed in the mentoring program without going through an orientation and training program.

Summary of the Mentor's Role

A mentor helps, guides, shares knowledge, and gets gratification from mentoring and coaching. Mentors need to be instructed to ask the mentees what they need help with in their work life. The mentor assists with putting a structure to work on the issues that the mentee needs assistance with developing. The mentor and mentee must determine when to schedule meetings that work with both of their schedules. The meeting can be over the phone, on the Internet, or in person. It is important to have face-to-face meetings to keep the relationship on track.

The relationship dynamic must be somewhere between a friendship and a teacher–student relationship. The mentee has to feel that he can speak to his mentor about any subject and the mentor will be open-minded and respond in an honest fashion. Early in the relationship, the mentor will most likely need to push the discussion to get all the issues out and to see where the mentee needs assistance. The mentor must hold the mentee accountable for making progress on the issues, habits, or skills that require attention and improvement. The mentor is primarily responsible for the growth of the mentee's capabilities and to push the mentee beyond his comfort zone.

How Long Does Mentoring Continue?

Some mentoring relationships end within months and some last a lifetime. Sometimes the mentee outgrows the mentor. The mentor must know when the role in the relationship has changed and if the mentee must be released or turned over to another colleague. The mentor should be a helper to the mentee and not a supervisor. The mentor should be on the mentee's side and look for opportunities to provide instruction and corrective action in a friendly manner. The advice dispensed by the mentor has to be tailored to the strengths and weaknesses of the mentee. Sometimes the mentor also has to provide the mentee with support in difficult situations. The mentor must also model the kind of behavior he wants the mentee to acquire and display. In addition, the mentor has to school the mentee on the behavior and standards the organization expects from all their employees.

Issues for the Mentor to Consider: Generation Gaps

The mentor must be cognizant of what population group the mentee belongs to in the organization. If the mentee is a senior, it is important to remember that seniors usually prefer mentors who are their peers, whom they respect and are willing to take direction and advice from in the course of their career. Baby boomers typically want to learn how to improve and want to be challenged to achieve more in their careers. Generation X might expect the mentoring relationship to be one of equals and that the mentor can learn as much from them as they can from their mentors. Millennial or Generation Y mentees expect every good organization to have a well-established mentoring program and to consider that there is no question the mentee is worth the investment.

If the mentee is older than the mentor, this can provide a challenge for the mentor in terms of navigating generational issues. Younger individuals in supervisory positions are no longer unusual. If a young mentor can work with an older mentee, it is likely that he can also function better in his own department with a diverse workforce. Diverse workplaces with people from various generations can exploit their strengths and minimize their weaknesses if they can work together.

The Mentee's Role

The mentee also has a big role to play in the mentor–mentee relationship. The mentees need to raise issues of importance to themselves and to actively seek the advice of the mentors. The mentees must also act on the advice and counsel given by the mentors. The mentee benefits from observing how the mentor operates and what skills and attributes make the mentor successful. The mentee can also learn from the mentor and other superiors what not to do by observing what styles and skills are not effective and should not be emulated.

Benefits to the Organization

You can expect many benefits from a well-designed and well-managed mentoring program. Donna Benardi Paul cites several examples of an effective mentoring program's benefits for public organizations (Paul, 2005). Mentoring programs can allow an organization to link career development, diversity, new employee orientation, and current strategic initiatives to create a seasoned and productive workforce. Specific benefits listed by Paul include the following.

- Increased productivity: An effective mentoring program enhances the performance of the mentee due to the acquisition of additional skills and resources. Additionally, the natural desire to perform well for both self-satisfaction and to live up to the mentor's expectations can result in increased motivation. Mentoring helps an individual development his or her full potential, not just learn tasks.
- Improved organizational communication: Mentoring provides networking at its best. As a result of the program, more accurate and positive communication occurs, often across departmental boundaries.

- Skill-based growth: Skill strengths and development needs become more evident, enhancing human resource planning and effectiveness. Positions are filled based on qualifications versus duration in a position.
- New employee orientation: Mentoring provides an efficient mechanism to orient new hires and enables them to function in a position.
- Recruiting advantages: Facilitated mentoring attracts talented new employees by demonstrating the organization's commitment to continuous learning. This is an extremely valuable feature in today's workplace.
- Cost-effectiveness: In an increasingly cost-conscious world, mentoring focuses on "in-house" resources, inexpensively spreads existing organization knowledge, can save time and money on recruiting and orientation, and can be customized to support organizational objectives that might otherwise require additional programs and funding. (Rhodes and Drahosz, 1997, pp. 5–6)

Scalability of a Mentoring Program

The size and distribution of the organization will impact the way the mentoring program is managed and directed. When the organization covers a large geographic area, it will require special efforts to keep the mentoring program active and relevant. The mentors and mentees might be separated by large distances and have few opportunities to interact on a face-to-face basis. When these conditions exist, then the staff assigned to the management of the mentoring program will need to be proactive in maintaining the program. The staff will need to contact all the mentors and mentees to see if the relationships are being actively maintained and beneficial to all participants. Also, there must be a concerted effort to ensure that mentor–mentee matches are in force and active. Regular assessments must be made of all the participants to ascertain if the goals and objectives of the program are being achieved. The staff must be of sufficient rank to contact high-level mentors and to provide direction to modify the program as necessary.

Mentoring Programs: Training and Communication

The organization will find it beneficial to create structures to keep the mentors and mentees in constant communication and for management and the organization to monitor how well the program is functioning. Training must be scheduled on a regular basis to provide refresher courses for existing mentors and mentees and for processing new mentors and mentees entering the program. web-based panel discussions can be made available to participants of the program and to people wishing to enter or learn about the program. A mentoring program should have regular one-on-one coaching to supplement the structured training program. Subject matter experts in the organization must be identified and made available to all the mentoring program participants. Also social media such as Facebook, LinkedIn, or Twitter can be used to distribute information to individuals in the mentoring program.

Where Do Mentors Come From?

While supervisors can be mentors for their employees, it is usually best for mentors to come from other operations or departments. This practice reduces concerns that the mentor will micromanage the mentee to prevent mistakes or will try to create replicas of themselves. Furthermore, this removes concerns that any disagreements a mentee may have with her mentor will impact her employment. A companion program to the formal mentoring program can empower employees to observe colleagues in their organization whom they admire and wish to emulate and to create their own mentor–mentee relationships for their own career development.

Informal mentor–mentee relationships can be as powerful and beneficial to an organization as the formal mentor–mentee program. All employees should be provided with soft skills training to help them understand that career advancement not only has to do with their education and experience but includes such characteristics as being well read, having good writing and presentation skills, and knowing how to interact with their supervisors effectively. This kind of training can provide an excellent supplement to an organization's formal mentoring program. In public organizations, employees need to be mentored on how to handle such issues as dealing with harsh treatment from elected and appointed officials during public meetings, ethics, media relations, working with elected and appointed boards, working with difficult people, and hiring the best people for the organization.

Author's Experience

Dr. Valcik has mentored several employees during his career, many of whom are from other countries. With many mentees, Valcik found they possessed excellent technical skills and could write excellent software applications but often had a difficult time understanding what the clients needed or how clients used the applications. Valcik spends quite a bit of time explaining how to interface with the functional users successfully to get a software application into production status where it can be used by the organization. These mentees also needed to learn how the American workplace operates from a cultural standpoint. These employees needed mentoring in communication and cultural issues more than they needed technical training to become successful employees in their future jobs.

Final Notes

As a part of the formal mentoring program, the organization must observe where it is getting the best results from the program. It will become clear which mentors are the most successful and which new and upcoming employees should be assigned a mentor. Also the mentors who have demonstrated a talent for effective mentoring should be assigned to counsel their colleagues on the ways to successfully mentor individuals. If the organization truly values the formal mentoring program, then mentoring should be recognized during employee performance reviews and compensation should reflect the additional responsibility.

Important Points to Remember

1. Mentoring programs are still relevant in this high-tech era because relationship management is a soft skill that becomes more valuable as individuals advance in an organization.
2. Mentoring produces positive outcomes such as improved productivity and retention of valuable employees.
3. Organizations benefit as well as employees from mentoring programs.
4. Both short-term and long-term mentoring are needed within an organization to address the needs of employees and the organization.
5. Peer-to-peer mentoring works best for the baby boomer generation.
6. When mentors and mentees are not able to be in close proximity, e-mentoring can be employed.
7. Reverse mentoring is beneficial when attempting to familiarize senior employees with the latest technological advances.
8. Mentoring is an excellent strategy for the integration of intergenerational teams.
9. It is important to avoid mentor burnout by providing the opportunity to have new mentoring relationships and through constant training.
10. Mentoring helps organizations and employees adapt to the constantly changing environment of public service.

CASE STUDY 10.1
Difficult Transition in a Forensics Department

SITUATION FOR CASE STUDY 10.1

You have just been hired as a director for a small but important office with a city forensic science unit. The department had three experienced employees quit or terminated before you took over. You have hired three people to replace the former employees. One task requires specialized skills with a particular software application that none of the three new employees currently possesses. There is no money in the budget to hire another person to perform this task, so your options are fairly limited.

Two of the new employees have good technical skills, but you are not sure if they can learn this software application. You decide to ask for volunteers to take on the assignment. One of the new employees, Julie, volunteers to train herself on the software to produce the critical data needed for the operations of the forensics department. You hired this person to perform a completely different task but realize that someone will need to step up and take on this responsibility or your organization will fail to perform one of its primary functions. You know that Julie has a master's degree and can pick up software skills fairly easily, but you also know that there is a learning curve involved.

1. Did the director make the right decision?
2. What happens if Julie fails at the assignment? How will this appear to the administrators about the director's decision?
3. How do you propose to mentor Julie through the learning process for this skill set?

Julie learns how to use the software and gradually gets operations back to normal. Julie sometimes comes to you with questions or to propose ideas on how to resolve technical issues. You are more than happy to listen and discuss the issues with her even though you do not have a technical background to understand the details. You decide the best thing to do is to send Julie to training with the original software vendor to see if Julie can learn the new skills better through an outside organization. You are a big proponent of training. Even though it may be fairly costly in the short term to send employees to training, you consider it to be a long-term benefit.

1. Should employees be sent to outside organizations for training if money is available?
2. Should employees be sent first to training before they begin their work or after they have worked for some time at their jobs?

WHAT ACTUALLY HAPPENED IN CASE STUDY 10.1

Over time, the department grew in size and importance. The organization has no mentoring program to this day. Administrators tended to mentor employees informally when they had time and if they felt a need to do so. Due to the mentoring she received and the skills she acquired, Julie was promoted within five years.

In the past, the organization tended to avoid sending personnel to training or would send personnel to training but have no means for those employees to practice the new skill set, which the employees soon forgot. The director promoted a policy of training employees outside the organization and mentoring them, which improved the employees' ability to perform tasks and resolve issues and ultimately benefited the organization.

KEY ISSUES RAISED IN CASE STUDY 10.1

The employees in this department are not atypical. It is common for employees to be assigned work additional to what they were originally hired to do. The director realized that she had to take care of gaps in the organization's operational capability and ensure that employees were trained for the skill set that they were now asked to perform. The additional responsibilities made the employees more accountable for the skills they were going to acquire. This meant that the employees in this case study needed additional training in order to succeed at their tasks. If the employees had not received training and encouragement from the director, the employees could have been set up for failure.

One mistake that many administrators make is to send their employees to training long before they are required to use those skills. When there is a gap of time between training and use of such skills, employees are likely to forget their new skills. It is sometimes better to send an employee to training right before the employee is supposed to use the skills or soon after the employee has started the work that requires the new skills. In this way, an employee who picks up some of the new work easily can skip introductory training and proceed to training that targets deficiencies.

Training needs to be set to the individual's actual needs. Too often employees are sent to training for skills that they will not use or to training at a skill level that is either too high or too low for their abilities. An initial assessment of an employee's skill level will prevent the employee from being demoralized and prevent a waste of the employee's time and the organization's resources.

WHAT COULD HAVE HAPPENED IN CASE STUDY 10.1

The director correctly handled a very difficult situation by identifying key personnel in the department that could adapt to a new situation and successfully fulfill key department operational requirements. After success with Julie's training, the director could have offered targeted training to other employees to make sure that all the new work was not placed solely on Julie.

CASE STUDY 10.2
Managing a Large-Scale Mentoring Program with Volunteers

SITUATION FOR CASE STUDY 10.2

A state public management association attempted to establish and manage a statewide mentoring program using volunteers. It was a wonderful program for the mentors and mentees, but it was a nightmare for the volunteers attempting to administer the program and achieve the results sought by the professional public statewide organization. The program had 80 mentors and 80 mentees, and they worked for jurisdictions all over the state. The program was administered by a five-person task force selected from the organization's membership. The first group of mentors was recruited from the membership by the statewide organization's board members, and almost all the individuals who were contacted agreed to be mentors. The individuals who were identified and recruited were honored to serve the organization in such an important assignment.

The association then solicited mentees from their membership roll through a variety of media channels. The mentees were primarily students and young professionals, with a few seasoned professionals. The vast majority of the mentors were experienced professionals with long tenures in the organization. The mentees had varied skills, but all were seeking mentorship to improve their chances of advancement in the profession and to increase their skills and knowledge. All the mentors and mentees went through an assessment processes to determine their strengths and weaknesses to improve the chances of successfully matching mentors and mentees. Once all the mentors and mentees were selected, they received training on expected roles, responsibilities, and duties as mentors and mentees. The five volunteers of the mentoring task force endeavored to run the program while doing their regular jobs—no easy feat considering the scale of the program.

WHAT ACTUALLY HAPPENED IN CASE STUDY 10.2

The program started off well, but the organization had underestimated how many changes would occur during the course of the year and the impact these changes would have on the mentoring relationships. People in the program quit their jobs, retired, transferred, and were reassigned, and all of these personnel actions impacted the effectiveness of the mentoring program. Mentors and mentees who had been close to each other were now in different parts of the state or had left the state. In many cases, the mentors and mentees used the Internet, social media, and the telephone to keep in touch, but the relationships were not as strong as they had been. No procedures had been established to transition mentors into new relationships with new mentees. In addition, many of the high-ranking officials serving as mentors found it difficult to allocate sufficient time to the mentor–mentee relationships to make them viable and useful. There were not enough volunteers to handle the daily administrative duties to keep the mentoring program running smoothly. Since the individuals administering the program were not being paid, they worked on the program only when their busy schedules allowed. This lack of full-time attention to the program quickly showed the weakness of the volunteer model.

The volunteers had to spend much more time than they had anticipated in keeping the mentors and mentees interacting and ensuring the relationships produced the desired results. The volunteers had to contact each mentor, generally with e-mails and phone calls, to ascertain the condition of the relationship and any issues that were developing. One of the most serious issues occurred when some mentees developed issues with their mentors who were prominent in the organization, and the issues had to be resolved by the volunteers. Fortunately, the volunteers were tenured professionals, personally knew all the mentors, and could discuss relationship issues without creating too much tension. In many cases, the volunteers learned that the mentees were not addressing relationship issues for fear that it would anger their mentors and endanger their future careers. Another problem that became apparent with the program was that there were not enough high-ranking women mentors to handle the demand of young women professionals wanting female mentors. The majority of the female mentors had two or more female mentees to sponsor.

KEY ISSUES RAISED IN CASE STUDY 10.2

The association realized that funds needed to be allocated to hire professionals to manage the administrative and logistical issues to keep the program functional. Also, additional funds were needed to provide ongoing training for the new mentors and mentees being brought into the program. Regular surveying of the mentors and mentees was needed to continually assess the program and to make modifications to maintain effectiveness. Paid staff was needed to contact the mentors and mentees to ensure that the participants were having regular contact and that both sides were benefiting from the mentor–mentee matches. The association's board needed regular reports on the status, results, and benefits of the program. It did not take long to realize that processes had to be established to ensure that matches that did not work out could be ended professionally and that new matches could be made without rancor or hurt feelings.

WHAT COULD HAVE HAPPENED IN CASE STUDY 10.2

The professional association should have provided the funds or raised funds from donors to have sufficient staff, materials, training funds, and other services to administer the program properly. It was appropriate for the five-person volunteer task force that established the program to provide oversight but not for this task force to have been responsible for the day-to-day administration of the program. The program should have started with a smaller number of individuals and allowed the program to grow slowly before running a full-service, state mentoring program. The duties of the mentors and mentees should have been more clearly outlined so that no one would be surprised as to what was expected from the participants.

Suggested Readings for Chapter 10

Johnson, W, and Ridley, Charles, 2004. *The elements of mentoring.* ISBN: 0-230-61364-0. New York: Palgrave MacMillan.

Shea, Gordon F., 1999. *Making the most of being mentored: How to grow from a mentoring partnership.* ISBN: 1560525460. Fredericton, New Brunswick, Canada: Crisp Publications.

Stone, Florence, 2007. *Coaching, counseling & mentoring: How to choose & use the right technique to boost employee performance.* ISBN: 0814473857. New York: AMACOM.

Chapter 11

Negotiating with Organized Labor

Impact of Organized Labor on Public Organizations

Public, nonprofit, and medical organizations in many states will inevitably need to negotiate with organized labor when making human resource decisions. With medical organizations in particular, professional organizations also can impact human resource policies and procedures. In some countries and U.S. states that have right-to-work mandates, the impact of labor unions is greatly diminished. However, even in right-to-work states, strikes can occur and impact public organizations. For example, the first statewide teachers' strike occurred in 1968 in Florida, which is a right-to-work state (UPI, 2010).

Where labor unions are strong, negotiations over employment can have dire consequences for public organizations if a compromise is not met between the two parties. In the United States, the first labor strike recorded was by the Polish craftsmen in the colony of Jamestown in 1619. In 1918 and 1919, a police strike in Britain was successful when the issues of wages, pension, and hours per week were raised by the National Union of Police and Prison Officers (Jones, 2010). The successful police strike in Britain is in sharp contrast to a strike conducted by Boston police officers in 1919, where the police were ultimately fired for "abandoning their post" (City of Boston, 1920). The phrase "abandonment of their post" would recur more recently when Hurricane Katrina and Hurricane Rita struck the Gulf of Mexico and some first responders left the city instead of performing emergency services. However, a police strike in 1974 in Baltimore had a happier result; concessions were made and the police returned to work (Berger, 2007).

Public organizations should keep in mind that other city employees have been known to go on strike. In 2002, firefighters in the United Kingdom went on strike for better pay (BBC News World Edition, 2002). In 2008, the National Union of Teachers (NUT) in Great Britain went on strike for 24 hours over a salary dispute, which impacted many public schools (Bunkall, 2008). In 1966, more than 35,000 workers from the New York City Transit Authority went on strike, completely shutting down the buses and the subway system and preventing commuters from getting to work (*New York Teacher*, 2005). This strike resulted in the passage of the Taylor law in the State of New York, which placed strike limitations on public employees while preserving collective bargaining for compensation (*New York Teacher*, 2005). International strikes have also been held in the public transportation sector, which can cripple the infrastructure. This was demonstrated by the strikes in France in 1995 (Warner, 1995). A labor strike occurred in 2007 when South African public schoolteachers and hospital workers went on strike because 600 hospital nurses were terminated and because the staff wanted a pay increase (BBC News One Minute World News, 2007).

The U.S. federal government has also seen its share of strikes throughout history. In 1970, U.S. postal workers staged a strike that led directly to the employees being allowed to bargain collectively with the federal government, a right they previously did not enjoy (American Postal Workers Union, 2010). However, a turning point occurred for labor unions in 1981 when President Ronald Reagan fired more than 11,000 striking federal air traffic controllers from their positions and further banned them from reapplying to any federal position (Early, 2006). This action from President Reagan dealt a crippling blow to organized labor unions not only in the public arena but also in private industry as well (Early, 2006). While Theodore Roosevelt may have been known as the "trust buster" in his administration, Ronald Reagan would be known as the "union buster" for his action against the air traffic controllers.

Higher education institutions are not immune to strikes. In 1967–1968, the faculty at St. John's College in New York voted to strike (Kelly, 1992). Faculty in the higher education sector can organize through unions and can bargain through the tenure system. Institutions that provide faculty with tenure status create an organized labor force that can counter decisions made by administrators through a vote of no-confidence.

Organized labor unions can strike for reasons other than compensation. Unions have been known to strike about working conditions and benefits, and in protest to layoffs and working hours. The right to work in safe conditions resulted in a strike at Port Chicago in 1944 when African Americans in the U.S. Navy refused to work after an explosion resulted in numerous deaths and injuries (Seligson, 2005). The Port Chicago incident illustrates that organized labor will strike to demand safer working conditions and to contend with a high risk of liability. Unions have come to the aid of employees who have been disciplined or terminated by filing grievances against the organization or supporting litigation through civil court on an employee's behalf.

Preparing for Labor Negotiations

Preparation for any negotiation must start with development of the negotiating strategy. First, conduct a thorough review of previous negotiations. Work with human resources specialists and the departments that were involved in previous negotiations to review all past notes and documents to determine which actions were successful or not and the operational and financial impact of previous agreements to the organization. After reviewing previous negotiation efforts, develop an overall strategy that will address which issues will likely be raised by the labor union and which issues are considered critical to the organization. Finally, conduct an impact study of existing and prior labor agreements to assess the effect of these agreements on operating units and the efficiency and effectiveness of the organization when dealing with labor agreements. Data compiled by human resources should be compared with the data developed by departmental personnel to find commonalties and to ascertain if there any gaps in the data.

A key consideration for the management team is the selection of the labor negotiating team. This team will require a diverse set of skills, personalities, and backgrounds to make the team effective. It will be important for the team to identify with the needs of the opposing team while keeping in mind management's point of view in the negotiations. Determine how much decision-making authority will be granted to the negotiating team. In almost all negotiations, teams will reach junctures where only higher-ranking individuals can decide if a negotiating point can be agreed to or opposed. However, the negotiating team needs to have sufficient latitude and authority to make the deal or to come very close to one with only one or two remaining points to be decided.

The negotiating team will need to be armed with detailed and accurate data that can include the following regarding the upcoming negotiations:

- Wage data (history, base wages, wage rates)
- Benefits
- Labor costs for the units or department
- Number of employees by rank, job classification, and Fair Labor Standards Act (FLSA) exempt status per unit
- Special pay and benefits (shift differential, overtime, holiday, educational, training, ride up (Pay awarded to an employee of a lower pay grade that fills in for higher grade employee and is compensated at the higher pay rate of the employee for which he/she is filling in.))
- Language assignment pay
- Length of workday, including types and number of shifts, lunch breaks, and paid break periods
- Sick and vacation accumulation rules, including payment of sick and vacation balances
- Termination pay rules

All pay, benefits, and work rules must be compared with other local, regional, and national organizations that the agency competes against when recruiting or retaining personnel. Management needs to establish its position on pay, benefits, and work rules compared with other private and governmental units.

The final step in the process is to develop a plan of action for the negotiations and to establish the goals and objectives to be achieved during the negotiations. This will involve assessing the political and community strength of the labor bargaining units and their relationship with the elected and appointed members of the governmental entity. It will be necessary to understand how strongly the managerial lead negotiating team will be supported by the public and the elected and appointed individuals who supervise the governmental units.

Public sector management does not have market triggers that help private sector managers constrain salary and benefits costs. It is difficult for public organizations to move work offshore, hire nonunion labor, switch to contingent workers, or privatize operations.

Public managers must assess estimated revenue growth to determine how much they can allocate to salary and benefits increases in their labor negotiations for the upcoming years. Managers are under considerable pressure to maintain labor peace and not push labor issues up to the policymakers.

Public sector associations often have strong supporters on the other side of the negotiating table. The elected officials on the negotiating team or the managers hired by the elected officials that are handling the negotiations are interested in keeping the labor units happy. Many elected officials believe that one of the objectives of the organization is to create employment in the community and to pay living wages. Public managers have to deal with the good will generated by some labor units like police and firefighter labor organizations.

Public management personnel are limited when it comes to employing consultants to fill the skill gaps in the labor negotiation teams and supplement the organization's negotiation capabilities. Citizens and elected officials see hiring consultants as wasteful of public expenditures. Labor organizations, on the other hand, have no such restrictions. The Sunshine requirements for public agencies, while appropriate, make it more difficult for public managers to develop and execute their labor negotiation strategies because this must be done in an open and transparent manner.

Applied Techniques for Negotiating with Organized Labor

When negotiating with organized labor, an administrator must take into account many factors in order to reach a successful resolution for the organization. *Administrators should have all of the information available to them before negotiations begin:*

Before formal negotiations begin, the parties should identify the key issues and determine data needs. (Lewicki, Saunders, Minton, and Barry, 2003, p. 116)

If an administrator goes into a negotiation with information about the organization's budget, the workload requirements for the positions, and the comparative salary levels of the positions, then the administrator has a position of strength from which to negotiate:

> Beyond dependence and conflict, the potential for each side to engage in opportunistic interaction—less than fully open motives and methods, self-interested maneuvers—is associated with bargaining situations. When two or more people try to influence each others' decisions through negotiation, they usually guard some information, move to stake out favorable positions, seek to mold perceptions and aspirations, and the like. …
>
> All that is required is that people care about their own interests, some of which conflict with others', and pursue them by seeking to influence decisions, not cooperating fully, turning situations to their advantage, or even resisting outright. (Lax and Sebenius, 1986, pp. 10–11)

In the negotiation process, knowledge is power. With certain types of information, the organization should be able to compile more information than the opposing organized labor faction, which ensures that the administrator has an advantage.

Be calm, cool, and collected when negotiating. Do not negotiate through the media. An administrator needs to stay focused on the topic being discussed and realize that the other party has a different perception than the administrator at the other end of the table:

> Increased interdependence of diverse people virtually guarantees the potential for conflict. The interests and perceptions of people in different products, services, markets, programs, and functions—naturally become identified with their units. And this is even truer for third parties and those in other organizations entirely. In the words of the old saying, "Where you stand depends on where you sit." (Lax and Sebenius, 1986, p. 9)

Administrators should identify which points they are willing to compromise on to achieve an advantage on a different point. Some points of negotiation can obviously impact the organization more than others. For example, the issue of benefits can have far-reaching consequences to an organization in regards to costs:

Which issues are most important to you and which are not particularly important? Knowing the answer to that question will help you answer the next: On which issues should you stand firm and on which issues can you afford to concede? In other words, what issues are you willing to trade away? (Lewicki, Saunders, Minton, and Barry, 2003, p. 53)

If an administrator is in a position where he or she must concede on one issue to gain on another, it is better to concede an item that has little or no value to the administrator.

An administrator should research the labor organization before negotiations begin so that he will not be surprised by an action that the labor organization may attempt. Just as it is advantageous to be well informed on your own organization and what the organization can offer or concede, it is important to be well informed about the needs and goals of the labor organization. Any knowledge gained can provide an advantage to the administrator.

An administrator should be aware of all legal guidelines (i.e., state and federal) before negotiations begin. An administrator should rely on an attorney to avoid inflammatory or inappropriate comments that can ignite a volatile situation. The administrator should set guidelines before the negotiations begin that will allow policies and procedures to be followed during the negotiation process.

For any type of negotiation, have an attorney present. It is important to have legal representation present to ensure that proper negotiation procedures are being followed and that if an agreement is reached between the two parties, the agreement can be legally binding. Also an attorney can potentially prevent an administrator from making a declaration that an organization may not be able to legally implement.

Ensure that proper record minutes are kept of the negotiation meeting. An administrator should always keep documentation on any type of meeting for legal requirements and public records requests.

Work with the labor organization to resolve grievances before the discussion of negotiations is brought up by either party. Using these tactics may very well resolve disputes before they occur and end up having to go to arbitration or negotiation.

Look at different ways that resolutions can be agreed upon before a labor strike occurs. There is usually more than one option available to administrators. Some options might be desirable, others disastrous. It takes creativity to consider what options might work for the organization and the labor union. Setting one's mind to only one or two courses of action will limit what the administrator can accomplish and can risk a strike.

If an administrator is prepared to let organized labor strike, have a plan to fill positions temporarily. An administrator should always have a plan in place in case negotiations fail. The administrator should also be aware that if the plan fails, the failure could give organized labor more leverage in the negotiation process.

Human Resources Liability Management

Recent court decisions tend to hold human resource professionals, supervisors, and other decision makers personally liable for their actions. The courts have ruled that in certain areas of personnel management that pertain to hostile work environment, free speech rights, or property rights to a job position, supervisors can be held personally liable for their actions while employed by a public entity. Employees see personal lawsuits as a means to pressure public organizations to settle cases in the employees' favor, to gain additional compensation for damages, and to punish the manager who took the employment action against them. Various legal statutes have set the precedents that enable employees to successfully sue their supervisors. Section 1983 of the Civil Rights Act of 1871 prohibits "every person" acting under the "color of any statute, ordinance, regulation, custom or usage" of any state from depriving any individual of "any rights" or "immunities" provided by the U.S. Constitution. Discrimination claims involving public officials often allege that the officials violated this law. If a public official has the authority to administer the public employer's policies and make decisions consistent with applicable laws, the official may be personally liable for these decisions if they have a discriminatory effect on an employee. Several other federal and state employment laws that allow personal liability for violations include, but are not limited to, the Fair Labor Standards Act, the Equal Pay Act, the Family and Medical Leave Act, the Consolidated Omnibus Budget Reconciliation Act, the Employee Retirement Income Security Act, the Occupational Safety and Health Act, and the Immigration Reform and Control Act. State courts have also found supervisors and managers liable for tort claims for wrongful acts such as defamation, intentional infliction of emotional distress, invasion of privacy, negligent training, fraud, and misrepresentation.

The worst part of the liability risk is the actual defense process because it may take thousands of dollars and a great deal of time to defend against the accusations, even if the manager is found not guilty of the charges. Listed below are several important steps that all public agencies can take to limit their human resources liability risks:

1. Know the law and know your risks.
2. Keep your policies up to date and follow them.
3. Conduct regular training for all of your decision makers.
4. Don't make quick decisions.
5. Explain your decisions.
6. Document your actions.

Author's Experience

While working as a water safety instructor at a municipality, Dr. Valcik witnessed several incidents of fellow employees engaged in prohibited activities that could have led to injury or death. The swimming pool where Valcik worked used an old chlorine gas pump system. When working with the system, a lifeguard is supposed to wear protective goggles and a respirator. One day, a lifeguard checked the pump system without wearing any protective gear. A chlorine gas leak occurred, but luckily, the lifeguard quickly held her breath to avoid inhaling the deadly gas. However, her unprotected eyes were hit with the gas and her contact lenses melted onto her eyes. The contact lenses had to be surgically removed. The city eventually replaced the old chlorine gas system with a more modern liquid chlorine pump system.

Many weeks later, this same lifeguard, while participating in a lifeguard training exercise, dove into the shallow end of the pool where diving was strictly prohibited. The lifeguard hit the bottom of the pool, broke her jaw, and lost a couple of teeth. The other lifeguards placed the injured lifeguard on a backboard and took her to the hospital.

One morning, a supervisor entered the pool area and witnessed a hazing incident among the lifeguards. As part of the hazing ritual, each lifeguard jumped through a skylight in the ceiling of the facility into the pool below while naked. The ceiling was approximately 30 feet above the water and the depth of the pool was only 8 feet. Catastrophic injuries could have happened. The supervisor reported the incident to the head of the lifeguards, who promptly put a stop to the practice. No other action was taken against the employees.

Other activities increased the city's risk of liability. Although the municipality posted rules, the parks and recreation department did not provide close supervision over its employees. There was evidence of nepotism, failure to post advertisements for open positions, and blacklisting of perceived whistle-blowers in the aquatics program. In the 1980s and 1990s, the swimming instructors were independent contractors who had little power to complain about or prevent activities that were in violation of written municipal policies.

Final Points

Issues involving human resources liability management should never keep an administrator from taking decisive action to deal with all the personnel matters within the public agency. An administrator will need to develop a well-crafted strategy for liability exposure by identifying possible vulnerabilities and to reduce them as much as possible to provide a secure defense for the organization's human resources decision makers and the public organization.

Important Points to Remember

1. There must be a constant investment in maintaining good management–labor relationships.
2. The increasing use of contingent workers could lead to further public sector unionization.

3. Job insecurity is a large and growing issue among the public sector workforce and is impacting relations with management.
4. Management's leverage continues to grow due to economic and demographic factors.
5. There is clear decline in the negotiation strength of employees.
6. There will be a continuing resistance of police and fire uniformed personnel to workplace pay, benefits, and work rule adjustments; but there will be a continuing effort to control these costs due to the need to restrain the growth of public sector expenditures.
7. Costs, pressures, resistance to increasing taxes, and technological advancements will continue to exert downsizing pressures on the public workforce.
8. The trend to contain or reduce the pay and benefits of public employees will continue, will have a detrimental effect on morale, and will increase the pressure on public sector management to continue to be productive while economizing.
9. The current decline in public employee privacy rights will continue into the foreseeable future.
10. There will be an upswing in union organizing at all public sector levels as cost containment pressures increase.

CASE STUDY 11.1
Negotiations Are Never Really Done until the City Council Says They Are Done!

SITUATION FOR CASE STUDY 11.1

The city manager negotiated an informal labor agreement with the police and firefighter associations, primarily regarding pay issues. In this city, the police and firefighter associations do not have collective bargaining rights through an election process, and there is no meet-and-confer legislation in the state to permit formal labor negotiations. However, it had become standard practice for the city manager and the police and firefighter associations to have informal discussions and to develop an informal agreement on pay, benefits, and working condition issues.

Recently, the city has experienced difficulty in recruiting entry-level police officers but had not experienced a similar problem with entry-level firefighters. The city council learned, through a detailed salary survey for all uniformed positions, that the city manager had not recommended nor funded entry-level police pay that was competitive with local suburban communities. The city maintained a policy of pay parity between the uniformed police and firefighter positions and offered competitive pension, health benefits, leave pay, and special pay for all other police and firefighter classifications. In fact, the defined benefit pension plan for police and firefighters was superior to all the suburban competitors. The pay differential among the civilian employees was less pronounced than with the uniform classifications when compared with suburban classifications. Given these findings, the city council demanded that the city manager reopen salary negotiations with the police and firefighter associations. In addition, the city council privately scolded the city manager for offering generous pay raises for the civilian employees but not using available city revenues, like the telecommunications revenues, to fund a larger pay increase for police and fire officers.

1. How could the city manager convince the city council to find another option to deal with the pay disparities besides reopening negotiations?
2. Should the city manager actively oppose the city council's decision to reopen the police and firefighter labor negotiations?
3. Was the city manager wrong to give large pay increases to the civilian employees? Should he have allocated the telecommunication revenues to fund the police and firefighter pay raises?

WHAT ACTUALLY HAPPENED IN CASE STUDY 11.1

After many labor negotiating sessions with both uniform associations, both sides agreed to a 12% pay raise for all uniform pay grades, a 1% shift pay increase for police officers on third watch, and a 10% pay raise for all civilian employee pay grades. This agreement was incorporated into the city manager's budget. However, during the city council's budget review process, the major police association and the major firefighter organization approached the city council about increasing the pay for police and firefighters in all grades to 15% and to increase the shift differential pay increase from 1% to 2% for second and third watches in the police department. The associations proposed to the city council to pay for the additional pay adjustments by increasing the police department squad car replacement standard from 75,000 miles to 100,000 miles. The budget office estimated that the reconfiguration of the police squad replacement would only fund a 1% salary increase for all uniform pay grades and the 2% shift differential pay for second and third watches. The city council voted to increase the pay for all police and firefighter pay grades by 1% to 13% and the shift differential pay for second and third watches in the police department. The city council kept the pay increase for all civilian employees at 10% as was recommended by the city manager.

During a private meeting with the city manager, the mayor had made it clear that he felt the original negotiated pay adjustments were too generous. The city manager informed the mayor that the city council did not share the mayor's point of view. The mayor informed the city manager that he would convince the city council to only approve an 8% pay raise for the police, fire, and civilian employees. The mayor's strategy would be to take the savings from the reduced pay rates to lower the tax rate by 2 cents. However, the mayor was unable to get even one city council member to agree to his 8% pay raise idea.

KEY ISSUES RAISED IN CASE STUDY 11.1

The city council was not happy that the city manager did not negotiate larger pay adjustments to the police and firefighter associations. This forced the council to deal with the issue. Managers are hired to deal with daily issues so that their superiors do not have to. The city manager then placed his trust in the mayor's ability to change the city council's mind. A manager cannot give someone else their job responsibilities. The other person will either not do the job or will have their own agenda for getting involved that may or may not benefit the manager.

WHAT COULD HAVE HAPPENED IN CASE STUDY 11.1

The city manager should not have left the management of the city council on the labor deal in the hands of the mayor. The mayor is a politician, and a politician's support is only as good as the public support he or she receives. The city manager should have been more completely engaged in the labor negotiations until the budget process was completely done. As a postscript to these negotiations, the police association criticized the city manager in the media for the deplorable condition of the police squad car fleet and the aging and dangerous condition of the fleet as a result of the deferral of the police squad car replacement target from 75,000 miles to 100,000 miles. The city manager reminded everyone that it was the police department's idea to extend the life cycle of the police squad cars to 100,000 miles from 75,000 miles to pay for their increased salaries. In retrospect, the city manager said that he should have publicly announced his opposition to the budget strategy to fund the additional pay by deferring the replacement schedule for police squad cars.

CASE STUDY 11.2
Employee Accident

SITUATION FOR CASE STUDY 11.2

You manage a shipping and receiving department for Valcik College, a selective liberal arts institution with a reputation for quality. Valcik College has an enrollment of 4,500 students and is situated in the middle of a large downtown urban area. You have been managing the shipping and receiving department for more than 30 years and you plan to retire within 5 years. The vice president for business services, who is also your immediate supervisor, has been working at Valcik College for more than 2 years now. In that brief time, the vice president has earned a reputation for cultivating a private industry mindset, focusing on costs, and treating employees as (in his words) "expendable and replaceable." This has not endeared the vice president to the departments that report directly to him.

One of your longtime employees, Derrick, has been trained and certified to use heavy equipment. Derrick is a very good employee, and you have no problems with his work ethic or skill levels. You tell Derrick to load a series of pallets on a flatbed truck that is located behind the shipping and receiving department. The vice president happens to be visiting your facility when Derrick accidentally runs into the vice president's expensive BMW with a forklift, which causes massive damage.

The vice president is very upset and wants to know what you are going to do about your employee who damaged his brand new BMW. "If it were me I would fire him on the spot!" stated the vice president. You tell the vice president that you will investigate the issue and let him know what action is to be taken. The vice president suggests to you that it would be easy enough to find a younger manager for the shipping and receiving department. You know it would be wrong to terminate Derrick, but you are fearful that you will get fired instead if you disobey the vice president's wishes. After all, this vice president appears to be all-powerful, and the human resources department has yet to challenge him on any other issues that violated Valcik College policies.

1. What are the human resource issues involved?
2. What human resource actions should be taken in regard to Derrick?
3. How should the shipping and receiving manager deal with the pressure from the vice president to terminate Derrick from his position?

WHAT ACTUALLY HAPPENED IN CASE STUDY 11.2

Derrick was terminated from his position from the organization after the manager was directed to do so by the vice president. The manager knew that the organization's human resources department did not support termination for a first-time mistake. The manager also knew that there was a progression of discipline that managers were supposed to follow prior to any termination.

The manager did not have Derrick tested after the accident for drugs or alcohol, a requirement outlined in the policies and procedures established by the human resources department. Nothing happened to the vice president for violating the human resource policies, and the manager who terminated Derrick was allowed to keep his position until he could take retirement. Morale for the shipping and receiving department suffered because of Derrick's termination. The employees felt they were no longer as secure in their own positions. Over the next few years, the turnover rate in the shipping and receiving department increased, costing Valcik College more money in recruiting and training.

KEY HUMAN RESOURCES ISSUES RAISED IN CASE STUDY 11.2

The manager of the department was told by the vice president to terminate Derrick from his position or else the manager would face termination himself. Since the manager of the shipping and receiving department did not want to be terminated so close to retirement, he felt he had no other option but to comply with the vice president's orders. Derrick's termination created a morale problem inside the department.

Derrick had no problems on his employment record before the accident, and there was no progression of discipline to justify his termination. As a result, the college has just exposed itself to a lawsuit for terminating an employee without justification. This can result in a significant financial judgment against the organization. In addition, the organization had no proof that drugs or alcohol were involved in the accident since they did not have the employee tested after the accident occurred. From an organizational liability standpoint, the vice president did not follow policy and procedures set by their human resources department, which would compromise their justification for terminating the employee.

WHAT COULD HAVE HAPPENED IN CASE STUDY 11.2

The manager could have had Derrick tested for drugs and alcohol after the accident according to the organization's human resource policies. In addition, Derrick could have been disciplined instead of terminated according to the organization's own human resource guidelines. After the termination occurred, the vice president could have been sanctioned for not following policies and procedures, which could have resulted in a financial loss for the organization.

CASE STUDY 11.3
Wrong Fuel, No Run

SITUATION FOR CASE STUDY 11.3

You are the sheriff of Benavides County, Texas, and have been elected to four terms consecutively by the residents. You want to make sure that you are sheriff for a fifth consecutive term. To accomplish this, you need to make sure that costs are controlled for your department. The sheriff's department has an exceptional reputation for upholding the law and having fast response times in the large rural areas of the county. The sheriff's department maintains a large jail that services the county and nearby cities and towns that do not have the resources to have their own detention center. Your department is responsible for a wide variety of law enforcement programs that requires maintaining specialized units like DARE, the antipollution unit, the mental health unit, and so on. All of these functional areas require sworn law enforcement officers and support personnel, like secretaries and janitors, to function. You have offset some of these costs by applying for and receiving state and federal grant money for these programs. Your department is also responsible for patrolling several small towns that do not have the resources to maintain a police force. Although the tax base to support your department is strong compared with other counties in the state, your resources are still valuable and you do not need to have any of your resources wasted unnecessarily. The fiscally conservative people of Benavides County hold elected officials to a very high standard in terms of controlling costs and making the most use of their tax dollars.

The patrol vehicles are valuable resources that must stay in a high readiness status at all times for patrolling and quick emergency response. To ensure that your vehicles remain in a high state of readiness, you have employed several mechanics for your motor pool staff. These mechanics are highly trained and certified to work on your vehicles and are very expensive to employ. However, you can justify the costs if in the long run your well-maintained vehicles prevent death or injury to the citizens of Benavides County and their deputies.

One of your most trusted and experienced deputies, Scott, accidentally pumped diesel fuel into his patrol car instead of gasoline. The deputy drove toward the motor pool exit, when he suddenly noticed the engine knocking. The car stalled, blocking the exit. No other sheriff's department vehicles could drive around the stalled patrol car. The officer was extremely embarrassed when he realized his mistake. Several motor pool employees saw the deputy make the mistake and did not say anything. The employees were seen laughing when the officer began to drive out of the motor pool area. This incident has just cost your department over $2,000 in repairs to your patrol car and has taken one vehicle out of your patrol. You are not laughing.

1. What should the sheriff do to the motor pool employees who witnessed the event?
2. What are the issues involved?
3. Are there any preventive programs that can be initiated to reduce accidents?

WHAT ACTUALLY HAPPENED IN CASE STUDY 11.3

The sheriff is an elected official with the responsibility to ensure that county assets under the department's auspices are well maintained and used for the appropriate purposes. When county equipment becomes damaged and employees could have prevented that damage from occurring, the sheriff must take the appropriate disciplinary action. The sheriff's deputy felt ridiculous, but it was an honest mistake. However, the motor pool employees who could have stopped the deputy from putting the wrong fuel into the vehicle are a different matter entirely. The stalled vehicle created a dangerous situation because the motor pool was blocked, preventing first responders from being dispatched to emergency calls. The sheriff filed written reprimands on the maintenance workers for their misconduct because they could have prevented damage to a county vehicle.

KEY HUMAN RESOURCE ISSUES RAISED IN CASE STUDY 11.3

Not only did the employees cause damage to a government-owned vehicle by not preventing the wrong fuel being used, but they also put the officer's life in danger by depriving the officer of a well-functioning vehicle. This presents a liability issue stemming from property damage and potential injury or death to the officer or others. Furthermore, the taxpayers are now out $2,000 for a repair that was completely preventable.

WHAT COULD HAVE HAPPENED IN CASE STUDY 11.3

Better training may or may not have prevented the officer from using the wrong fuel pump, but a sign posted to remind people to verify that the right type of fuel is being used could be a good preventive measure. In addition, the employees who service vehicles could be encouraged to prevent damage and accidents from occurring with an incentive bonus plan. Money saved from averting damage or injury can offset the costs of a bonus program.

CASE STUDY 11.4
After-Work Issues

SITUATION FOR CASE STUDY 11.4

You have been an assistant director for a large state agency for five years. Before becoming an assistant director you worked for the state agency in an entry-level position and were promoted after demonstrating extremely good interpersonal skills. One of the agency's many responsibilities is to oversee state, county, and local elections to ensure that the elections are run in accordance with federal and state laws.

Your department has been designated to make random inspections on various polling locations around the state. You are understaffed and underfunded for the task. You are in the middle of a campaign season, and the workload for your 10 employees is quite heavy because the job really requires at least 40 inspectors to ensure a thorough job. The employees who work in your department must make frequent trips to various locations to ensure that voting equipment is working and compliant with the election laws.

You have learned that two of your employees, Dawn and Linda, have been seen drinking heavily after work. Both of them are responsible and do not drive while intoxicated. You are getting worried, however, because they both stay out late at night and barely make it to work on time the next morning. Otherwise, both employees are model employees and accomplish their work efficiently and efficiently. Lately, Linda and Dawn have been calling in sick more than usual, particularly when compared with other employees.

Another employee, Andrea, is very conservative and is active in the Republican Party. However, Andrea does not discuss her political viewpoints with coworkers or engage in political activities during work hours. After work hours, Andrea freely expresses her political opinions with others, including her coworkers. Sometimes those opinions offend other people. You have heard several employees complain about all three employees regarding incidents that occurred after business hours and away from the workplace.

1. What are the human resource issues?
2. Can or should the assistant director intervene with the employees?
3. Can the assistant director take issue with Linda and Dawn taking frequent sick leaves?

WHAT ACTUALLY HAPPENED IN CASE STUDY 11.4

The supervisors said nothing to the three employees because their actions were not affecting their work and did not occur during work hours. There is very little that can be done to public employees if their actions do not occur at work, do not violate organizational policies, and do not involve organizational assets. Regarding sick leave, it is a common policy at many public organizations to required a doctor's note if employees miss a certain number of consecutive days. Since Dawn and Linda were calling in sick for only one day at a time, they did not need a doctor's note. Andrea's actions could be actionable only if she attempted to lobby politicians using her affiliation as the employee of a public organization, used work assets for campaigning, or campaigned during work hours.

KEY ISSUES RAISED IN CASE STUDY 11.4

Where is the line drawn between work and personal business? This is a difficult decision for administrators in all organizations. Administrators should ask themselves the following question: "Are the after-hours activities affecting job performance?" If the answer is yes and the behavior is against human resources policy, then the administrator can intervene. If the activities are off site and are not affecting their work performance, then the administrator should be watchful but should not intervene unless the situation deteriorates. In Dawn and Linda's case, the main issue was that they were calling in sick quite frequently, which indicates that their heavy drinking may eventually lead to a work performance issue. However, if the employees have earned sick leave and vacation time, they are entitled to take that time according to organizational guidelines.

WHAT COULD HAVE HAPPENED IN CASE STUDY 11.4

Administrators should be careful about enforcing workplace policies on employees' personal time. Not only are many of those policies unenforceable outside the workplace, but they can also lead to legal action if an employee is terminated for a noncriminal action that occurred when they were not at work.

Since these incidents occurred on the employees' personal time and did not impact their work or violate any policies, the administrator correctly refrained from intervening. The administrator should closely observe all three employees to ensure that they continue to follow workplace policies and that their actions do not negatively impact the workplace. If Linda and Dawn call in sick on a more regular basis, the assistant director should contact the human resources department for guidance on the options for contending with such a situation.

Suggested Readings for Chapter 11

Belmon, Dale, Gunderson, Morley, and Hyatt, Douglas, 1996. *Public sector employment in a time of transition*. ISBN: 0-913447-67-6. Madison, Wisconsin: Industrial Relations Research Association.

Carrell, Michael, and Heavrin, Christina, 2009. *Labor relations and collective bargaining: Cases, practice, and law*. Eighth edition. ISBN: 0136084354. New York: Prentice Hall.

Coleman, A.,1990. *Managing labor relations in the public sector*. ISBN: 9781555422455. San Francisco: Jossey-Bass.

Kearney, Richard, 2001. *Labor relations in the public sector*. Fourth edition. ISBN: 0-8247-0420-7. New York: Marcel Dekker.

Chapter 12

Morale and Motivation in the Workplace and Managing Personnel through Transitions

Morale and Motivation in the Workplace

Good employee morale and motivation in the workplace is very important to the well-being of any organization. The motivation factor in public and non-profit organizations has an even bigger impact than normal because salaries are, on the whole, lower than their private industry counterparts and the employees of public and nonprofit organizations rarely shift missions or organizational purpose. It is therefore important to keep morale and motivation high to ensure that a high-quality output continues even when times are difficult for an organization. Having good morale and motivation in the workplace also helps to ensure that retention is high, which enables public, nonprofit, and medical organizations to improve over time. With medical organizations, it is important to keep motivation and morale high to maintain quality patient care because employees often work with extremely difficult circumstances on a regular basis, which in turn can erode motivation and morale.

Burnout

Burnout can occur in any organization, private or public. Burnout can occur for a number of reasons, which can be related to either the job or personal issues away from work. Burnout due to the job can be a result of some of the following causes:

- Being saturated with work responsibilities
- Working long hours
- Being required to work a position with little or no training
- Working below the employee's skill level
- Working with difficult or demanding administrators or coworkers
- Contending with life-and-death situations on a daily basis (medical, first responder)
- Being asked to work above the employee's level of proficiency

Administrators should be very watchful of their employees' performance on the job. Administrators have the capability to intervene if an employee's work performance begins to suffer due to burnout. Actions that can be taken by an administrator include the following:

- Redistribute the employee's work to other employees who are not as overburdened
- Send an employee to training if the current job skill set is an obstacle
- Transfer an employee to another department if mental stress is apparent
- Make sure that employees take their vacation time when needed instead of feeling indispensable at the job site
- Most importantly, provide positive and reassuring support with frequent communication

If an administrator takes no action to prevent burnout, then the employees' work will deteriorate or they will begin to look for another position elsewhere. A deterioration of work quality will disrupt the organization and force the administrator to redistribute the work to other employees anyway, which can lead to bigger morale issues. If the employee quits, the administrator is forced to begin the costly and time-consuming recruiting, hiring, and training cycle with the risk that a new employee might not perform as well as the previous employee.

Doing More with Less

Doing more with less essentially means the organization will not receive additional resources but will be expected to take on additional responsibilities. If necessary, this approach may work in the short term, but it is not healthy for the organization in the long term. After a certain point, employees will begin to wear down and eventually seek employment elsewhere. Additionally, some of the newly added responsibilities may require training or skill sets that the organization simply lacks, which can cause morale and motivation problems for the organization's employees. Administrators at some point will be forced to find additional resources or will be forced to drop some responsibilities or face work quality deterioration.

Backfill Positions

Backfill positions are intended to be filled by temporary employees while permanent employees are assigned to a short-term organizational project. Although a backfill position may sound like a reasonable approach to a temporary situation, it can cause more work for existing employees because it takes time to train backfill position employees. Some skills are so specialized that certain responsibilities cannot be transferred to the temporary employees. This means that employees who were reassigned to the new project will continue to fulfill old responsibilities on top of the new responsibilities. Backfill positions, however, can prove to be useful if utilized correctly. For example, temporary workers who have limited skill sets can be assigned to simple, time-consuming tasks that will free existing employees to focus on the more advanced tasks. Backfill positions are also useful in evaluating temporary employees who may be good candidates for permanent positions if those positions become available at a later date.

Leadership Change

For those organizations that have had problems with leadership, a change of leadership may give the organization a boost in both morale and motivation. Initially, employees are much more likely to comply with the new administrator's vision and operational changes without too much resistance. If the new administrator proves to be capable and understands the impact of good leadership on an organization, then the employees will begin to support the new administrator and his or her plans to implement changes in the organization. However, a new administrator who replaces an administrator that was popular with employees and had good leadership abilities will find the employees much less likely to support the vision of change for the organization. When replacing an effective administrator, one should first take stock of the business processes and personnel that exist within the organization. If an administrator does intend to make changes in personnel or procedures, these changes should be made very slowly to ensure that the administrator has stakeholders' support in any changes. Bad decisions can undermine the administrator's credibility among the stakeholders in the organization, especially if the administrator acted without stakeholder support. An administrator could face plummeting morale and motivation if his or her credibility is called into question.

Layoffs and Terminations

Layoffs and terminations are never good for morale or motivation because the employees who are left are usually fearful for their positions and in some cases feel guilty that their friends, coworkers, or supervisors have been let go while they still have a job. Layoffs and terminations tend to be counterproductive to quality and quantity of work output by those employees remaining. Organizations might view a layoff as an opportunity to get "deadwood" (employees who are seen as low performers or have personnel issues) out of an organization. However, layoffs can have the opposite effect, particularly if an organization retains employees due to political considerations. When layoffs occur, an organization must have unbiased procedures for identifying personnel who are to be separated from the organization. An organization should also be very supportive of employees who have not been laid off in an effort to retain their talent. If employees feel that their positions are in jeopardy, they will begin to seek employment elsewhere. Ultimately, if care is not taken in a layoff situation, bad morale and declining motivation can potentially damage the organization.

Scandals

A scandal can damage an organization's reputation as well as morale. For example, if an organization appears to external constituents to have elements of corruption, unethical practices, or discriminatory procedures integrated into its structure, then the employees, whether they are involved with those issues or not, will be associated with the bad character of the organization. An example of this would be the Abu Ghraib Iraqi prisoner scandal in the U.S. Army in 2005 (Hettena, 2005). While the incident involved only a few military personnel, the entire military organization in the Middle East was tainted by the scandal.

The morale and motivation of such an organization will diminish, and exemplary employees will begin to seek employment elsewhere. An administrator who inherits such a problem should take drastic steps to identify the reasons the organization's reputation is being damaged and to ensure that those types of behaviors are not tolerated again. These steps may include everything from reprimands to termination for employees who are violating organizational policy. Once an administrator officially assumes control, an audit should be conducted on operational procedures, employee capabilities, and fiscal operations of the department. An audit will document current procedures and practices and discover preexisting problems that can hurt the organization in the future.

Transitions

Transitions are natural in the evolution of an organization. Organizations that do not experience transitions become static and eventually cease to exist. Transitions can occur quickly or very slowly over a long period of time. Often in public or nonprofit organizations, transitions can result when an organization is given a new mission or function. During transitions it is especially important to keep motivation and morale high to ensure a successful transition.

Rarely do public organizations cease to exist because their missions are almost always unfulfilled and never ending. However, there are examples of public organizations ceasing to exist, as in the case of mergers into another public organization or abolishment through political mechanisms (e.g., State of Texas Legislature—the Sunset Advisory Committee) (State of Texasi 2011). In some cases, one public organization can be absorbed by another due to public mandate, as in the case of Pleasant Grove, Texas, being annexed by City of Dallas (Maxwell, 2010). If the mission of a public organization is fulfilled, the result can be the disbanding of the organization. In higher education institutions, this most commonly occurs when research centers are disbanded because grant funds are exhausted or the research project has come to an end.

An excellent example of an organization that experienced a major transition due to mission change and absorption is Los Alamos National Laboratory, which has transitioned on many occasions since the laboratory's inception in 1941. After World War II, Los Alamos had technically fulfilled its mission by developing the atomic bomb that brought an end to the war (Rhodes, 1986). However, there was a new foe, the Soviet Union, which resulted in the laboratory's involvement in the development of the hydrogen bomb (Rhodes, 1995). Los Alamos was moved from the auspices of the military to the Department of Energy, which retained the University of California system as an operator of the laboratory. When security breaches occurred in the first few years of the 21st century, the contract for operating the laboratory was opened for bid and the University of California partnered with Bechtel Corporation to win the bid against the University of Texas system and its private industry partner (Broad, 2005). The new contract reorganized the laboratory's administrative structure and employee benefits (Broad, 2005).

The military itself has transitioned and downsized several times since the end of the Cold War primarily through base closures, unit disbandment, and unit reorganizations. An example is the Strategic Air Command (SAC), which came into existence in 1946 and was combined in 1992 at the end of the Cold War into the military organization USSTRATCOM (U.S. Strategic Command), which controlled nuclear weapons for the U.S. military (Strategic Air Command, 2010; SAC Elite Guard, 2010). Once a prime deterrent to the Soviet Union, SAC's main mission ceased to exist after the Soviet Union collapsed. Those assets in SAC were reallocated and reorganized into an umbrella organization that oversaw nuclear weapons for the U.S. Air Force as well as the U.S. Navy (SAC Elite Guard, 2010).

What to Do during a Transition

If the administrators know that a transition is about to occur, they should prepare their employees to make adjustments that will enable them to complete work that is essential to the operation of the organization. As William Bridges states:

> Before you can begin something new, you have to end what used to be. Before you can learn a new way of doing things, you have to unlearn the old way. Before you can become a different kind of person, you must let go of your old identity. So beginnings depend on endings. The problem is, people don't like endings. (2003, p. 23)

Proper mental preparation of employees is very important to any successful transition. If an organization's employees understand ahead of time that a transition is going to occur and that they must do business processes differently than in the past, the employees will have time to adjust mentally. If an administrator gives no notification prior to implementation of a transition, the employees will be shocked, confused, and overworked as they try to learn the business processes and will be tempted to retain as many of the old practices as possible during the transition.

Besides providing employees with training, having the proper documentation on hand is critical to the success of a new business process. For example, if a new information system is being implemented, the data contained in the old system will still be required for day-to-day job functions, but the way in which the data are entered, extracted, shared, and utilized will change. Even if the quality of the data provided by the new system is superior to the old system, employees might be resistant to using the new system effectively because they were accustomed to the steps they took with the previous system to obtain and use the data. To prevent employees from using the old processes for data input and retrieval on the new system, thus introducing errors and inefficiencies, the organization must provide clear, easy-to-understand instructions on how to use the new system and how others within the organization are dependent upon proper procedures to do their jobs. For example, the employees who input data into the system need to understand how these data will be used downstream for reporting and analysis, thus motivating them to follow the new procedures.

Transition and Administration Communication

Communication is the key to winning employee support for a successful transition and reducing resistance, overt or otherwise. An administrator will need to understand that employees fear change. Will I have a job when the implementation begins? What will I be doing during the implementation? I really love my job now; how will this transition impact what my role is in the organization? Do I have the skills needed for the upcoming implementation, or am I too old to learn new skills? What will happen if I cannot master the new skill set required?

The administrator should realize that employees have concerns about how transitions will impact not only their role in the organization but also their performance.

A mistake that an administrator can make during an implementation process is to assume either that he knows everything that is required to make the transition successful or that outside consultants can be hired to make the transition successful. An administrator should be willing to listen to stakeholders and employees because many times the administrator has a global view on how an implemented plan should work but lacks the technical expertise to know what specific steps are required to achieve implementation and avoid obstacles.

Forcing a business change upon several organizations at once can have disastrous consequences because organizational cultures have different perspectives and needs that have to be accounted for with any implementation plan. While a written document may define and outline an implementation plan, an administrator must be prepared to honor the conditions in the document and work closely with employees to ensure that the implementation proceeds smoothly. Failure to do so will jeopardize the success of the transition and cause the stakeholders to have doubts about the administrator's leadership abilities. They may even find ways to work around the project plan to accomplish operational objectives. Thus the original implementation plan that is set forth by the administrator fails in intent.

Consultants

Consultants present a very different challenge. Often administrators will bring consultants into projects due to their perceived expertise in a particular area. In some cases administrators are justified in hiring consultants if the organization lacks the skill sets necessary to implement a particular segment of a transition. However, consultants may not be familiar with the organizational culture or the details of an organization's operational requirements, which can create tension between the administrators and the stakeholders or employees and lead to frustration and disillusionment with the overall objective of the administrator. Administrators should always keep in mind that the consultants' main objective is to make money. The consultants will not have to live long term with any changes or procedures that they implement. If items that were supposed to be implemented do not go as planned, the consultant always has the option of walking away from the contract leaving the organization to "fix" the initial implementation process.

Cooperating with Other Organizations during Transitions

Often, during massive economization efforts at the federal, state, or local level, several organizations are targeted at once to undergo a transition from one process to another to save money, to provide some type of enhanced capability, or to increase an agency's overall control over other organizations. If an administrator in charge of an overall implementation plan has failed to take into account different organizational cultures (as well as different organizational skill levels), the ability to transition to an overall implementation plan may be difficult or impossible to achieve. Additionally, an effort that initially succeeds in one or more areas of implementation may ultimately fail if the organizations see that there is no benefit to following an implementation plan or if the overseeing organization is unable to force an organization to follow the implementation plan. Over time, the organizations that are loosely coupled will begin to drift from the "ideal" coalition to "reality," in which the different organizations once again begin to operate independently. To succeed, the overseeing administrator must be able to provide a workable implementation plan that will allow a successful transition for the organization to the new business process without losing capability. If capability is diminished by the new process or operational requirements are not met by the new business process, organizational drift will begin, which will deviate from the "ideal" standard that the overseeing organization had in the beginning of the implementation plan.

During the cooperation stage, different organizations will initially cooperate and collaborate to attain general operational standards for a business process. However, if cooperation and collaboration break down, the different organizations will employ several tactics to halt the transition effort. If an established organization does not wish to change its business processes to align with the other organizations' processes, it can halt the transition effort by delaying the decision-making process as long as possible to wear down the other organizations. While this can work successfully for a short time, this strategy can also backfire if the other organizations are not willing to concede to the resistant organization. This forces the established organization to either split off from the coalition or begin to concede points in order to attain standards. A strategy for smaller or less-skilled organizations that do not want to change is to pit the other organizations against each other. Conflict among organizations can result in cancellation of the transition effort or can backfire and cause the coalition to organize against the holdout. Ultimately, any effort to stop, delay, or sabotage transition efforts will only create friction among the groups involved. When collaboration projects are undertaken, it is in the best interest of all stakeholders to be willing to change and listen for the benefit of all.

Author's Experience

Dr. Valcik was working at Nortel Networks when one of his managers was transferred from her position to a different position in the country. The staff was never informed why this occurred and what it meant for the department. Within hours of the announcement, headhunters had contacted everyone who worked for that manager and began to recruit them. Within a couple of days, the department had a new manager, but the uneasiness and tension lasted for months while the new manager assessed what was going on in the department and worked to take the department in a new direction. Soon after Valcik left the department to work for the University of Texas at Dallas, the department was absorbed by a larger department, and his former coworkers left the company.

Final Notes

Morale, motivation, and transition are intertwined in public, nonprofit, and medical organizations. Without good morale and high motivation, a transition has very little hope of success. The following are a few points that are worth remembering:

- Treat employees as you want to be treated yourself.
- Be aware of your employees' mental well-being not only during times of organizational change but also during normal operating levels for the organization.
- Keep events in perspective. For some organizations, making deadlines is critical and a matter of life and death (i.e., hospitals). However, most public and nonprofit organizations do not (and should not) have that type of pressure placed upon employees to perform.
- An administrator with a good staff that operates with good morale and high motivation is invaluable to an organization. Do not take those employees for granted. During times of crisis, these employees will perform at an optimum level for the organization.
- Realize that most employees care about their positions and their organizations and have a good work ethic. Treat them with respect.

As far as transitions are concerned, an interesting question posed is, "What would organizations that were primarily focused on cancer research do if cancer was cured?" Organizations such as the University of Texas MD Anderson Cancer Center would either need to find a new mission or essentially be forced to disband. An administrator should always have a transition plan in the event that a mission changes, the administrator resigns from the post, or the organization needs to adapt to an ever-changing environment. If there is no plan in place, a transition has a good chance of failing. A successful transition plan, coupled with continuous management of morale and motivation, will enable an organization to successfully transition to a new phase in its existence and provide a model for other organizations to follow.

Important Points to Remember

1. It is crucial to have good morale in the organization in order to have a stable, productive workforce.
2. An administrator should never ask an employee to do a mundane task that he either has not done in the past or would not be willing to do himself. Lead by example.
3. An administrator should always keep in close contact with employees. If an administrator appears to be distant or uncaring, employee morale could decline.

4. Transitions often cause uneasiness among employees in the organization. It is important to gain support from employees for any major transition that may occur in information systems and/or business processes. Without this support, resistance to change from employees will be more likely.

5. Do not expect consultants to solve organizational problems or implement transitions successfully. Consultants can help, but a successful transition will be dependent on the organization's personnel.

6. Administrators should maintain open communication with their employees and should be willing to listen to their employees as well as distribute information.

7. Administrators should always stay focused on their organization's mission and purpose and avoid taking on too many responsibilities, which can drag down the organization or burn out employees.

8. Transitions in the organization should be well planned before they are implemented. If the plans are not well laid out or communicated to employees, many potential problems can arise.

9. Administrators should consider all aspects of a transition when in the planning stages. There will need to be many benefits, and there may be disadvantages as well, to any transition or transformation that is being planned.

10. It is important to remember that employees can sense their administrator's attitude and behavior, so it is important to stay motivated and upbeat as much as possible.

CASE STUDY 12.1
Forced into a Supervisory Position

SITUATION FOR CASE STUDY 12.1

You are a director for a large federal research center that employs around 500 people and is charged with developing technology critical for national defense. You are an electrical engineer by profession and do not want to be a director since you are very goal oriented at the project level. Due to circumstances, you are now told that you must lead a research center that previously lacked any direction or leadership. Morale is bad and many of your top engineers are fighting over petty items (e.g., tables, supplies). Most of the personnel under your auspices hold doctorate degrees, manage their own research laboratories and offices, and are used to running their research in the manner that they see fit.

You understand that gaining control over the situation will be a huge obstacle to resolve before getting the defense systems into production. In addition, you have several high-ranking military individuals that you must interface with, and there is a possibility that you will now be deployed as a civilian in a war zone to oversee testing of advanced systems that your team is responsible for producing. Additionally, you have the to safe guard and secure research and information that is produced from your research center since the research, if obtained by foreign operatives, could compromise national security. There is no money in the budget for raises, and the research projects are critical for the nation's defense.

1. How will you raise morale in your department?
2. What skills should you develop to manage your personnel effectively?
3. How will you retain your current employees?
4. How will you deal with high-ranking officials in the military?

Due to the recent conflicts, your staff and research center is finally allocated some additional funds for research and development. Fortunately, you were able to send another person in your place to the combat zone, which allowed you to stay and supervise your organization more effectively. When the conflict ends, you discover that you are a full-time manager who no longer conducts any research of your own. Instead of projects, you are managing people.

1. How do you contend with an unauthorized and unknown person attempting to gain confidential information?
2. What policies and procedures should you have in place to safeguard your organization's information?
3. What policies and procedures should you have in place to protect your employees from being abducted if they are traveling abroad?

WHAT ACTUALLY HAPPENED IN CASE STUDY 12.1

While the director managed to get results from his professional staff, it was not without stressful situations. The project that the director was responsible for was actually tested and deployed in Desert Storm. Details pertaining to how the director was able to resolve the personnel issues are, by necessity, lacking, but the director was able to overcome the issues of bad morale and bickering to produce a successful product for the military.

After the morale of the department improved, the director was sent by the organization to Europe. As an interesting side note, while the director was having lunch outside at a café with three of his colleagues, they were approached by an unknown person. The unknown person knew all the names of the employees and knew what organization they worked for in the United States. The unknown person was wearing a Soviet Union submariner's watch. This incident occurred after the breakup of the Soviet Union and the person appeared to be Russian. The director and his colleagues said nothing to the person, and he eventually left the café after gaining no information. When the director finally retired, the research center asked him to stay on for a little longer past retirement to help with the transition to a new director.

KEY ISSUES RAISED IN CASE STUDY 12.1

A major issue raised in this case study is having someone put into a management and leadership position who has not been adequately trained as a supervisor. While the administrator in this case study was able to overcome a lack of training on personnel management and get the project team under control, having training to perform supervisory tasks over large groups of people would have been helpful. The transition process from having no management to having a person that upper administrators felt could handle such a role would have been difficult and stressful to all of the organization's employees. Without any type of management supervision, chaos could have ensued, which would have been counterproductive to the organization. The supervisor's primary challenge was organizational fragmentation and personnel not working well as a team. The other issue in the case study contends with sending a civilian supervisor into a potentially dangerous situation.

WHAT COULD HAVE HAPPENED IN CASE STUDY 12.1

The organization could have provided the supervisor with more support and training when they forced him to become a manager. The supervisor could have documented unprofessional behavior and counseled the employees on how to act professionally in the workplace. The supervisor did a good job getting the research center's morale and productivity improved.

CASE STUDY 12.2
State Property

SITUATION FOR CASE STUDY 12.2

As a chief financial officer (CFO) of a state agency that employs more than 2,000 people, you are responsible for accounting programs that report data to the director of your agency. Your organization is located in a large metropolitan city and has difficulty recruiting, hiring, and retaining talented individuals who have a high degree of technical skills because the surrounding businesses in the community can afford to pay highly skilled employees much more than your organization can. Furthermore, the work environment is more stressful because the agency has to report data to state and federal oversight agencies, which are unforgiving of mistakes. Consequently, you attempt to keep the stress to a minimum by establishing stable work hours and consistent policies and procedures.

Your agency still uses a mainframe that has space allotted for your department's programs. However, there is no restriction currently that prevents an employee in your department from altering another person's program that they may be using for their reports. There is also no departmental policy on who can alter programs, but there is an agency disclaimer that states that no employee will damage or disclose information or programming on the agency's computer systems.

An employee, Emma, has developed a set of programs that your department relies on heavily for financial planning and reporting. These programs have taken months to develop and are a huge investment of labor hours for your department. Another employee, Ben, needs to modify the programs for his own purposes. Rather than copy the program to his library, Ben violates policy and modifies the original programs without permission from Emma. Emma reports Ben's action to you and is livid that the programs will now have to be repaired. Ben is well aware of committing the violations but claims that the programs were accessible and that he needed to use them for his own reports which alone justified his actions. You respond to Ben that these programs are not his personal property but those of the agency. The programs will have to be reconstructed by Emma, which will take days, if not weeks, to fix. The rest of your employees are extremely upset with Ben.

1. What are the issues involved?
2. As the CFO, how will you deal with Ben?
3. How will you placate Emma?
4. What do you do to address your staff on this issue?

WHAT ACTUALLY HAPPENED IN CASE STUDY 12.2

The agency had no internal written policies on this type of action. However, each employee signs a form that states that they will not tamper with, damage, or destroy data or computer systems at the agency. Originally, the CFO was not going to pursue disciplinary action against Ben. Instead, the CFO held a departmental meeting to refresh everyone's familiarity with agency policies and procedures. Ben showed no visible sign that he understood that he had violated policy and that he should not have altered the programs without permission. Several employees were upset by the lack of disciplinary action taken by the CFO and later voiced their concerns to the CFO. The CFO then gave Ben a verbal warning and told him not to modify any more programs.

KEY ISSUES RAISED IN CASE STUDY 12.2

The issue raised in this case study is essentially unauthorized use of state property as well as unauthorized alteration of a tool used for state reporting. By altering the programs, Ben actually cost the agency more money since those programs had to be repaired by the original programmer. This does not include state deadlines that might have been missed because this program had to be fixed. Ben added to the programmer's workload, which would impact their other projects. The case study illustrates how difficult it can be for public organizations to hire highly skilled employees when the employment market in the surrounding community is competitive. In a competitive job market, public organizations must find other ways to compensate for lower wages by offering better benefits, a set 40-hour workweek, or training to improve technical skills. New employees who are hired need to understand the policies, procedures, and culture of the organization so that they can successfully transition into the organization. Allow some time for new employees who come from private industry backgrounds or from a different level of public organizations to acclimate to their new environment.

WHAT COULD HAVE HAPPENED IN CASE STUDY 12.2

Not only did Ben commit an offense that was against organizational policy, but Ben also committed an offense against state policy. The fact that the programs were no longer in their original state for reporting and audit purposes could have potentially damaged the organization. In private industry, an employee who does this would very likely be terminated for such an offense. However, in a public organization, a written reprimand against the employee's actions and documentation of the incident would be the standard course of action. If the supervisor had called Ben into his office, reprimanded Ben for his actions, and written him up for the offense, it would have preserved the morale of the office and the trust they had in their supervisor. Ben could have been ordered to repair the damage he caused, thus sparing the original programmer from doing the extra work.

CASE STUDY 12.3
Morale

SITUATION FOR CASE STUDY 12.3

A long-term employee at a public agency in the southwest had become the chief executive officer (CEO). The CEO had been with the agency long enough to qualify for retirement and receive a pension. The CEO informed the elected board that if the opportunity presented itself, she would secure a high-paying position elsewhere and retire unless she was compensated enough to care for her elderly parents. The elected board wanted to keep their CEO because the agency was going through severe fiscal stress and needed continuity to keep the organization on track until better times returned and orderly transition in the executive suite could be arranged. To keep their CEO, the board decided that its members and six assistant executive officers would sell their unused sick leave balances at the end of each calendar year back to the agency. This contract stipulation was approved unanimously by the elected board as a strategy to retain their top management team. However, this action was taken during a severe economic downturn, and very few of their employees at any level were leaving the organization. The employees had not received any pay adjustments for the last three years, during which the top executives were able to sell back their accrued sick leave. The top executives had received on average $250,000 each over a three-year period while the chief executive officer received $350,000 during the same time.

WHAT ACTUALLY HAPPENED IN CASE STUDY 12.3

During the first two years of the buyback program there was no controversy or media coverage. However, after three years of no raises and increasing health benefit costs, some of the employees who knew of the sick pay program went to the media to complain. The media coverage of the buyback program generated large backlash from the workforce. The rank-and-file employees believed that the sick leave buyback program was unfair and could not be justified in such a stressful economic environment. The employees succeeded in generating negative media coverage of the buyback program for the top executives. The elected members of the board defended their actions and stated that the program was needed to retain top staff during a time when strong and consistent leadership was vital for the agency to navigate through stormy economic waters. All the top executives who took advantage of the sick leave buyback program were long-term employees and had accumulated large sick leave balances.

KEY ISSUES RAISED IN CASE STUDY 12.3

The sick leave buyback program created a great deal of animosity between the rank-and-file employees and the agency's top management. Many of the employees believed that although the executives had earned the sick leave, they should only be compensated for the sick leave balances upon retirement. They pointed out that the top executives were well compensated and that there was no need to provide additional inducement to encourage them to stay with the agency. It also provided a poor example to the organization for the top executives to accept the sick leave buyback pay at a time when lower-level employees were not receiving pay increases and their take-home pay was actually declining due to the increasing cost of the health benefits. Many of the employees felt that if the buyback program had not been in effect, the funds spent on the top executives could have saved 40 to 45 employees who had been laid off during the three years. The sick leave buyback provision made it very difficult for the CEO to ask for ongoing budget reductions to deal with the continuing economic stress still affecting the organization. The employees felt the CEO and her top assistants were capable but not indispensable.

They believed that because of the economic downturn, there were plenty of qualified candidates who could have led the organization and it would not have damaged the organization to replace the CEO.

The CEO should have been aware that leading a public organization, even during good times, is a very challenging endeavor. If the CEO needed additional funds to care for her parents, she should have informed the board of her intentions to retire and work elsewhere and not accepted a deal that would have deprived the organization of funds. Then the board could have taken the necessary steps to replace the CEO.

Employees in all organizations pay attention to what their leaders do and not what they say. Good leadership requires leading by example and with character. Once a leader loses the respect of her organization, it is almost impossible to regain that respect and lead that organization effectively.

WHAT COULD HAVE HAPPENED IN CASE STUDY 12.3

The elected board could have suspended the sick leave buyback program until the economy had recovered and the employees of the organization were able to receive regular pay adjustments for merit performance and/or cost-of-living adjustments. If the elected body had not suspended the program, the CEO should have forgone exercising the pay plan provision that allowed reimbursement of unused sick leave pay until economic conditions had improved. In addition, the CEO should have disclosed to the public and the employees how much her assistant CEOs were being paid under the sick leave buyback and when the payments were going to be made.

The board's decision to pay the executives substantially more than the lower-level employees was just an indication that they were deaf to concerns regarding the pay differentials between the rank-and-file employees and top managerial employees. While public agencies strive to be responsive to new managerial trends, it is still important for all public employees to be treated fairly and equally. The egalitarian nature of public service will be one of the last virtues of public service to disappear.

Suggested Readings for Chapter 12

Anderson, Dean, and Ackerman-Anderson, Linda, 2001. *Beyond change management: Advanced strategies for today's transformational leaders.* ISBN: 0-7879-5645-7. San Francisco, California (CEO). The HE : Jossey-Bass/Pfeiffer.

Bazerman, Max H., 2002. *Judgment in managerial decision making.* Fifth edition. ISBN: 0-471-39887-X. New York: John Wiley & Sons.

Bridges, William, 2003. *Managing transitions: Making the most of change.* Second edition updated and expanded. ISBN: 0-7382-0824-8. Cambridge, Massachusetts: Da Capo Press.

Senge, Peter, Kleiner, Art, Roberts, Charlotte, Ross, Richard, Roth, George, and Smith, Bryan, 1999. *The dance of change: The challenges to sustaining momentum in learning organizations.* ISBN: 0-385-493223. New York: Doubleday.

Chapter 13

Conclusion: Trends in Human Resources Issues for Public Organizations

This book has afforded the authors an opportunity to discuss key human resource topics through case studies based on actual events for readers to review. The intention of this book is to provide readers with practical information on a wide array of topics and advice on how to contend with personnel issues when they occur. Whether the readers are supervisors or employees, this book is intended to give a perspective on how to deal with difficult situations as well as how to interact with people in their organization.

Often a supervisor will be faced with several complicated issues instead of one simple problem. There may not be any "perfect solutions" in a real-life situation. The administrator's goal should be to reduce liability to the organization and to avoid decisions that will irritate the situation even further; that will violate federal, state, or local statutes; or that will cause additional tension among employees. It is important to control one's emotions when dealing with human resource issues, advice that applies to administrators and employees alike. Above all, administrators should listen to their employees. The ability to listen can be extremely valuable for defusing a potentially volatile human resources issue.

Public, nonprofit, and medical organizations should have a robust set of policies and procedures to contend with human resource issues. Unless an organization is extremely small, there is usually a dedicated human resources department where administrators can seek assistance and guidance on difficult personnel issues. Some organizations also retain an attorney for legal advice and services. If administrators have such resources available to them, they should use them to the fullest extent possible. Other administrators who do not have access to a human resources department or an attorney should evaluate the policies and procedures that other organizations of similar size and scope have for certain situations that can occur.

Lawsuits

Medical organizations in particular have always been vulnerable to malpractice lawsuits. Malpractice lawsuits can cause severe damage to organizations through bad publicity and financial ruin. Often, malpractice suits can be brought in civil courts and, if the plaintiff wins, can result in substantial financial loss for an organization. There is also the risk of criminal charges brought against medical personnel if authorities uncover enough evidence to justify charges against an individual or group of individuals. Organizations that have a medical component to their mission need to make sure that their employees have proper policies and guidelines to abide by and that proper training is given to all personnel who interface with patients. If an organization does not take those steps, a successful lawsuit, or worse, a criminal charge, could potentially damage the organization long term.

Generational Workforce Issues

Currently, four generations are in the American workforce. Each generation has workforce characteristics and stereotypes that have been given them. Almost every organization still retains some seniors (those are individuals born in 1945 or earlier) in their workforce. Called the "greatest generation" by the journalist Tom Brokaw and sometimes inclusive of the smaller "silent generation" born between the Great Depression and World War II, seniors are the gatekeepers for public organizations. Standard characteristics of this generation include a belief in hard work and frugality when it comes to the expenditure of public organization funds and holding respect for organizational structure and authority. Some negative stereotypes that have been ascribed to them include being behind the times, rigid, autocratic, and averse to change and risk.

The baby boomers are the largest demographic group in America's workforce. They were born between 1946 and 1964. There are about eight million of these individuals and they have been the moving force in our public service workforces for the last 50 years. One can say that this generation prefers to "live to work" and is very career driven. Stereotypes used to describe them include being self-centered, unrealistic, political, power-driven, and workaholic. They were expected to rotate out of the workforce to allow the younger generations to take more prominent roles in public organizations. However, the recent economic downturn and the increasing cost of health insurance have resulted in many boomers staying on the payroll to deal with the costs of life.

The following two generations are significantly smaller than the preceding two. Generation X, those generally born between 1965 and 1981, tend to be very interested in work–life balance. Many of them grew up as latch-key kids because they were the children of the first generation of women to enter en masse into the workforce. Their early independence has made them self-reliant and pragmatic. Stereotypes used to describe them include being unmotivated slackers, selfish, impatient, and cynical.

Generation Y employees, those generally born between 1977 and 1994, are now entering the workforce in substantial numbers and competing with Generation X employees for middle manager and executive positions in public service organizations. Generation Y has been characterized as fast paced and fun seeking. They are generally technology savvy, sometimes to the point of being overly dependent upon technology to solve all challenges. They think nothing about answering a cell phone or texting during a meeting. Stereotypes used to describe them include having a short attention span, spoiled, entitled, and disrespectful.

How all four generations handle their exit and entry into the workforce will be highly critical to the effective management of America's public organizations. Employers will be challenged to get these different generations of employees to work as a team, to be productive, and to serve their citizens effectively.

Employee Recruiting and Networking

Currently, the employer is in control because the demand for jobs is significantly greater than the number of jobs that are available. However, this will quite likely change as the older generations transition from employment to retirement. The baby boomers number about 87 million individuals and will not be easy to replace in the government workplace. The total number of Generation X and Generation Y will attempt to fill the void in our governmental workforces, but there does not appear to be sufficient new workers to fill all the vacancies. In addition, public organizations are struggling to replace their most experienced workers and developing the new cadre of workers to take on the roles filled by retiring seniors and boomers. The competition for workers will be worldwide, recruiting new employees will be very competitive, and there are concerns that the United States is not producing sufficient workers for jobs in engineering, accounting, medical fields, and mathematics. The increased competition for skilled workers will force public organizations to develop new and innovative recruiting strategies to fill their organizational vacancies. For example, school districts all over the United States are either actively recruiting or thinking about recruiting Spanish language, science, and mathematics teachers from foreign countries to fill their needs for teachers in those specialties. This is especially true in school districts with very diverse populations that need teachers fluent in dozens of languages. Also employees and employers are using new techniques, like social networking venues such as Facebook, Twitter, and LinkedIn, to find new employees and work opportunities.

Work–Life Balance

While public and nonprofit organizations currently struggle to fill positions because it is difficult for them to provide salaries competitive with the private sector, these organizations will become more competitive in the future because public organizations are traditionally more stable and have a set workweek with compensated overtime. Public and nonprofit organizations typically have 40-hour workweeks along with generous sick and vacation leave and various federal holidays. On a per hour basis, public employees are likely to fare just as well as their private industry counterparts in regard to salary because they work fewer hours per week and have the ability to take more personal leave than their private industry counterparts. Employees who seek a better work–life balance will find these traits desirable and are more likely to choose public organizations over private industry organizations as a result. Given that the younger generations tend to value work–life balance over traditional career advancement and high salary, public organizations can more easily compete with the private sector for the most talented employees even without the ability to offer high salaries.

Technology

Technology is already increasing the capabilities of many public, nonprofit, and medical organizations. An example of advanced technology is the requirement for hospitals now using i-Stat to use iStat—a handheld medical testing device used for point-of-care service—for laboratory tests in place of using a hospital laboratory (Abbott, 2011) if the hospital is designated as a Level II trauma center (Valcik, 2010). The transition to using iStat has reduced the need to use medical technologists for laboratory tests and enables employees trained on iStat to carry out laboratory tests in the emergency room through this handheld device (Valcik, 2010).

Technology allows organizations to improve productivity while reducing manpower through automation and simplification of tasks, which enables lower-paying positions to perform more specialized job functions. The trend toward increased reliance on technology and automation to reduce overhead costs will only continue in public, nonprofit, and medical organizations in the foreseeable future. Public organizations will need to analyze how they need to be structured to accommodate new technology and how they should retrain existing employees to carry out other organizational mandates.

Training and Development

The new skills that the workforce will need to learn will change at a very rapid pace. Training in the future will more likely be provided through new technological methods such as podcasts, teleseminars, online learning, and webinars in addition to, or instead of, traditional classroom training. A great deal of training, particularly compliance training in agency policy and state and federal laws, will be self-directed through computer interfaces. In the future, traveling to receive training or to learn the latest techniques in a particular profession or specialty will be replaced with online training, mentoring, and coaching strategies.

Rising Health Care Costs

The continually rising cost of health care and health insurance is affecting what employers can provide in terms of benefits for their employees. The rise in employee premiums, the practice of seeking insurance first from a spouse's employer, increased premiums for covered family members, and higher health care provider co-pay fees are ways in which employers try to contain overhead costs when providing benefits. An increasing trend among government organizations is to increase the share of health benefit cost to the employees and limit the funds expended on dependents and retirees. It is no longer unusual to see public service organizations dropping employees' health benefits after they retire. The recent passage of health care legislation by the U.S. Congress will surely affect how public agencies provide health care coverage for their employees. Health benefit costs in 2009 were 17.6% of the total national domestic product of the United States (U.S. Department of Health and Human Services, 2009). This is an unsustainable level of public expenditures for local, state, and federal government agencies.

Diversity

This issue has been in the forefront of our society since the civil rights era and will gain new importance as an aging population is replaced by Generation Y employees, who as a group consider diversity a positive attribute and take it as a given that the workforce, like their private associations, is culturally, racially, and ethnically diverse. Furthermore, the U.S. population is projected to be minority-majority (a term used to describe a U.S. state or other jurisdiction whose racial composition is less than 50% white) by 2050 (Nasser, 2008). As the workforce becomes increasingly diverse, public organizations will need to recruit and hire a more diverse workforce to meet their goal of maintaining a workforce that reflects the community as a whole. The recent election of our first black president is just another indication that diversity is being embedded into the very fabric of our public workforces.

Outsourcing

Outsourcing, or privatization of public service functions, is a growing trend in public organizations in the United States. As financial resources become scarcer and the willingness of the public to raise taxes and other revenue streams is eroding, there is a push to find new ways to provide public agency services in new, cost-effective ways. The most likely services to be outsourced include human resources, water and sewer services, convention and visitor services, building inspection, engineering, architectural services, equipment and building services, financial services, legal services, landscaping, and maintenance. These issues impact the cost of hiring public employees since health benefits, pension costs, and training are associated with permanent employees. Recruiting and work rules can cause public agencies to turn to private providers to provide public services.

Sometimes private companies can provide economies of scale to reduce costs for citizens. For example, a company that provides water treatment services globally has access to skilled employees from all over the world and can have greater purchasing power than smaller governmental entities. In another example, an equipment services agency that maintains public agency vehicles often cannot compete for resources such as new facilities, new equipment, new computer software and hardware, and skilled employees to provide high-quality services against a private firm that specializes in the provision of such services.

Safety in the Workplace

Chapter 8 went into some detail on violence in the workplace. With all of the states looking at giving the right to carry for people who have a concealed handgun license, the issue of carrying weapons to the workplace (including higher education institutions) will be a source of debate for years to come. The issue of Second Amendment rights versus the liability to a public organization and safety considerations will be the crux of future policy and political debates. Threats of terrorism and mass shootings in the workplace will challenge administrators to develop new ways of keeping employees safe from violence that can potentially occur in the workplace.

Economic Downturns—Public Backlash against Public Employee Salaries

Recent layoffs and pay reductions in the private sector have placed pressure on the public sector to do likewise. Public employees who are union members have borne the brunt of citizen frustration over a perception of low work output, excessive job security, generous benefits, and high salary compared with private sector employees. In 2010–2011, public unions began to lose political power. The union leaders started conceding to salary freezes and benefits cuts in the face of severe political opposition (Powell, 2011). In 2011, New York's governor announced a one-year wage freeze for unionized state employees (Confessore, 2011). How this action will impact labor relations in New York remains to be seen. The action does appear to indicate that executive leaders and politicians are more likely to confront public unions in tough economic times since public support for such actions are increasing.

How public organization leaders will recruit and hire in tough economic times remains to be seen. The main advantages that public organizations have traditionally had over private industry—a set 40-hour workweek and good benefits—are in danger of disappearing due to public outcry. Without those advantages, public organizations will have a more difficult time recruiting and retaining good employees.

Final Notes

Managers and human resources personnel should continually evaluate the trends that are occurring in the workplace. By staying current with trends in human resources, administrators of public, nonprofit, and medical organizations will be able to keep organizations flexible enough to accommodate changes in areas such as technology, legal statutes, and economic conditions. Failure to take new trends into account can lead to problems in recruiting, hiring, and retraining the personnel that will allow an organization to stay viable, efficient, and effective to carry out its mandates. If the organization does not stay viable, then the administration faces the possibility of being replaced by a new set of administrators. Additionally, if the organization fails to take human resources trends into account, then retention and hiring could become an issue since some applicants and employees will attempt to avoid working for an organization that is out of touch with the current work environment. Although the manufacturing sector has been able to maintain and even improve productivity by replacing people with machines, service industries, which include public and nonprofit organizations, cannot function without people. Therefore, it would serve administrators well to remember that an organization's employees are its most valuable asset.

References

Abbott, 2011. "Abbot Point of Care, i-Stat and the Laboratory." Retrieved April 11, 2011.

American Postal Workers Union (APWU), 2010. APWU history. Retrieved on March 8, 2010. http://www.apwu.org/about/history.htm

Barro, Josh, 2010. "is Public Sector Wage Growth Moderating?" RealClearMarkets.com, May 4, 2010. Retrieved July 22, 2010. http://www.realclearmarkets.com/articles/2010/05/04/is_public_sector_wage_growth_moderationg_9844.html.

BBC News, 2004. Attackers storm Russian school. Retrieved on February 23, 2010. http://news.bbc.co.uk/2/hi/europe/3616868.stm

BBC News One Minute World News, 2007. Strike escalates in South Africa. BBC. June 14, 2007. Retrieved on March 8, 2010. http://news.bbc.co.uk/2/hi/africa/6747061.stm

BBC News World Edition, 2002. Fire strike would threaten Iraq action. BBC. September 5, 2002. Retrieved on March 8, 2010. http://news.bbc.co.uk/2/hi/uk_news/2238303.stm

Berger, Jane, 2007. There is tragedy on both sides of the layoffs: Privatization and the urban crisis in Baltimore. *International Labor and Working-Class History*, 71: 29–49. Retrieved on March 8, 2010. http://journals.cambridge.org/action/displayFulltext?type=1&fid=1354444&jid=ILW&volumeId=71&issueId=01&aid=1354436

Bridges, William, 2003. Managing transitions: Making the most of change. Second edition, updated and expanded. ISBN: 0-7382-0824-8. Cambridge, Massachusetts: Da Capo Press.

Broad, William J., 2005. California is surprise winner in bid to run Los Alamos. *The New York Times*. December 22, 2005. Retrieved on March 12, 2010. http://www.nytimes.com/2005/12/22/national/22alamos.html?_r=1

Bunkall, Alistair, 2008. PM remains firm over teacher strike. *Sky News*. April 24, 2008. Retrieved on March 8, 2010. http://news.sky.com/skynews/Home/Sky-News-Archive/Article/20080641313845

Campbell, Duncan, 2001. *Top Gun* versus *Sergeant Bilko*? No contest, says the Pentagon. *The Guardian*. August 29, 2001. Retrieved on March 25, 2010. http://www.guardian.co.uk/world/2001/aug/29/media.filmnews

City of Boston, 1920. Annual report of the police commissioner for the City of Boston. Retrieved on March 8, 2010. http://www.archive.org/stream/annualreportofpo1919bost#page/n5/mode/2up

Confessore, Nicholas, 2011. Cuomo plans one-year freeze on state workers' pay. *The New York Times*. January 2, 2011. Retrieved on January 3, 2011. http://www.nytimes.com/2011/01/03/nyregion/03cuomo.html?_r=1&emc=eta1

Copeland, Larry, 2005. I could tell he was going to shoot everybody. *USA Today*. March 13, 2005. Retrieved on July 22, 2010. http://www.usatoday.com/news/nation/2005-03-1 3-ga-courthouse_x.htm

Coral Springs, 2007. Ugly America: Katrina brings out the worst of New Orleans. CoralSprings.com. Coral Springs, Florida. September 7, 2005. Retrieved on March 26, 2010. http://coralsprings.com/frontpage/katrina.htm

CNN, 1997. "CIA Shooting Suspect Held Without Bond," CNN Interactive.com. June 18, 1997. Retrieved on April 12, 2011. http://edition.cnn.com/US/9706/18/cia.shooting/index.html

Dallas Morning News, 2005. The *Dallas Morning News* Robert Miller column: BR&Gt, Cancer center has big goal. *Dallas Morning News*. December 29, 2005. Retrieved on December 10, 2010. http://www.redorbit.com/news/health/343204/the_dallas_morning_news_robert_miller_column_brgtcancer_center_has/index.html

Dallas Morning News, 2009. Case studies. *Dallas Morning News*. Local/News, Science/Medicine. October 11, 2009. Retrieved on March 25, 2010. http://www.dallasnews.com/sharedcontent/dws/news/healthscience/stories/DN-medboard_cases_11pro.ART.State.Edition1.4c12166.html

Early, Steve, 2006. An old lesson still holds for unions. *The Boston Globe*. July 31, 2006. Retrieved on March 8, 2010. http://www.boston.com/news/globe/editorial_opinion/oped/articles/2006/07/31/an_old_lesson_still_holds_for_unions/

Edwards, Chris, 2010. "Employe Compensation in State and Local Governments," Cato Institute Tax & Budget Bulleting No 59, January, 2010. http://www.cato.org/pubs/tbb-59.pdf

Einarsen, Stale, Hoel, Helge, Zapf, Dieter, and Cooper, Cary L., 2005. Workplace bullying: Individual pathology or organizational culture? In *Workplace violence: Issues, trends, strategies*, edited by Vaughan Bowie, Bonnie S. Fisher, and Cary L. Cooper. ISBN: 1-84392-134-0. Portland, Oregon: Willan Publishing.

Employer-employee.com, 2010. Sexual harassment and discrimination. http://www.employer-employee.com/sexhar1.htm

Foley, Ryan, 2007. As faculty leave, some worry University of Wisconsin slipping. Associated Press. May 30, 2007. Retrieved on March 26, 2010. http://www.gazetteextra.com/facultyfleeswisconsin053007.asp

Genomeweb LLC, 2010. Alabama shootings. The Daily Scan. February 15, 2010. Retrieved on July 22, 2010. http://www.genomeweb.com/blog/alabama-shootings

Grimme, Don. Top ten tips to attract, retain and motivate employees. Speakers Platform. http://www.speaking.com/articles_html/DonGrimme_889.html

Healthfield, Susan M., Five tips for effective employee recognition. About.com. Retrieved on February 6, 2010. http://humanresources.about.com/od/rewardrecognition/a/recognition_tip.htm

Hettena, Seth, 2005. Reports detail Abu Ghraib prison death: Was it torture? MSNBC. February 17, 2005. Retrieved on March 12, 2010. http://www.msnbc.msn.com/id/6988054/

Hockley, Charmaine, 2005. Staff violence against those in their care. In *Workplace violence: Issues, trends, strategies*, edited by Vaughan Bowie, Bonnie S. Fisher, and Cary L. Cooper. ISBN: 1-84392-134-0. Portland, Oregon: Willan Publishing.

Hope, Katie, 2010. Pay rises for public sector despite recession. *Moneywise*. February 18, 2010. Retrieved on January 3, 2011. http://www.moneywise.co.uk/news-views/2010/02/18/pay-rises-public-sector-despite-the-recession

Ingraham, Patricia Wallace, 1995. *The foundation of merit: Public service in American democracy.* ISBN: 0-8018-5111-4. Baltimore, Maryland: The Johns Hopkins University Press.

Internet Center for Management and Business Administration, Inc., 2010. Frederick Taylor and scientific management. NetMBA. Retrieved on June 15, 2010. http://www.net-mba.com/mgmt/scientific/

Jacoby, Jeff, 2010. Public-sector pay, private-sector backlash. *The Boston Globe.* January 27, 2010. Retrieved on January 3, 2011. http://www.jeffjacoby.com/6872/public-sector-pay-private-sector-backlash

Jones, Owen, 2010. The 'Spirit of Petrograd'? The 1918 and 1919 police strikes. *What Next?* Retrieved on March 8, 2010. http://www.whatnextjournal.co.uk/Pages/Latest/Police.html

Kelly, George A., 1992. Catholic higher education: Is it in or out of the church? *Faith & Reason.* Retrieved on March 8, 2010.

Kimery, Anthony L., 2007. US oil complex vulnerable to attack. *Homeland Security Today.* November 27, 2007. Retrieved on July 22, 2010. http://www.hstoday.us/content/view/13/128/

Kulik, Carol T., 2004. *Human resources for the non-HR manager.* ISBN: 0-80-58-4295-0. Mahwah, New Jersey: Lawrence Erlbaum Associates.

Lax, David A., and Sebenius, James K., 1986. *The manager as negotiator.* ISBN: 0-02-918770-2. New York: The Free Press.

Lewicki, Roy J., Saunders, David M., Minton, John W., and Barry, Bruce, 2003. *Negotiation.* ISBN: 0-07-242965-8. Boston, Massachusetts: McGraw-Hill Higher Education.

Loveland, Laurie J., 2010. Performance management. North Dakota Human Resource Management, North Dakota State Government. April 4, 1986. Retrieved on August 2, 2010. http://www.nd.gov/hrms/managers/guide/discipline.html

Macleod, Marlee, 2010. Charles Whitman: The Texas tower sniper. Tru Crime Library. Retrieved on July 22, 2010. http://www.washingtonpost.com/wp-rv/national/long-term/shooting/archives2.htm

Managing employee retention and separation, 2010. Retrieved on August 2, 2010. http://www.google.com/webhp?hl=en&tab=nw#hl=en&source=hp&q=managing+employee+retention+and+separation&aq=0p&aqi=g-p1g9&aql=&oq=mana&gs_rfai=CiCcnDFtGTKmjBo-GNKHCgNoMAAAAqgQFT9AbXKE&fp=fb153a59cce8ec69

Maxwell, Lisa, 2010. *The handbook of Texas online.* Texas State Historical Association. Retrieved on March 12, 2010. http://www.tshaonline.org/handbook/online/articles/PP/hvp57.html

May, Janet, 2002, March. Disciplining employees: Avoid the procedural pitfalls. Association of Washington Cities. Olympia, Washington. Retrieved on August 2, 2010. http://www.awcnet.org/documents/pnewsmar02.pdf

McCraken, Peggy, 1997. City manager's job draws 20 candidates. *Pecos Enterprise.* January 31, 1997. Retrieved on February 23, 2010. http://www.pecos.net/news/arch97/013197p.htm

Memmott, Larry, 2010. Retaining and motivating employees, 2002. Washington State University—Tree Fruit Postharvest Conference. Retrieved on August 2, 2010. http://scholar.google.com/scholar?q=retaining+and+motivating+employees,+Larry+Memmott&hl=en&as_sdt=0&as_vis=1&oi=scholart

Miller, Laurence, 2008. *From difficult to disturbed: Understanding and managing dysfunctional employees.* ISBN: 978-0-8144-0922-0. New York: AMACOM—American Management Association.

MSNBC.com, 2007. Worst U.S. shooting ever kills 33 on Va. campus. NBC News. April 17, 2007. Retrieved on July 22, 2010. http://www.msnbc.msn.com/id/18134671

Murchison, Stuart, 2010. Uses of GIS for homeland security and emergency management at higher education institutions. In *New directions for institutional research: Institutional research and homeland security*, edited by N. Valcik. Volume 146, Chapter 7. Summer 2010. ISBN: 978-04709-03148. Hoboken, NJ: John Wiley & Sons.

National Right to Work, 2011. "Right to Work States." Retrieved on April 11, 2011. (Used to construct Figure 2.2) http://www.nrtw.org/rtws.htm

Nasser, Hay El, 2008. U.S. Hispanic population to triple by 2050. *USA Today*. February 12, 2008. Retrieved on April 12, 2011. http://www.usatoday.com/news/nation/2008-02-11-population-study_N.htm

New York Teacher, 2005. The history of the Taylor Law. Labor Spotlight. June 9, 2005. Retrieved on March 8, 2010. http://www.uft.org/news/teacher/labor/taylor_law/

Oklahoma City National Memorial and Museum, 2010. Retrieved on February 23, 2010. http://www.oklahomacitynationalmemorial.org/

O'Leary, Rosemary, 2010. Guerilla employees: Should managers nurture, tolerate, or terminate them? *Public Administration Review*. ISSN: 0033-3352. American Society for Public Administration. January–February 2010, Volume 70, Number 1. Hoboken, New Jersey: Wiley Services, Inc.

Padilla Jr., Ramon, 2005. Six rules for motivating and retaining good government employees. *Tech Republic*. May 9, 2005. Public Employee Discipline, Medical Educational Services, Inc. Retrieved on February 2, 2010. https://www.meds-pdn.com/continuing_education.php?seminar_id=370

Paterik, Richard C., 2007. Effective strategic succession planning through mentoring. Waters Consulting Group.

Paul, Donna Bernardi, 2005. *The value of mentoring. What do protégés look for in a mentor? Results of three experimental studies.* Society for Human Resource Management.

Perlmutter, Philip, 1999. *Legacy of hate: A short history of ethnic, religious, and racial prejudice in America.* ISBN: 9780765604064. Armonk, New York: M.E. Sharpe.

Powell, Michael, 2011. Public workers face outrage as budget tightens. *The New York Times*. January 2, 2011. Retrieved on April 12, 2011.

Rhodes, D. C., and Drahosz, K. W., 1997. Dynamic mentoring: A guide to building successful mentoring partnerships. (pp. 5–6). Trammel Crow Company Report.

Rhodes, Richard, 1986. *The making of the atomic bomb*. ISBN: 0-671-44133-7. New York: Simon and Schuster Paperbacks.

Rhodes, Richard. 1995. *Dark sun: The making of the hydrogen bomb*. ISBN: 978-0-684-80400-2. New York: Simon and Schuster Paperbacks.

SAC Elite Guard, 2010. SAC Elite Guard. Retrieved on March 12, 2010. http://www.saceliteguard.com/USSTRATCOM.html

Seligson, Tom, 2005. Isn't it time to right the wrong? *Parade*. February 6, 2005. Retrieved on March 8, 2010. http://www.parade.com/articles/editions/2005/edition_02-06-2005/featured_1

Sexual Harassment at Work, 2010. Know your rights: Sexual harassment at work. Retrieved on January 3, 2011. http://www.equalrights.org/publications/kyr/shwork.asp

Sexual Harassment Fact Sheet, 2010. Preventing sexual harassment: A fact sheet for employees. Retrieved on January 3, 2011. http://www.dotcr.ost.dot.gov/Documents/complaint/Preventing_Sexual_Harassment.htm

Sexual Harassment Support, 2010. What is sexual harassment and why is it so difficult to confront. Retrieved on January 3, 2011. http://www.sexualharassmentsupport.org/

Snacks, Hort, 2010, January. Involving employees in the business (retaining and motivating). Government of Alberta, Canada, Agriculture and Rural Development.

State of Texas, 2010. Texas Penal Code, Section 22.011. Sexual assault. Retrieved on July 22, 2010. http://law.onecle.com/texas/penal/22.011.00.html

State of Texas, 2011. Sunset Advisory Commission. Retrieved on April 12, 2011. http://www.sunset.state.tx.us/

Strategic Air Command, 2010. Strategic-Air-Command.com. Retrieved on March 12, 2010. http://www.strategic-air-command.com/intro/SAC-Intro.htm

Texas Mental Health Code, 2010. Texas Statutes – Subtitle C: Texas Mental Health Code, Section 573.001: Apprehension by Peace Officer without Warrant. Retrieved on April 12, 2011. http://codes.lp.findlaw.com/txstatutes/HS/7/C/573/A/573.001

Tahmincioglu, Eve, 2010. Women still reluctant to help each other. MSNBC.com. July 7, 2010. Retrieved on August 2, 2010. http://www.msnbc.msn.com/id/38060072/ns/business-careers

Tynan, Dan. 25 ways to reward employees (without spending a dime). *HR World*. Retrieved on February 6, 202110. http://www.hrworld.com/features/25-employee-rewards/

United States Court of Appeals for the 5th Circuit, 1998. Deffenbaugh-Williams v. Wal-Mart Stores, Inc., 156 F.3d 581, No. 97-10685 1998.

United States District Court for the Southern District of New York, 1998. Fierro v. Saks Fifth Avenue, 13 FSupp. 2nd 481 1998.

UPI, 2010. 1968 year in review. UPI.com. Retrieved on March 8, 2010. http://www.upi.com/Audio/Year_in_Review/Events-of-1968/Pope-Paul-VI/Garbage-Strike/12303153093431-7/

United States Supreme Court – No. 97-282, 1997. Faragher v. City of Boca Raton, 524 U.S. 775 1997.

United States Supreme Court – No 97-549, 1997. Burlington Industries, Inc. v. Ellerth, 524 U.S. 742 1997.

U.S. Department of Health and Human Services, 2009. National health expenditure fact sheet. https://www.cms.gov/NationalHealthExpendData/25_NHE_Fact_Sheet.asp

U.S. Supreme Court, 1967. *Garrity v. New Jersey*, 385 U.S. 493 1967.

U.S. Supreme Court, 1975. *NLRB v. Weingarten, Inc.*, 420 U.S. 251 1975.

U.S. Supreme Court, 1985. *Cleveland Board of Education v. Loudermill, et al.*, 470 U.S. 532.

Valcik, Kristi L., 2010. Medical technologist at Medical Center of Plano.

Valcik, N., and Lavin-Loucks, D., 2006. Hogtied! The Texas stalking law. *Conservative Justice Digest*. Retrieved on January 3, 2011. http://conservativejusticedigest.blogspot.com/2006/12/hogtied-media-public-policy-and.html

Vasu, Michael L., Stewart, Debra W., and Garson, G. David, 1998. *Organizational behavior and public management (public administration and public policy)*. Third edition. ISBN: 0824701356. Boca Raton, Florida: CRC Press.

Warner, Margaret, 1995. Winter of discontent. PBS. December 8, 1995. Retrieved on March 8, 2010. http://www.pbs.org/newshour/bb/europe/france_12-8.html

Washington Post, 1998. Shootings at the Capitol: From the shootings to the investigations. Retrieved on July 22, 2010. http://www.washingtonpost.com/wp-srv/national/long-term/shooting/archives2.htm

Webb, Eugene J., Campbell, Donald T., Schwartz, Richard D., and Sechrest, Lee, 2000. *Unobtrusive measures.* Revised edition. ISBN: 0-7619-2012-9. Thousands Oak, California: Sage Publications.

Webb, James R., 2010. Executive defense. Retrieved on July 22, 2010. http://www.dallaskenpo.com/executive_defense.html

WEBCPA, 2010. Daughter of IRS attack pilot praises him. WebCPA. February 22, 2010. Retrieved on July 22, 2010. http://www.webcpa.com/news/Daughter-of-IRS-Attack-Pilot-Praises-Him-53347-1.html

White, Mary, 2010. About performance reviews. eHow.com. Retrieved on June 15, 2010. http://www.ehow.com/about_4579757_performance-reviews.html

Whitty, Monica T., and Carr, Adrian, N., 2005. Cyber-harassment in the workplace. In *Workplace violence: Issues, trends, strategies*, edited by Vaughan Bowie, Bonnie S. Fisher, and Cary L. Cooper. ISBN: 1-84392-134-0. Portland, Oregon: Willan Publishing.

Wikipedia, 2011. "At Will Employment" Retrieved on April 11, 2011 (Used to Construct Figure 2.1). http://en.wikipedia.org/wiki/At-will_employment

Williams, Phillip, 2004. Dozens killed in Russian hostage crisis. ABC News Online. September 4, 2004. Retrieved on July 22, 2010. http://www.genomeweb.com/blog/alabama-shootings

Youaskme, 2010. How to set up coaching and mentoring programs. Retrieved on March 1, 2010. http://www.ehow.com/how_5596825_setup-coaching-mentoring-programs.html

Index